Vicarious Vagrants

Order from: Whitehurst & Clark, Book Fulfillment
1200 County Road, Route 523
Flemington, NJ 08822
http://www.wcbks.com
wcbooks@aol.com
1-908-782-2323 ('phone)
1-908-237-2407 (fax)

Price US$45.00. NJ residents add seven percent sales tax.
All major credit cards accepted. Mail-in orders from
individuals must include a check or money order. Libraries
and library wholesalers will be invoiced. All foreign orders
must be pre-paid. Domestic orders must include a postage
and packing fee of $4.50 for the first copy or title and $3.00
for each additional copy or title. For orders from outside the
U.S.A., the postage and packing charge is US$13.00.

Vicarious Vagrants:

Incognito Social Explorers and the Homeless in England, 1860–1910

Edited, with Annotations and an Introductory Essay
by Mark Freeman and Gillian Nelson
University of Glasgow

The True Bill Press
Lambertville, NJ

The True Bill Press
P.O. Box 0349
Lambertville, NJ 08530-0349
http://www.TheTrueBillPress.com
SAN 852-4807

Printed and bound in the United States of America.

First printing.

1 3 5 7 9 8 6 4 2

Library of Congress Cataloging-in-Publication Data

Vicarious Vagrants: Incognito Social Explorers and the Homeless in England, 1860-1910. Edited, with annotations and an introductory essay by Mark Freeman and Gillian Nelson. Lambertville, NJ: The True Bill Press, 2008. p. cm.
Includes bibliographical references and index.

ISBN-13: 978-0-9791116-2-4
ISBN-10: 0-9791116-2-5

1. Homeless persons—England—History—Case studies.
2. Poor laws—England—History—Case studies.
3. Tramps—England—History—Case studies.
4. Workhouses—England—History—Case studies.
5. England—Social conditions—19th century.
6. England—Social conditions—20th century.
I. Freeman, Mark, 1974- II. Nelson, Gillian, M.Phil.
III. Title.
HV 4546.A3 V52 2008
LCCN 2008900095

This book was set in 11.5 pt. Janson Text type.
Interior and cover design by
Michelle Lawlor, OTTN Publishing

Table of Contents

Editors' Introduction
Mark Freeman & Gillian Nelson

I n 1910, writing under the pseudonym Denis Crane, the journalist Walter Thomas Cranfield published a book entitled *A Vicarious Vagabond*, an account of his experiences in disguise among the homeless of London. Dressed in a soiled cap, a tattered and collar-less shirt, a secondhand coat and shoddy boots—and with four days' growth of facial hair—Cranfield temporarily "became" a vagrant. He described the people he met, the places in which he slept, and the feelings he experienced. He stayed in a workhouse and various shelters for the homeless; he begged and sold matches in the street; he attended the out-patients' department of a hospital, pretending to suffer from colitis; and he visited churches to experience the "ordeal" of being in a congregation among well-dressed, respectable people.[1] Cranfield emphasized that his book was a "record of personal

---

1. Crane, Denis. *A Vicarious Vagabond*. London: Hurst & Blackett, 1910, *passim* and p. 193 (quoted). A photograph of Cranfield is reproduced at the end of this section.

experiences in regions inaccessible or repugnant to the majority of people": a journey into the London underworld, carried out incognito in order to see at first hand the conditions in which the homeless spent their lives, and to try to convey, instead of an external perspective, something of "the poignant knowledge of the victim" (pp. ix, viii). According to Cranfield, the use of disguise gave him access into both the surroundings and the outlook of the vagrant: "Always possessed of some facility for assuming a role with an intensity of feeling that makes it almost real, during those days among the poor I not only played, but experienced, my part" (p. 26).

Cranfield was just one of many social explorers who ventured among the poor in disguise. Many kings are reputed to have done so: for example, James V of Scotland was famed in folklore for his exploits in the guise of the "Gudeman of Ballangeich," and in modern times Kings Hussein and Abdullah of Jordan were reported to have gone among their people *incognito*.[2] In the twentieth century, George Orwell's *Down and Out in Paris and London* (1933) was perhaps the best known example of an ongoing tradition of *incognito* social exploration; and more recently the *Guardian* journalist Polly Toynbee has gone undercover to explore a variety of low-paid occupations. Barbara Ehrenreich has done the same in the United States.[3] However, the period 1860-1910 was the heyday of the undercover social investigator. The best known are James Greenwood—whose pamphlet *The Amateur Casual, or A Night in the Workhouse*, first published in 1866, is reprinted in this collection—and Jack London, the American novelist whose *The People of the Abyss*

---

2. Stephenson, David. "'The Gudeman of Ballangeich': Rambles in the Afterlife of James V." *Folklore*, 115, (August 2004), pp. 187-200, especially p. 189. James V's incognito adventures were often prompted by amorous intentions.

3. Toynbee, Polly. *Hard Work: Life in Low-Pay Britain*. London: Bloomsbury, 2003; Ehrenreich, Barbara. *Nickel and Dimed: Undercover in Low-Wage USA*. London: Granta, 2002. Other examples include Davies, Nick. *Dark Heart: The Shocking Truth about Hidden Britain*. London: Chatto and Windus, 1997; and, in a more academic vein, Hall, Tom. *Better Times than This: Youth Homelessness in Britain*. London: Pluto Press, 2003.

(1903) was an important influence on Orwell.[4] This collection reprints the work of several writers who, like Cranfield, Greenwood, and London, used disguise to explore the social underworld. They include a Church of England clergyman, a Congregationalist minister's wife, a socialist campaigner, a working-class woman acting under the direction of a medical man, and a number of professional journalists. These vicarious vagrants, as we have termed them, echoing Cranfield's title, had different motivations, and drew different conclusions from their work, but all were participants in a long-standing tradition of undercover social exploration. They wrote in a period when vagrancy was increasing—according to one estimate, the number of vagrants in Britain increased tenfold between 1850 and 1910[5]—and when methods of social investigation were undergoing considerable refinement. The emergence of "scientific" social research stimulated new understandings of a range of social problems, which were increasingly addressed by reforming legislation, especially in the early twentieth century. However, in many respects the vagrant "underclass" lay outside the spectrum of the new social research, and remained one of the most intractable problems facing the social reformers of the period. Therefore, the vicarious vagrants whose work is reprinted in this book were an important feature of social investigation in this period.[6]

*   *   *   *   *

4.   London, Jack. *The People of the Abyss.* New York: Macmillan, 1903.

5.   Vorspan, Rachel. "Vagrancy and the New Poor Law in Late-Victorian and Edwardian Britain." *English Historical Review*, 92, (January 1977), pp. 59-81, at 59, citing the Royal Commission on the Poor Laws and Relief of Distress, which reported in 1909.

6.   See Freeman, Mark. "'Journeys into Poverty Kingdom': Complete Participation and the British Vagrant 1866–1914." *History Workshop Journal*, 52, (Autumn 2001), pp. 99-121.

The problem of homelessness has pervaded the history of British social policy: indeed, one scholar has remarked that it "is a phenomenon which we still have not cured in our own immeasurably more sophisticated age."[7] An enduring theme within official policy has been—and remains—the need to strike a balance between the provision of relief on the one hand, and the deterrence of vagrancy on the other. Anglo-Saxon rulers had attempted to secure the social order of England by imposing strict regulations as to places of settlement and residence on the population, but also, mainly through religious institutions, organized the provision of material relief to the homeless poor.[8] In the fourteenth century, when the ravages of the Black Death ushered in an age of labor mobility and assertiveness, legislative responses were designed to shore up the feudal social order. The Ordinance of Labourers in 1349 and the Statute of Labourers in 1351 restricted laborers' geographical mobility, and attempted to stop the provision of any assistance to those who moved around the country, trying to force people into productive labor. The first of these declared:

> "Because that many valiant Beggars, as long as they may live by begging, do refuse to labour, giving themselves to Idleness and Vice, and sometimes to Theft and other abominations; none upon the ... Pain of Imprisonment, shall under the colour of Pity or Alms, give any thing to such, which may labour, or presume to favour them (towards their desires), so that thereby they may be compelled to labour for their necessary Living" (quoted in Humphreys 1999, p. 26).

Another Statute of Labourers, in 1388, reiterated the restrictions on mobility, although, according to Humphreys, it implied a

---

7. Rose, Lionel. *'Rogues and Vagabonds': Vagrant Underworld in Britain 1815-1985*. London: Routledge, 1988, p. 13.

8. Fourth-century sources on Roman Britain mention the problem of vagrancy: Humphreys, Robert. *No Fixed Abode: A History of Responses to the Roofless and the Rootless in Britain*. Basingstoke: Macmillan, 1999, p. 16.

slightly more liberal attitude towards the provision of relief. This statute prohibited labor migration unless the individual concerned was in possession of "letters patent" issued under the king's seal by justices of the peace, and stipulated a different penalty for vagrancy:

> "If any servant or labourer is discovered in a city, borough, or elsewhere as a vagrant from some other place, without a letters patent in his possession, the mayors, bailiffs, stewards, or constables shall immediately arrest him and put him in the stocks, and keep him prisoner until he finds surety to return to his service in the town from which he has come, or to go back there and be a servant or labourer, until for some good reason he has a letter to depart."[9]

The statute drew an implicit distinction between the vagrant who "takes to the road as a beggar, although able to serve and labour," and those "who are unfit for service"; the former, as noted above, were to be dealt with punitively, whereas the latter could be removed to their place of birth (Bagley & Rowley 1966, p. 219). This can be viewed as an early version of the settlement laws, which were to become an important feature of poor relief, and the treatment of vagrancy, in subsequent centuries.

In the fifteenth century, increasing efforts at a local level to provide for the poor reflected the worsening economic conditions in many areas, which precipitated vagrancy and undermined social stability. The poor were assisted by religious charity, often provided through the agency of monks and friars, and following the dissolution of the monasteries in the sixteenth century, a plethora of parochial and municipal charities emerged to fill the charitable vacuum that was left. Official policy—an early example was an Act of Henry VII in 1489—was concerned both to curb the indiscriminate provision of relief, and to ensure that sufficient provision was made for the destitute in order to preserve social

---

9. Reprinted in Bagley, J. J. & Rowley, P. B. *A Documentary History of England, Volume I: 1066-1540.* Harmondsworth: Penguin, 1966, p. 216.

order in an age of violence. As Humphreys has explained, "a two-pronged approach to the very poor" was designed both to repress vagrancy and to provide for genuine need. This resulted in the evolution of a distinction between three categories of vagrant: the genuine work-seeker, "the increasing number who moved around to satisfy subsistence needs," and "the sturdy rogue who shunned conventional work" (Humphreys 1999, p. 33). Distinctions of this kind proved remarkably persistent, and, with modifications, underpinned most subsequent legislation, at least for the next three hundred years. They reflected a mixture of humanitarian concern and a preoccupation with social discipline that was embodied in sixteenth-century legislation, culminating in the Acts of 1597-1601 that created the machinery of the English poor law. This legislation made explicit the distinction between the "able-bodied" and "impotent" poor. The first of these Elizabethan Acts was styled an "Acte for the Punyshment of Rogues, Vagabonds and Sturdy Beggars," among other purposes; it required parishes to administer a public flogging to vagrants, and then remove them to their last place of residence; however, at the same time it insisted that parishes provide relief for the poor, financed by a local rate (Bagley & Rowley 1966, pp. 53-54). Houses of correction had also emerged in the sixteenth century, encouraged by legislation in 1575-76: their functions included the incarceration of those convicted of offenses that attracted short sentences, and the temporary imprisonment of vagrants, as well as the fathers of illegitimate children.[10]

Therefore, at the beginning of the early modern period, harshness towards the lazy beggar was combined with the legal enshrinement of a right to poor relief. A clearer set of rules emerged after the passage of legislation in 1662 that tightened up the law of settlement and removal. All potential claimants of poor relief were to have a parish of settlement, which had a duty to relieve them, and to which they could be removed by the poor law authorities in another parish, if the latter believed them "likely to be chargeable" on the rates. According to Humphreys, the aim of

---

10. Henriques, Ursula R. Q. *Before the Welfare State: Social Administration in Early Industrial Britain*. London: Longman, 1979, p. 156.

the legislation was "to repress the travelling poor," who may have numbered around 30,000 at this point (1999, pp. 66-68). Settlement rights in a parish could be obtained by birth; by marriage for a woman, who took her husband's place of settlement; by renting property of a certain value; by paying rates in the parish; and by various miscellaneous qualifications.[11] It was difficult, if not impossible, for the travelling poor to obtain a settlement in any of these ways. Subsequent legislation in the late seventeenth century permitted licensed movement between parishes by paupers, who were required to wear badges denoting their pauper status and their parish of settlement.[12] More punitive measures were introduced in the eighteenth century, and the laws of settlement and removal remained "a persistent constraining influence on the mobility of poor people" (Humphreys 1999, p. 75). By this time it was clear that labor mobility was necessary in a period of rapid economic change. Industrialization and economic development required a mobile labor reserve, and the capitalization of agriculture under the impact of enclosures pushed many small farmers off the land. A seasonal labor force emerged in agriculture, comprising many thousands of temporary in-migrants from Ireland by 1800, as well as townspeople who travelled on a seasonal basis to undertake harvest work. Another type of vagrant was the "tramping artisan," whose mobility was supported by trade unions, and who played an important role in the eighteenth and early nineteenth centuries.[13] At the same time, the vagrant population was

---

11. Snell, K. D. M. *Parish and Belonging: Community, Identity and Welfare in England and Wales 1700-1950*. Cambridge: Cambridge University Press, 2006, pp. 85-86.

12. Humphreys 1999, p. 70; Hindle, Steve. "Dependency, Shame and Belonging: Badging the Deserving Poor c.1550-1750." *Cultural and Social History*, 1, (January 2004), pp. 6-35.

13. Hobsbawm, E. J. "The Tramping Artisan." In Hobsbawm, E.J. (Ed.). *Labouring Men: Studies in the History of Labour*. London: Weidenfield and Nicolson, 1968, chapter 4.

swelled by demobilized servicemen, who often lacked skills that could be used in alternative employment, and who became particularly numerous in the years after the end of the Napoleonic Wars in 1815. Coupled with the impact of the post-war economic downturn, the problem of vagrancy seemed to reach new heights of urgency in the late 1810s and early 1820s, in a period when poor relief expenditure of all kinds was causing widespread uncertainty about the future of the Elizabethan system. A Select Committee on Vagrancy, reporting in 1821, "revealed the increasing burden of vagrancy control on the community," and widespread abuses of the systems of control that had emerged since 1601 (Rose 1988, pp. 9-10).

By this time, there was a three-pronged statutory definition of the "sturdy rogue." The law identified, in increasing order of their perceived social threat, the "Idle and Disorderly," "Rogues and Vagabonds," and "Incorrigible Rogues." By the early nineteenth century, magistrates could sentence the first of these classes to a month's imprisonment (usually in conventional jails, as houses of correction were falling into disuse), the second to six months and to be whipped; and the "Incorrigible Rogues" could be locked up for two years, whipped, and either transported or forced into the armed services (Rose 1988, pp. 3-5). However, alongside this harsh deterrent policy for habitual vagrants, a system of "walking passes" had evolved, whereby "respectable" vagrants were given tickets that allowed them freedom from prosecution. Although these were outside the framework of statute law, they echoed the letters patent of 1388. Moreover, many magistrates were unwilling to bring the full severity of the law down upon genuinely respectable vagrants (Rose 1988, p. 7). Partly as a result, the Vagrancy Act (1824), which confirmed and modified many of the provisions of legislation two years earlier, softened the punishments to which vagrants could be subjected: only "Incorrigible Rogues" could now be flogged, and terms of imprisonment were reduced. Begging was permitted, under license, for discharged prisoners and servicemen, and the Act cracked down on some of the abuses of the system of dealing with vagrancy. By 1832 the number of vagrants jailed per annum had more than doubled, but Rose argues that this was as much the result of worsening economic circumstances—and hence increased levels of vagrancy—as of the strictness of the Act (1988, pp. 12-14. See also Humphreys 1999, p. 83). Some of the costs incurred by parishes in removing vagrants back to their place of last residence were moderated by the 1824 reform, but, as Rose points out, the Act was criticized because, although it persisted with the identification of three categories of vagrant, it "made no distinction between the unfortunate and the ne'er-do-well" (1988, p. 16). This was left to charitable organizations which emerged in the same period, such as the Society for the Suppression of Mendicity, which attempted to restrict the provision of private relief to the "deserving" poor (Rose, 1988, chapter 3).

Vagrancy was not directly addressed by the reform of the poor law in England and Wales in 1834. This legislation merged the parishes into larger poor law unions, which built large workhouses and organized relief through an elected board of guardians in each union. However, the new central poor law authority—firstly the Poor Law Commission and then its successors, the Poor Law Board from 1847 and the Local Government Board from 1871—issued repeated directives to poor law unions, regarding the treatment of the "casual poor." The nature of vagrancy was such that outdoor relief (poor relief given to the recipient in his or her own home, without requiring admission to a workhouse) could not be paid, and in any case one of the aims of the reform of 1834 was to end the payment of outdoor relief to the able-bodied, into which category the majority of vagrants fell. Admission to one of the new union workhouses would, of course, be unattractive to a vagrant, and it was not possible to force individuals into workhouses against their will. The problem was exacerbated by the laws of settlement and removal: the cost of relief was supposed to be borne by a pauper's parish of settlement, to which he or she could be, and often was, removed. However, in the case of a vagrant, the determination of her, or more usually his, parish of settlement was often difficult or impossible. Nevertheless, poor law authorities were required to relieve the poor, and therefore to make provision for vagrants. For vagrants in London, the Metropolitan Houseless Poor Acts (1864-65), which required poor law authorities to provide relief for all homeless people, without reference to their place of settlement, was, in Seth Koven's words, "a kind of bill of rights for vagrants," and as a result was attacked by many ratepayers who were concerned about the increased costs that might ensue from the legislation.[14]

Increasingly, provision for vagrants was made in the form of a separate workhouse ward, the casual ward, known among its users as the "spike." Here, vagrants could apply for admission to spend one night only in the ward. One of the intentions of the reform of 1834 had been to segregate different categories of pauper, but in practice it took some time before specialist accommodation, including casual wards, was widely constructed. By the late 1870s, of 643 poor law unions, 572 had constructed a casual ward (Vorspan 1977, p. 61). The peak of casual ward construction was in the 1860s and 1870s, when a large program of workhouse construction was undertaken, usually taking the form of modifications to existing workhouses.[15] One of the reasons for these alterations was to expand workhouse provision in the context of a contemporaneous "crusade against outdoor relief," which was launched by the Poor Law Board in an attempt to cut the growing costs of the poor law.[16] Another feature of this period was a growing campaign, motivated by humanitarian considerations, to expose and improve workhouse conditions. Groups such as the Workhouse Visiting Society, established by the reformer Louisa Twining in 1858,[17] pressed for better conditions, and the unhealthy conditions in some metropolitan workhouses were exposed in a series of articles in the medical journal, the

---

14. Koven, Seth. *Slumming: Sexual and Social Politics in Victorian London.* Princeton, NJ: Princeton University Press, 2004, pp. 33-34.

15. Driver, Felix. "The Historical Geography of the Workhouse System in England and Wales 1834-1883." *Journal of Historical Geography*, 15, (July 1989), pp. 269-86.

16. See McKinnon, Mary. "English Poor Law Policy and the Crusade Against Out-Relief." *Journal of Economic History*, 47, (September 1987), pp. 603-25.

17. See Twining, Louisa. *Recollections of Life and Work, Being the Autobiography of Louisa Twining.* London: Arnold, 1893; Grenier, Janet E. "Twining, Louisa (1820-1912)." *Oxford Dictionary of National Biography*, 55, (2004), p. 726.

Lancet, in the mid-1860s. Other medical campaigners also pressed for workhouse reforms.[18] There was a determined effort to distinguish between the "deserving" and "undeserving" poor, embodied in the establishment of the Charity Organisation Society in 1869, which attacked the evils of "indiscriminate charity," and aimed to coordinate private and public welfare provision, by restricting charity to the "deserving" and poor relief to the "undeserving."[19]

Rachel Vorspan (1977) has shown that this distinction was widely applied to the vagrant population, as well as to the poor more generally, and that official policy on vagrancy was driven by it. The central poor law authorities, and legislation of the period, were underpinned by the distinction between the respectable vagrant, tramping in search of employment, and the degraded and work-shy "habitual tramp." The creation of casual wards was partly encouraged as a way to segregate homeless paupers from other, more permanent, inhabitants of workhouses, and there was a gradual attempt to impose harsher conditions in casual wards. A vagrant who spent the night in a casual ward would be expected to perform a work task in the morning, usually a disagreeable one such as picking oakum, breaking stones or operating a crank to grind corn.[20] In 1871, legislation required that vagrants be detained in the workhouse until 11 A.M., to ensure that the stipulated work task was carried out. This was rather counterproductive, since those inmates who were genuinely seeking work would not be able to find any as late as 11 A.M. This statute also attacked the "habitual tramp" by requiring work-houses to detain for three nights any casual pauper who visited the same ward three times in

---

18. See Richardson, Ruth & Hurwitz, Ben. "Joseph Rogers and the Reform of Workhouse Medicine." *History Workshop Journal*, 43, (Spring 1997), pp. 218-25.

19. On the C.O.S. see Lewis, Jane. *The Voluntary Sector, the State and Social Work in Britain: The Charity Organisation Society/Family Welfare Association since 1869.* Aldershot: Edward Elgar, 1995.

20. The latter was the work task performed by James Greenwood in Lambeth workhouse in 1866. See below, pp. 71–72.

a month. In 1882, the Casual Poor Act required *all* vagrants to be detained for two nights, or for four nights if it was their second application to the same place in a month. However, many poor law unions did not enforce the strict requirements of the law, being keen to move the vagrants out of their jurisdiction as quickly as possible. From 1892, official policy was relaxed, allowing vagrants to discharge themselves at 5:30 or 6 A.M. as long they claimed to be "desirous of seeking work" (Vorspan 1977, p.70). On the other hand, some workhouses made conditions less agreeable by introducing solitary confinement in casual wards, which was thought to lessen the chances of respectable work-seeking vagrants being morally contaminated by the more numerous "habitual tramps." A majority of poor law unions had adopted this policy by the early twentieth century (Vorspan 1977, pp. 68-69). Other unions policed vagrancy with a system of "way-tickets," which effectively served as a license to travel and a ticket of entitlement to relief, and the system was also used by voluntary agencies (Humphreys 1999, pp. 109-10). Again, the historical foundations of this policy can be seen in the Statute of Labourers of 1388 (see above, pp. 10–11).

The story of vagrancy in this period, then, is one of attempting to distinguish between categories of tramp, and to deal with them accordingly using the institutions of poor relief. However, although the issue of vagrancy is unavoidably seen through the lens of poor law history, it is important to bear in mind that the users of casual wards formed only a small proportion of vagrants, certainly on any one particular night. According to the report of the Royal Commission on the Poor Laws and the Relief of Distress in 1909, "the casual pauper is but an incident of vagrancy; and vagrancy, at one time swelling, at another shrinking in volume, merges into a shifting and shiftless fringe of the population in such a way as to elude definition" (quoted in Vorspan 1977, p. 63). According to a police census in the 1860s, about 15 percent of the vagrant population slept in a casual ward on any night (Vorspan 1977, p. 64). Some poor law authorities, lacking casual wards of their own, paid for vagrants to be housed in lodging houses, and these private institutions were used by many others, who begged the small sums necessary to gain entrance. Rose—basing his account on some of the sources reprinted in this book—describes a typical lodging house, with its "communal kitchen cum dining room cum day room in the basement," sleeping accommodation upstairs, and poor toilet facilities. Lodging houses, like casual wards, had separate male and female sleeping quarters, but the sexes often mixed during the day. They were susceptible to "gatecrashing" by people who had not paid, and theft and violence were common, especially in the nineteenth century, although there had been "some improvement" by the 1900s, when the "pervading atmosphere was one of dinginess rather than danger."[21] After 1908, old-age pensions supported some people's lives in lodging houses (Rose 1988, p. 72). Other vagrants were housed temporarily by charitable organizations, such as the Salvation Army or Church Army, while in the summer months many spent whole nights out of doors. These vagrants often got very little sleep: it was difficult, especially in London, to sleep on the streets at night without being woken up and "moved on" by the police. Jack London described a night "carrying the banner"— wandering around the metropolis all night—and thus explained why so many tramps slept in the capital's parks during the day (1903, chapter 10). Another social explorer, Howard Goldsmid, recalled: "Often have I met a man and his wife, each with a sleeping child in their arms, walking aimlessly about the streets, as they have walked through all the weary hours of the long, silent night ... to these poor wretches anything would be better than tramping the hard flags, whose resonant echoes mock their heavy footfalls."[22] Despite the sympathy elicited by cases such as this, vagrancy remained a crime, and many reformers believed that it should be entirely removed from the remit of the poor law and turned over the police (Vorspan 1977, pp. 74-75). Again, this suggestion reflected the harshness of contemporaneous attitudes to the "undeserving" poor.

The distinction between the "deserving" and "undeserving" vagrant reflected the ubiquity, especially from the 1880s, of the

---

21. Rose 1988, pp. 67-9, citing Everard Wyrall, Mary Higgs, and George Z. Edwards.

22. Goldsmid, Howard. *Dottings of a Dosser, Being Revelations of the Inner Life of Low London Lodging-Houses.* London: T. Fisher Unwin, 1886, p. 76.

concepts of the "residuum" and, later, the "unemployable." In both Britain and the United States, according to John Welshman, there was a "sudden interest in the residuum in the 1880s";[23] this interest, perhaps, peaked with the publication, in 1890, of William Booth's *In Darkest England and the Way Out*, which famously described the "submerged tenth" of the population.[24] Of course, the distinction between the "deserving" and "undeserving" poor, between the "respectable" and the "residuum," has a longer history, but it carried particular force in the context of the social crises of the 1880s. Gareth Stedman Jones has argued that the importance of the idea of the residuum lay in contemporaneous fears of the revolutionary potential of an alliance between the residuum and the respectable; the latter were susceptible to contamination by the residuum, and the apparent effects of this contamination could be seen in the Trafalgar Square riots of 1886 and the London dock strike of 1889.[25] Andrew Mearns's pamphlet, *The Bitter Cry of Outcast London*, published in 1883, described squalid housing, deep poverty and gross immorality in the slums of London. *The Bitter Cry* caught the popular mood, and prompted a rush of similar pamphlets, which competed with each other to reveal the worst horrors of working-class life in London and elsewhere. Vagrants were a growing part of the residuum, and increased attention was given to the problem of vagrancy by the social investigators of the 1880s; there are some examples in this book. Although it seems highly unlikely that lodging houses could ever have encouraged or sustained a revolution, this fear was widely expressed in the 1880s, for example by Howard Goldsmid, who urged reform of London's "doss-houses" in order to prevent revolution (Rose 1988, pp. 74-75; Goldsmid 1886, pp. 136-67). Public and private agencies gave detailed consideration to

---

23. Welshman, John. *Underclass: A History of the Excluded 1880-2000.* London: Hambledon Continuum, 2006, p. 2.

24. Booth, William. *In Darkest England and the Way Out.* London: Salvation Army, 1890, part 1, chapter 2.

25. Jones, Gareth Sledman. *Outcast London: A Study in the Relationship between Classes in Victorian Society.* Oxford: Clarendon Press, 1971, chapter 16.

methods of dealing with vagrancy: there was even a published guide for "Christian workers," which introduced aspects of tramps' behavior and culture, and translated their slang.[26]

The same concerns, and social distinctions, pervaded the social discourse of the 1900s, when the term "residuum" fell out of favor, but the idea of the "unemployable" was widely floated.[27] Rising unemployment in the early 1900s, together with the return of servicemen from the second Boer War (1899-1902) gave rise to increased levels of vagrancy, and attention was turned to local poor law officials, who—or so it was thought at the Local Government Board—were too lax in their administration of the law, and "were not applying the rules regarding casual applicants with sufficient rigour" (Humphreys 1999, p. 113). In particular, the terms of the Casual Poor Act were not being adhered to, and compulsory detention beyond one night was not being enforced. The result of these concerns was the appointment in 1904 of a Departmental Committee on Vagrancy, which reported in 1906. Echoing the mantras of the Charity Organisation Society, the report blamed "indiscriminate dole-giving" for the existence of vagrancy, and recommended, among other things, that the police assume responsibility for vagrancy, that labor colonies be established in which vagrants could be compulsorily detained for six months or more, and that lodging houses and voluntary shelters be more strictly regulated (Humphreys 1999, pp. 113-15). Although not all these recommendations were accepted, the tenor of official policy remained harsh. This did not prevent the number of vagrants relieved in casual wards from increasing during the Edwardian period, from around 5,000 each night in 1900, to more than 7,000 in 1902, about 9,000 in 1905, and almost 10,000 by 1910 (Humphreys 1999, p. 115). Again, it must be remembered that those sleeping in casual wards represented only a small proportion of all vagrants in England on any single night.

---

26. Newton, William. *Secrets of Tramp Life Revealed, Or a Guide to the Public.* Ashton-under-Lyne: J. B. Sharpley, [1886], p. 7.

27. Welshman, John. "The Concept of the Unemployable." *Economic History Review*, 59, (August 2006), pp. 578-606.

The Committee's recommendation of labor colonies reflected a widely shared social reform agenda of the period. The labor colony as a tool of social policy was advocated across the political spectrum, although in practice very few such institutions were actually established. The social investigator Charles Booth "very tentatively" suggested using labor colonies to remove the lowest social classes from London and thereby free the more respectable sections of the working classes from the labor competition of the residuum;[28] and the Salvation Army labor colony was William Booth's suggested "way out" of Darkest England. Although different people meant different things when they proposed the establishment of labor colonies, the idea was usually based around removing people from an urban environment, and setting them to work in agricultural or other rural employment, away from the dirt and vice of the city. The degree of compulsion in labor colony proposals varied considerably: for some, such as William Booth, the labor colony was a place to which people should go voluntarily; for others, it was a place where the "unemployable" classes should be forcibly taken and set to work. For the Webbs, William Beveridge, and Seebohm Rowntree, some form of compulsion was necessary for the unemployable class: Rowntree, for example, had "no doubt" that labor colonies would be suitable places in which "treatment" of members of the "work-shy" class could take place.[29] Even the Labour Party, in its "New Unemployed Bill" published in 1907, advocated forcing the work-shy to labor. Section 3 of the Bill, as Ramsay MacDonald reported, proposed:

> "When the local unemployment authority are of opinion that unemployment in any case is owing to deliberate and habitual disinclination to work, they may report the case to a court of summary jurisdiction, and the court may issue an order which shall permit the

28. Welshman, *Underclass*, p. 12; Brown, John. "Charles Booth and Labour Colonies 1889-1905." *Economic History Review*, 21, (August 1968), pp. 349-60.

29. Rowntree, B. Seebohm & Lasker, Bruno. *Unemployment: A Social Study*. London: Macmillan, 1911, p. 199.

local unemployment authority to enforce control over the person named in the order for a period not exceeding six months, which period must be passed in the performance of reasonable work under the supervision of the local unemployment authority."

Commenting on this provision, MacDonald's account further remarked:

"However little one may like it, such a provision is necessary in any comprehensive measure like this. Some men are born loafers, more still are made loafers by evil social conditions; but, whatever may be his origin, the loafer exists and has to be dealt with. He must not be allowed to damage the claims of the deserving temporarily unemployed. So long as he is mixed up with the unemployed his little ways and escapades will be palmed off, as though he were a typical example of the mass, upon a public only too willing to hear unfavourable things about the poor unfortunate out-of-work."[30]

A stint in a labor colony would help to improve the character of the "habitual" loafer. This bill, along with much else in this period relating to unemployment, did not directly address the issue of vagrancy; however, similar distinctions, and a similar focus on character, were evident throughout the literature on vagrancy.

*   *   *   *   *

Distinguishing between the various social and economic problems of the period lay at the heart of the growth of systematic social investigation in the late nineteenth and early twentieth century. The social surveys of Charles Booth and Seebohm Rowntree, focusing on the problem of urban poverty, together with the increasing involvement of government in social research, repre-

---

30. MacDonald, J. Ramsay. *The New Unemployed Bill of the Labour Party.* London: Independent Labour Party, 1907, pp. 10-11.

sented the emergence of a 'scientific' approach to the understanding of social problems.[31] However, vagrants were not easily
susceptible to this kind of social inquiry. For example, the census,
although it recorded those who spent census night in a casual ward
or lodging house, could not accurately enumerate those who spent
the night sleeping out of doors. Similarly, the house-to-house
poverty surveys used by Seebohm Rowntree and other social
investigators in the Edwardian period were, obviously, of little use
in the study of homelessness. Anne Crowther has argued that
knowledge and understanding of vagrant life was peculiarly
dependent on literary and descriptive sources: vagrancy, "more
elusive than most social problems," "remained an issue where the
creative writer offered as much guidance as a blue book [i.e. an
official report], especially as the basic tools of the reformer—
plausible statistics—were lacking."[32] Moreover, even where statistics were available—for example, nightly tallies of admissions to
casual wards—such information illuminated only the scale of the
problem, and said little about its causes or potential remedies.
There were some accounts of tramp life "from the inside," either
genuinely or purportedly, but these were uncommon, and those
who wrote them were atypical of the vagrant population, such as
the tramping poet W. H. Davies, whose *Autobiography of a Super-
Tramp* was published in 1908. Therefore, the tradition of
impressionistic social description, which was used to such powerful
literary and dramatic effect in the mid-nineteenth century by men
such as Henry Mayhew and John Hollingshead,[33] to convey the
lifestyles of the metropolitan underworld, remained an important

---

31. Booth, Charles (Ed.). *Life and Labour of the People in London*. London:
Macmillan, 1902. 17 vols.; Rowntree, B. Seebohm. *Poverty: A Study of Town Life*.
London: Macmillan, 1901.

32. Crowther, M. A. "The Tramp." In Porter, Roy (Ed.). *Myths of the English*.
Cambridge: Polity, 1992, pp. 91-113, at 101, 110.

33. See Wohl, Anthony S. "Social Explorations among the London Poor:
Theatre or Laboratory?" *Revue Française de Civilisation Britannique*, 6, (février 1991),
pp. 77-97.

feature of middle-class efforts to illuminate the Victorian and Edwardian vagrant subculture, and to explore possible remedies for the growing problem of vagrancy.

The social explorers whose work is reprinted in this volume all have one thing in common: they operated incognito. This strategy enabled them to communicate directly with the investigated population, without having to negotiate the barriers of social class that were encountered by those who met the working-class population in other ways. The very difficulty of communicating with the investigated population enhanced the importance of adopting suitable methods of investigation, and of conveying to the reader the sense that these methods had successfully yielded results. Anthony S. Wohl explains that

> "the emphasis on the urban poor as sullen or aggressive savages, leading very different lives from the writers unearthing them, could raise an awkward question in the minds of the reader [sic]: how could these authors possibly get close enough to these strange natives to win their confidence and so write about them with any authenticity? The interview technique [as used by Mayhew] was vital here, for it suggested that an intimacy with the slum-dwellers had been achieved, and that denizens of the slums were relaxed enough to tell all, to hold back nothing, however shocking. And as the genre developed, another dramatic device was used, one that planted in the mind of the reader an extra element of terror to the enterprise of penetrating the slums—that of the writer daringly going down to the slums in disguise" (1991, pp. 91-92).

This method was applied to many social groups. Beatrice Webb worked incognito as a "plain trouser hand" in the East End of London while investigating the tailoring trades for the Industry series of Charles Booth's survey; and Booth himself spent three separate periods as a lodger in a working-class London street. Richard Jefferies, a popular writer on rural life, adopted clandestine techniques of investigation; and Christopher Holdenby's *Folk of the Furrow* (1913) told of the pseudonymous author's undercover work as an agricultural laborer, although the extent of his incognito status was rather questionable.[34] Olive Malvery, one of the most widely read social explorers of the Edwardian period, spent long periods living incognito among the poor, taking various jobs in factories and shops.[35]

However, vagrants were undoubtedly the most widely investigated social group using the incognito technique. The authors of our texts came from a wide range of backgrounds, and dealt with different geographical areas—London, the north of England, and rural Hertfordshire—but many common themes run through their accounts. The texts represent three distinct periods of social concern: the 1860s, when the problem of vagrancy appeared to be worsening, and the conditions within workhouses, as well as the apparently spiralling costs of poor relief, were the subject of widespread debate; the 1880s, when the issue of the social "residuum" was at the forefront of political discussion; and the 1900s, when vagrancy was once again an important issue, as large-scale unemployment and concerns about "national efficiency" were high on the political agenda.[36] In the last period, the landslide election victory of a reforming Liberal government in 1906 gave a further spur to debates about vagrancy, as did the report of the Departmental Committee on Vagrancy in the same year, and the Royal Commission on the Poor Laws, which sat from 1905 to 1909. Only one text in this book dates from outside these three periods: J. R. Widdup's *Casual Ward System*, which was published in 1894.

---

34. Freeman 2001, pp. 114-15; Freeman, Mark. *Social Investigation and Rural England.* Woodbridge: Boydell & Brewer, 2003, pp. 63-64, 147; Holdenby, Christopher. *Folk of the Furrow.* London: Smith, Elder, 1913. Holdenby's real name was Ronald George Hatton.

35. Malvery, Olive. *The Soul Market, with which Is Included "The Heart of Things."* London: Hutchinson, 1906; Cohen, Susan and Fleay, Clive. "Fighters for the Poor." *History Today,* 50, (January 2000), pp. 36-37. Malvery also explored vagrant life using the incognito method.

36. See Searle, G. R. *The Quest for National Efficiency: A Study in British Politics and Political Thought 1899-1914.* Oxford: Blackwell, 1971.

James Greenwood is the best known of the vicarious vagrants in this book. Greenwood (1832-1929), known as the "Amateur Casual," was the brother of Frederick Greenwood, editor of the *Pall Mall Gazette*, a London newspaper ("written by gentlemen for gentlemen") with a small circulation that was started in 1865. Greenwood's three articles in the *Gazette*, published in 1866 under the title "A Night in a Workhouse," told of his experience, disguised as a vagrant, in the casual ward of Lambeth workhouse in south London. In a period when workhouse conditions were giving rise to widespread public concern, the articles struck a chord with the reading public: the *Gazette*'s circulation doubled immediately in their wake.[37] The problem of vagrancy in London had been highlighted in the popular press during the cold winter of 1865-66, when the provisions of the Metropolitan Houseless Poor Acts were beginning to take effect. Greenwood's articles were reprinted in *The Times*, and in pamphlet form. They described the squalid conditions endured by the occupants of the casual ward, and, in many cases, their uncouth behavior and laziness when faced with the compulsory work task in the morning. Greenwood, who was paid the considerable sum of £30 for his articles, was accompanied on the venture into the workhouse by a friend, a stockbroker named Bittlestone, who was "erased entirely" from the text of *A Night in a Workhouse* (Koven 2004, pp. 33-36; Stead 1893, p. 144). W. T. Stead, who later carried out incognito investigations of his own,[38] wrote in 1893: "from that one night spent in the casual ward of the Lambeth Workhouse may be traced the beginning of the reform of our Poor Law" (p. 145).

Although this was a rather exaggerated claim, another remark by Stead does capture the impact of Greenwood's articles on investigative journalism: "To us, to-day, after all the immense development of journalism, the exploit of the 'Amateur Casual' may seem a little thing; but to the journalists of a quarter of a

---

37. Stead, W. T. "The 'Pall Mall Gazette.'" *Review of Reviews*, 7, (February 1893), pp. 139-56, at 144.

38. See Simpson, Antony E. (Ed.) *The Maiden Tribute of Modern Babylon.* Lambertville, NJ: The True Bill Press, 2007 (orig. 1885).

century ago it seemed something almost super-human" (1893, p. 144). The articles, and the incognito method, certainly caused a stir. We reprint one example of the widespread attention that Greenwood provoked: a versified summary of his night in Lambeth workhouse, written by "M.A." (it is not clear who "M.A." was). There were also theatrical versions of Greenwood's exploits, and "Daddy," the workhouse inmate who oversaw admissions to the casual ward, became an overnight hero.[39] The scandalous activity in the casual ward—some implicitly sexual—prompted a popular outcry (Koven 2004, chapter 1). There were a number of imitators of Greenwood, two of whom were arrested, and one of these imprisoned, for obtaining poor relief by deception. One imitation that found its way into print, rather than into the reports of the police court, was an investigation initiated by J. H. Stallard, which is reprinted in this volume. Stallard was a member of the Royal College of Physicians, and a prominent advocate of reform of charity, sanitation, and the poor law.[40] Stallard wished to investigate conditions in women's casual wards, but believed that, although the "Amateur Casual" and other men could explore the workhouse from the inside, a middle-class woman's sensibilities would not allow her to carry out the necessary deception: her disgust at the conditions would be bound to show through her disguise (see below, p. 82; Koven 2004, pp. 54, 186). Instead he engaged a working-class widow, who used various names including Ellen Stanley and Jane Wood, to travel in disguise to a London casual ward. Apparently, even this woman found it difficult to convince the authorities that she was a genuine vagrant (see below, p. 101). The published account of this exploration, entitled *The Female Casual and Her Lodging*, is written from the points of view

---

39. Koven 2004, pp. 51-4, 63-5. "Daddy" was a pauper named Budge, who was able (temporarily) to leave the workhouse with the money he earned by posing for a photograph and by participating in a stage version of the "Night in a Workhouse."

40. See for example Stallard, J. H. *Pauperism, Charity and Poor Laws, being an Inquiry into the Present State of the Poorer Classes in the Metropolis, the Resources and Effects of Charity, and the Influence of the Poor-Law System of Relief, with Suggestions for an Improved Administration.* London: Longmans, Green, Reader and Dyer, [1868].

of both Stallard and the widow: once the descriptions of conditions have been given in the latter's words, Stallard resumes the authorial voice, discussing his own visits, in his medical capacity, to casual wards. In many respects, the story was similar to Greenwood's, focusing on the vermin, disease and foul language that were encountered in the casual ward; however, as Koven explains, in other respects,

> "Stanley's *incognito* exploration may have been inspired by Greenwood's, but the story she told was far different from his … In contrast to Greenwood's coy staging of his descent into the casual ward ... Stanley's narrative is utterly devoid of titillating pleasures. Where Greenwood lingers over his description of the bodies of the beautiful youths he encounters, Stanley feels horrified empathy for the nude, lice-infested female bodies she sees." (Koven 2004, p. 187; see below, pp. 86–87, 96, 102**).**

The Female Casual and Her Lodging is an example of "how class and gender shaped" the experiences and representations of vagrant life; and the mixture of narrative voices in the text emphasizes the fact that Stallard's experience of it was doubly vicarious: vicarious in the sense that Stanley herself was undergoing a pretense to gain access to the casual ward, and vicarious in the sense that Stallard had, necessarily, sent an investigator into the casual ward instead of venturing there himself.

The night in Lambeth workhouse in 1866 not only gave rise to imitators; it also enhanced Greenwood's own fame, and launched his career as the most daredevil social explorer of the age, rivalled only by W. T. Stead, whose undercover investigations of child prostitution in 1885 (*The Maiden Tribute of Modern Babylon*) resulted in a short prison sentence. Greenwood went on to produce many more books and articles dealing with low life, notably *The Seven Curses of London* (1869) and *Low-Life Deeps* (1876). In this collection we also reprint his long pamphlet entitled *On Tramp*, published in 1883, which is a particularly valuable account of vagrant life outside the cities, and outside the casual ward. In this source Greenwood provided evidence of the various abuses of the system, and semi-criminal activities, with which tramps in Hertfordshire, just north of London, were associated; he also demonstrated many of the ethical difficulties faced by the incognito social investigator. For example, when a well-meaning gentleman gave the undercover vagrant a job weeding his garden, Greenwood ran off without completing it; and he tacitly condoned a felony when he joined a roguish pair of tramps who were eating a roast chicken that, in his opinion, was almost certainly stolen (below, pp. 165–168, 169–170).

On Tramp was one of many studies of vagrant life that appeared in the mid-1880s, in a period of renewed concern about the lives of the poor. We have seen how contemporaneous fears about the possible contamination of the "respectable" by the "residuum" generated widespread interest in the condition of the poor, especially in London, where social unrest was particularly acute. Mearns's *The Bitter Cry of Outcast London* provoked a flurry of slum journalism, in London and the provinces. One example of a pamphlet which owed its inspiration to Mearns was *Outcast Keighley* by C. W. Craven, published in 1887. Craven was a poet, based in the Yorkshire town of Keighley, whose poems (in an indication of their quality) were published by a local relative of Craven's. Craven also published his own writing, including a pamphlet entitled "A Night in the Workhouse" (also 1887), which is reprinted in this collection. A short account, which explicitly acknowledged Craven's debt to the "Amateur Casual" (below, p. 188), "A Night in the Workhouse" shows that social concern regarding vagrancy had moved beyond London and into the provinces. Craven claimed to have had "a desire for a long time to obtain an insight into the vicissitudes of a vagrant's life" (below, p. 181) and his description of a night undercover in the casual ward bears many similarities to Greenwood's.

F. G. Wallace-Goodbody was another vicarious vagrant from the 1880s (or at least, this was when his account was published). Wallace-Goodbody is a rather obscure character, whose idiosyncratic description of "The Tramp's Haven" appeared in the *Gentleman's Magazine*. This periodical had been running since 1731, and included a wide range of material, from current affairs to fiction. According to Wallace-Goodbody's account, his adventure in the casual ward came upon him by accident; there was no deliberate act of disguise. He explained that a doctor had given him a certificate for admission to a workhouse infirmary, but that this was full, and he had been advised to go to the casual ward. The workhouse was fictionalized: it was in central

London, apparently, but there is no such street as "Sinai Avenue." However, some aspects of Wallace-Goodbody's story are similar to those of Greenwood's, such as the workhouse bread that was "singularly provocative of thirst,"[41] and the dirty bath shared by all the occupants of the ward. Here, the morning's work task was oakum-picking, whereas at Lambeth workhouse in 1866 it had been corn-grinding, and Wallace-Goodbody was kept at the task until he had picked the allotted amount, which meant that in total his stay in the ward amounted to 20 hours. Unlike Greenwood, neither Craven nor Wallace-Goodbody gave any indication of the sexual behavior of the inmates of the casual ward, and neither provoked the same popular outcry as their predecessor.

Our next vicarious vagrant is J. R. Widdup, whose pamphlet *The Casual Ward System: Its Horrors and Atrocities* (1894) told the story of the night spent by the author in the casual ward of Burnley union workhouse, in Lancashire. According to the title page of the pamphlet, the story had first been printed in *The Socialist and North-East Lancashire Labour News*. Widdup was the editor of this newspaper, which lasted from 1893 to 1896: there is no indication that its circulation was significantly boosted by Widdup's articles, as the *Pall Mall Gazette*'s had been by Greenwood's. The *Socialist*, published in Burnley, was an unofficial organ that supported the Social-Democratic Federation, and competed with the Federation's official newspaper, *Justice*.[42] As a socialist campaigner, Widdup had a natural sympathy with the plight of the inmates of the casual ward, but when he attempted to discuss socialism with his cell-mate (this casual ward had shared cell accommodation), the latter fell into silence (below, pp. 196). Many of the experiences related in this pamphlet echoed those of the vicarious vagrants of the 1860s and 1880s, although at Burnley,

---

41. Greenwood, although he did not taste the bread he was given, remarked that it seemed, like the oatmeal porridge or "skilly" that was served in the workhouse, to "provoke thirst." See below, p. 63.

42. Crick, Martin. *The History of the Social-Democratic Federation*. Keele: Keele University Press, 1994, pp. 110, 112, 120 n. 27.

the work task that Widdup was given was sawing timber. A short appendix offered detailed, if fairly modest, proposals for reform of the casual ward regime; Widdup squarely blamed the "horrors and atrocities" that he encountered on the capitalist system.

Our last three vicarious vagrants wrote their accounts in the Edwardian period. The best known of these is Mary Higgs (1854-1937), wife of a Congregationalist minister, Thomas Kilpin Higgs, of Greenacres Congregational church in Oldham, Lancashire. Higgs was a friend of W. T. Stead (as was another *incognito* social explorer, Olive Malvery), and it is probable that her undercover social researches, which began in 1903, were inspired by Stead's example. Higgs published a pamphlet entitled *Three Nights in Women's Lodging Houses* in 1905, and a collection of her social explorations, entitled *Glimpses into the Abyss*, in 1906. She gave evidence to the Departmental Committee on Vagrancy in 1906, and was an important founder member of the National Association for Women's Lodging Houses in 1909, as well as addressing a range of other social problems in her published work.[43] The article reprinted in this volume, "The Tramp Ward," was published in the *Contemporary Review* in 1904, and also appeared in pamphlet form; it was reprinted in *Glimpses into the Abyss* under the title "A Northern Tramp Ward." It is a description of a single (two-night) visit to a female casual ward in a northern workhouse, and focuses on the inhumanity of workhouse officials, on the characters who populated the casual ward, and on proposals for reform of the system.

Higgs was a well-known campaigner and social explorer, but few in 1909 would have been familiar with Everard Wyrall, whose first book, published in that year, was *The Spike*. Wyrall was born in 1878, and died in 1933, having become a prolific military historian, focusing on the First World War. *The Spike* was originally published serially, in the *Daily Express* in 1908, and it is a classic of the genre, which has not been reprinted before. The first part of *The Spike* is set somewhere in the suburbs of London (Wyrall travelled on a train from London Bridge station for twenty minutes); the events of the

---

43. See Chadwick, Rosemary. "Higgs [née Kingsland], Mary Ann (1854-1937)." *Oxford Dictionary of National Biography*, 27, (2004), pp. 78-79; [Higgs, Mary K.], *Mary Higgs of Oldham*. Wells: Clare, 1954.

second part took place to the south-west of the metropolis (he told a policeman that he was on his way to Portsmouth); and thirdly and lastly, Wyrall visited a workhouse casual ward in London itself. The last section has many unmistakable echoes of the "Amateur Casual," although Greenwood's exploits had taken place more than four decades earlier. Wyrall emphasized the need to improve casual ward accommodation, and admired the efforts of the Church Army, which housed vagrants, provided them with work, and hence improved their self-respect; thus, Wyrall thought, the Church Army's work with vagrants contrasted favorably with the "strong-hearted brutality" of the casual wards (below, pp. 273–278). Wyrall's story is an exciting one, full of dramatic intensity: at any moment, the reader feels, his disguise will be found out, and his adventures will end. Indeed, at the last workhouse he visited, he was discharged early, and believed that his real identity and purpose had been discovered (below, p. 262).

The pamphlet by George Zachary Edwards, with which this collection ends, is a much less colorful document, although, like the others, it is based on the author's incognito experiences among vagrants. As the title, *A Vicar as Vagrant*, makes clear, Edwards was a Church of England clergyman, vicar of Crossens, near Southport. A graduate of the University of Durham, Edwards had been a curate at North Meals, also near Southport, before moving in 1904 to the vicarage at Crossens, which he left for nearby Ainsdale in 1911. Accompanied by a friend, Edwards spent four days "on the road" in April 1910, staying in lodging houses. His pamphlet analyses the problem of vagrancy based partly on his own experiences, and partly on other sources, such as the minority report of the Royal Commission on the Poor Laws, which was published in 1909 (below, pp. 305–308). Predictably, Edwards discerned an important role for the church, which he exhorted, rather vaguely, to study the problem of vagrancy and, more concretely, to establish labor colonies for vagrants. In common with many Edwardian social reformers, he cited the example of Germany, where colonies were being used to address the problem.[44] Like Walter Cranfield, Edwards attended a church service in his vagrant costume (above, p. 7, below, pp. 301–302).

---

44. See below, pp. 229–230, 312. For a recent Anglo-German comparison, see Hennock, E. P. *The Origin of the Welfare State in England and Germany 1850-1914*. Cambridge: Cambridge University Press, 2007.

*   *   *   *   *

Together, the experience of these vicarious vagrants demon-
strates the popularity of incognito social exploration, and the per-
sistence of the "dramatic device" of disguise in social exploration
(Wohl 1991, p. 92). However, the usefulness of disguise extended
beyond its dramatic qualities. It was widely held that the incognito
method enabled the social explorer to find out what conditions were
like, and how poor law and charitable institutions treated the casual pauper, in a way that would not have been possible for an overt
social investigator. The exposure of the surroundings and treatment
of the vagrant was itself a powerful motivation for going undercover. Greenwood's first declared reason for visiting Lambeth workhouse was "to learn by actual experience how casual paupers are
lodged and fed" (below, p. 54). Widdup's primary concern was with
"what sort of treatment the fellows were subjected to who went
inside" the casual wards (below, p. 190). Similarly, Wyrall's *Who's
Who* entry declared him to be "one of the few who voluntarily have
donned rags and gone into casual wards of workhouses, breaking
stones and picking oakum, in order to see how the State treats
down-and-outs."[45] It was obvious to Stallard that the official visits of
a workhouse doctor, or other official, could not yield the same kind
of information as a visit in the guise of a pauper. Higgs thought that
poor law guardians had little knowledge of the conditions within
their own casual wards, and suggested that they should send undercover investigators to each others' workhouses in order to learn
more about them (below, p. 207). Reviewing Higgs's *Glimpses into
the Abyss* in the *Economic Journal*, William Beveridge saw considerable value in the alternative perspective on poor law institutions that
Higgs's researches provided:

> "For the most part, knowledge as to this class has to
> come through the various institutions that provide for
> it—that is to say, from the accounts of those in charge
> of casual wards, shelters, and common lodging-houses.
> Mrs Higgs is able to show the homeless life from

---

45. "Wyrall, Reginald Everard [1878-1933]." *Who Was Who, 1929-1940.*
London: Adam and Charles Black, 1947, p. 1,499.

another point of view, and to supplement the study of the vagrant through the institutions as they appear to the vagrant."[46]

The effectiveness of this approach is suggested by many observations that are common to most of the texts. The cruelty of workhouse officials was often commented upon. Wallace-Goodbody's violent "tramp-master" was just the worst example of the many villainous characters that appear in this book, although Greenwood's "Daddy" was a notable exception, as was the kindly male official encountered by Stallard's investigator, at Whitechapel, who allowed her to wear her own clothes instead of the verminous workhouse uniform (below, p. 95). The vermin encountered in casual wards was another common theme, as was the poor bedding, the dryness of workhouse bread and the saltiness of the oatmeal porridge or "skilly," and the ill health—symptomized by incessant coughing—of the vagrant population. These features of the casual ward regime shocked the sensibilities of these middle-class vicarious vagrants.

Of course, the factual information that they presented is not susceptible to verification, and some of their claims may have been exaggerated. Their bravery is not in doubt—following Greenwood's exploits, one commentator remarked that he deserved a Victoria Cross for his bravery[47]—although, according to Vorspan, their sanity might be.[48] There is no way of verifying their accounts, which were clearly, in some cases, selective. For example, Koven has focused on Greenwood's complete removal from his account of his

---

46. *Economic Journal,* 16, (December 1906), pp. 581-83, at 581.

47. Keating, Peter (Ed.). *Into Unknown England 1866-1913: Selections from the Social Explorers.* Manchester: Manchester University Press, 1976, pp. 15-16. The Victoria Cross is a military medal; the George Cross would have been a more suitable suggestion.

48. Vorspan 1977, p. 67: "their experiences in the casual wards were so uniformly horrific that they prompt one to speculate upon the psychology of the participants in these experiments."

friend Bittlestone, who accompanied him into Lambeth workhouse (2004, p. 36). Other omissions were deliberately highlighted to emphasize the awfulness of the conditions that had been encountered. Greenwood ended his pamphlet with the sentence: "I have some horrors . . . infinitely more revolting than anything that appears in these papers" (below, p. 75). Koven has strongly suggested that this referred to homosexual activity in the casual ward, a feature that appears close to, but still beneath, the surface of much of Greenwood's account (2004, chapter 1). Other aspects of tramp life reported by the vicarious vagrants may have been exaggerated, and Vorspan has suggested that they may have deliberately sought out the most notorious casual wards in order to enhance the dramatic qualities of their accounts, although Higgs avoided the worst places because of concerns about her personal safety (Vorspan 1977, p. 68; Higgs 1906, pp. 175-76). Moreover, they were writing from memory: it would undermine their disguise if they made notes while "in the field." The long sections of reported speech in some of the accounts could be, at best, approximations of what was actually said.

The vicarious vagrants sometimes claimed that they had been able to communicate more freely with those under investigation than would have been the case if they had been overt social researchers. This was at least as important as discovering the conditions in which the casual pauper was lodged. For example, Stallard announced: "Association on the footing of equality is as necessary to secure the confidence of the vagrant as it is to disarm official caution; and considerable address is required to pass through the wards without arousing the suspicion of the police and the attendants, and without exciting the jealousy and anger of the paupers themselves" (below, p. 81–82). Once the disguise had been successful, and the vicarious vagrant admitted to the ranks of the casual poor, useful information was easily available. Higgs claimed that it was impossible to spend time as a tramp among tramps "without eliciting confidence," and boasted that she came to know her fellow inmates of the casual ward "intimately," and "extracted much information and confirmation of personal histories and social condition" (below, pp. 216, 222, and 225). When Widdup was in the timber yard at Burnley workhouse, one of the many talkative paupers "with childlike simplicity told me all about himself" (below, p. 202). The accounts in this book are peppered with ethnographic insights that appear to reflect a sensitive interaction with the investigated population. Craven, for example, learned from one inmate of the Keighley casual ward that he never went out on Sundays, because he disliked the way in which the respectable inhabitants shunned him in the street (below, p. 185). Wyrall, almost as soon as he had donned his tramp's clothes, learned "how deeply one can be made to feel poverty," finding himself shunned by passers-by and feeling an overwhelming desire to hide himself away (below, p. 233). The vicarious vagrants, then, were eager to signal themselves as having obtained unrivalled access to the vagrant underworld, and to have shared in the feelings as well as the lifestyles of their subjects.

However, their experience of the vagrant underworld was usually transient, and did not reflect the realities as experienced by the people under investigation. They were usually accompanied or protected in some way.[49] As noted above, Greenwood was accompanied by his friend Bittlestone; Wyrall, when visiting one particularly notorious "spike," took a friend with him; and Edwards was accompanied by a young companion, who was an experienced boxer, as a result of which the vicar "felt more than safe in his care in whatever rough and wicked company we got" (above, p. 27, below, pp. 256 and 281). Higgs usually travelled with a companion, and on one occasion when she could find nobody to travel with her, she arranged to be shadowed by a plain-clothed policeman.[50] Moreover, with some exceptions, their experience of the vagrant underworld was brief. Greenwood and Craven based pamphlets on just one night in a workhouse, although Greenwood later went on longer tramping expeditions: *On Tramp* is one example. Higgs undertook only short stints in the 'abyss'; her account reprinted here is of a single visit to a northern casual ward. Her longest journey was one of five days and five nights. Wyrall's tramping experiences appear to have been confined to three short episodes. Edwards and his companion spent four days "on the road," staying in lodging houses. Edwards described the experience of spending the whole night out of doors, but made it clear that the experience was his companion's, and not his own (below,

---

49. See Brunt, Lodewijk. "The Ethnography of 'Babylon': The Rhetoric of Fear and the Study of London 1850-1914." *City & Society*, 4, (June 1990), pp. 77-87.

50. Higgs 1906, pp. 250-51. For other examples, see Freeman 2001, p. 109.

pp. 294–297). The vicarious vagrants who went to the casual wards often found that the food was of such poor quality that they did not eat it, making a choice that was not available to their fellow casuals.[51] Greenwood's (and Bittlestone's) relief at enjoying a glass of sherry and a bath at the end of his visit to the casual ward can easily be imagined.[52] The depth of their penetration of the abyss, therefore, can be called into question.

On the other hand, it was possible for even a brief exploration of the vagrant underworld to yield useful and interesting information. Higgs claimed that it was "surprisingly easy" to become a vagrant (below, p. 207). Tramp life was relatively accessible, compared with the closed domestic world of the urban working classes. Contemporaries who attempted participant-observation studies of the "respectable" working classes found significant barriers between themselves and the objects of their investigation, and the experience of work or home life among the poor required a longer-term and more dedicated spell of social exploration.[53] In a later period, George Orwell remarked: "Nothing is easier than to be bosom pals with a pickpocket, if you know where to look for him; but it is very difficult to be bosom pals with a bricklayer."[54] The Liberal journalist and politician C. F. G. Masterman explained that, in the working-class district of south London in which he went to live as a social investigator, "[t]here is no speech or language, no manifest human intercourse," and that "next-door neighbours are strangers to each other; in the midst of this human hive many walk solitary."[55] By

---

51. Wallace-Goodbody, however, ironically recalled having "enjoyed a banquet composed of brown bread and water," below, p. 135.

52. See below, p. 73 for the glass of sherry; Stead 1893, p. 144 for the bath.

53. See for example Reeves, Maud Pember. *Round About a Pound a Week*. London: G. Bell and Sons, 1913; Reynolds, Stephen. A *Poor Man's House*. London: John Lane, 1909; Freeman 2001, p. 110; Freeman 2003, chapter 5.

54. Orwell, George. *The Road to Wigan Pier*. Harmondsworth: Penguin, 1962 (orig. 1937), p. 135.

55. Masterman, C. F. G. *From the Abyss: Of Its Inhabitants by One of Them*. London: R. B. Johnson, 1902, pp. 86, 33.

contrast, tramps were talkative, and there were many occasions in their lives at which a conversation might be struck up. Queuing, which the vagrant had to do frequently in the course of obtaining food or shelter, was one: for example, Wyrall conversed with other vagrants in the queue for admission to a doss-house, and Craven waiting for breakfast (below, pp. 264–267 and 186). The morning work task in the casual ward provided another opportunity: as noted above, Widdup found his companions talkative in the morning, although they had been much quieter in the bathroom the previous night (below, pp. 199–200 and 192). Shared sleeping accommodation and eating areas provided opportunities for social interaction, and, once a vicarious vagrant had gained a little experience, he or she was able to share information about the quality of food or accommodation in particular casual wards or lodging houses: Higgs provides an example (below, p. 216–218).[56] Cranfield pointed out that "[o]ne of the first noticeable features of low life is its gregariousness," and another explorer identified a "freemasonry of want," to which the vicarious vagrant could be speedily admitted.[57] Even the act of disguise itself brought about subtle changes in experience. Later, Orwell remembered similar feelings:

> "My new clothes had put me instantly into a new world. Everyone's demeanour seemed to have changed abruptly … Clothes are powerful things. Dressed in a tramp's clothes it is very difficult, at any rate for the first day, not to feel that you are genuinely degraded. You might feel the same shame, irrational but very real, your first night in prison."[58]

Of course, Orwell did not know what the first night of a prison sentence was like, but could only say that one "might feel" in the

---

56. See also Freeman 2001, pp. 110-11.

57. Flynt, Josiah. *Tramping with Tramps: Studies and Sketches of Vagabond Life.* New York: Century, 1899, p. 67; Crane 1910, pp. 105-06.

58. Orwell, George. *Down and Out in Paris and London.* London: Secker and Warburg, 1986 (orig. 1933), p. 130.

way that he described. This captures both the limitations and the strengths of vicarious vagrancy. In a modern context, Tom Hall has emphasized the limited extent to which undercover slum journalists can really "tell us anything about what it really is to be poor," given the inherent "artificiality" of the exercise. However, he goes on to argue that

> "it would be depressing to conclude that just because we cannot *be* another person we cannot know their life in some meaningful way. The truth, surely, is that you don't have to get under anyone's skin in order to forge an understanding. Alongside will do ... [The social explorer] may not know what [her subjects'] lives really *are*, but this does not stop her finding out a bit about what they're *like*."[59]

To this extent at least, the work of social explorers, whether they operated incognito or not, was capable of conveying insights of potential interest and value into the lives of another social class or group; and in this respect they fulfilled an important social and political function.

*   *   *   *   *

The social reportage of this period, including vicarious vagrancy, has attracted a large body of scholarship; however, as Wohl notes, literary scholars have been the most active in the field, focusing on the language used to represent the urban poor (1991, p. 81). With some exceptions,[60] few have seen the late nineteenth- and early twentieth-century vicarious vagrants as forerunners of

---

59. Hall, Tom. "Through a Glass Darkly: Undercover in Low-Pay Britain and America." *Sociology*, 38, (July 2004), pp. 623-30, at 626. Original emphases.

60. See Brunt 1990; Freeman 2001; Parssinen, Carol Ann. "Social Explorers and Social Scientists: The Dark Continent of Victorian Ethnography." In Ruby, Jay (Ed.). *A Crack in the Mirror: Reflexive Perspectives in Anthropology*. Philadelphia: University of Pennsylvania Press, 1982, pp. 205-19.

modern sociological or anthropological researchers, or even of today's journalists who travel into the slums to report on the conditions that they encounter there. Whereas Charles Booth and Seebohm Rowntree have been assimilated into the historiography of modern quantitative social research,[61] one can search in vain for references to the incognito social explorers of the same period in accounts of the development of participant observation methodology. The tradition of urban social description was very deliberately excised from the historiography of British empirical sociology in the 1930s. For example, the social researcher and historian A. F. Wells, in a study of social surveys published in 1935, denied Henry Mayhew a place in his canon of social investigators on the grounds that his method was "essentially non-statistical: it is rather the concrete descriptive method of a journalist or novelist. His spiritual relatives are Dickens and Defoe." Wells claimed that quantitative survey work was required to substantiate the accounts of investigators such as Mayhew, and that "the journalistic method when used by itself is unsafe, even dangerous."[62] The association of slum journalists such as Greenwood and Jack London with working-class fiction has compounded this exclusion from the history of social research; this is epitomized, for example, by John Marriott and Masaie Matsumura's characterization of this kind of writing as "semifactual."[63] Our own examples make it clear that social research often crossed over into descriptive literature: Wallace-Goodbody's text, in particular, provides evidence of this. However, although social exploration has many literary qualities, it can also be associated with the emerging social science of the period. Those who studied the lives of the poor were aware that different methods of investigation were available to them. Carol Ann Parssinen draws an

---

61. See, for example, Kent, Raymond A. *A History of British Empirical Sociology.* Aldershot: Gower, 1981.

62. Wells, A. F. *The Local Social Survey in Great Britain.* London: Allen and Unwin, 1935, p. 14.

63. Marriott, John, and Matsumura, Masaie. *The Metropolitan Poor: Semifactual Accounts 1795-1910.* London: Pickering and Chatto, 1999. 6 vols.

analogy between the social explorers of our period and "professional ethnographic research": like modern researchers, "they charted
an essential methodology in seeking first-hand knowledge of the
poor and, in some cases, living among their subjects for short periods of time" (1982, p. 206). This does not mean that we have to
believe every word that the vicarious vagrants wrote; however, if we
accept that they had a clear methodological awareness, we can view
them as participants in an evolving project of social investigation,
and thereby reintegrate them into the longer history of social
research methodologies.

Their contemporaries did not always draw a rigid distinction
between the emerging "scientific" social survey and alternative
methods of information-gathering. Some participant observers
themselves identified an antagonism between impressionistic social
description and quantitative research, preferring their own methods
to those of the new caste of researchers whom Cranfield sneeringly
dismissed as "sociological students" (Crane 1910, p. viii). Another
incognito explorer declared his contempt for "gentlemen who have
academic positions, and say 'sociology'" (quoted in Freeman 2001,
p. 116). Nevertheless, many in this period recognized that there was
room for a variety of approaches to social inquiry: for example,
Reginald Bray, a social investigator of the period, remarked:

> "we are in an age which desires exact knowledge;
> and that desire, in its craving after satisfaction, takes
> many forms. It may find its fulfilment in long columns
> of statistics; it may see itself realised in an intricate
> chain of reasoning; or it may win its goal in a series of
> impressionist studies. Any one of these deserves the epi-
> thet scientific, provided the result is an accurate picture
> of facts."[64]

Similarly, William Beveridge praised Mary Higgs for showing
"homeless life from another point of view," in impressionistic
accounts which, importantly, "carry the stamp of truth, and are

---

64. Bray, Reginald. Review of Reynolds, *A Poor Man's House. Sociological Review*,
2, (April 1909), pp. 196-98, at 196.

indeed completely in accord with other evidence."[65] The similarity of many of the vicarious vagrants' experiences enhanced their trustworthiness, and hence their place in the canon of sociological or "scientific" research. Higgs herself even declared that "exploration" was "the method of science" (Higgs 1906, p. vii; quoted in Keating 1976, p. 28).

It is certainly possible to use insights from modern sociological literature to help us, as historians, to interpret the methods of the vicarious vagrants. Like modern ethnographers, the vicarious vagrants encountered the problem of constructing an ethnographic narrative from their experiences, although they often structured their narrative differently from today's practitioners of the method (Parssinen 1982, p. 214). For Parssinen,

> "In choosing to adopt the disguise of a native, Greenwood and [Jack] London were obliged to grapple with the paradox that lies at the heart of participant observation. That is, they had to stand both inside and outside their experience and then make what they had discovered coherent for others" (1982, p. 208).

Modern academic ethnographers often structure their texts thematically; this undermines the dramatic quality of the work and enhances the authority of the research. However, journalistic versions of participant observation research tend to adopt the kind of narrative deployed by the social explorers of a century ago. Thus, for example, Polly Toynbee's account of life on low pay in modern Britain begins by explaining the motivation for her venture into social exploration, and then goes to on to describe the unpleasant experience of moving into a flat in a rundown area. Toynbee then narrates her experiences episodically, in the same way as the vicarious vagrants in this book. There is one "heart pounding" moment when, just like Everard Wyrall nearly a century earlier, Toynbee fears that her disguise might be seen through, in this case by leading political figures whom she knows from her work as a *Guardian*

65. Beveidge, William. Review of Higgs, *Glimpses into the Abyss. Economic Journal*, 16, (December 1906), pp. 581-83, at 581, 583.

journalist (2003, pp. 120-21). The basic project of modern undercover explorers is the same as that of those who disguised themselves in our period, and often the language used is strikingly similar, although new media have broadened the means of dissemination. In 1976, Peter Keating remarked:

> "No week now passes without the story of some voyage of social exploration being carried into the homes of millions of viewers, including the homes of those being explored. And because the problems have shifted rather than changed, the methods employed to provoke attention are little different from those pioneered by the Victorians and Edwardians" (p. 31).

The methods are similar; however, as Lodewijk Brunt argues, there are important differences between the social explorers of the nineteenth and early twentieth centuries and those of today. Brunt concludes that social explorers used a particular "rhetoric of fear," which was "relatively specific to the second half of the 19th century, to England, and to the class the social explorers belonged to" (1990, pp. 83-84). The distinctiveness of our vicarious vagrants lies in the historical circumstances in which they operated. Social problems, as Keating avers, may have "shifted rather than changed," but the shift is not inconsiderable, and the problem of vagrancy was explored in the specific context of the Victorian and Edwardian institutional arrangements for dealing with it. Hence there was a heavy focus on casual wards, even though only a minority of vagrants used them.

Brunt's "rhetoric of fear" pervades this book, and in particular the fear that the "habitual tramp" would contaminate the more respectable members of the vagrant class. Brunt argues that a distinctive feature of the literature of urban social description in this period was the distinction between "good" and "evil" members of the poorer classes of society, or what John Hollingshead in 1861 called the "patient, hard-working poor" and the "noisy crowds" below them (Brunt 1990, p. 85). Such distinctions took more sophisticated form under the terms "respectable" and "residuum," or "deserving" and "undeserving." Similarly, Vorspan argues that the central message of the vicarious vagrants was that respectable casuals were treated with undue harshness by the system, and that they were morally contaminated by the disreputable majority that frequented the casual wards and lodging houses (1977, pp. 68-69). She notes that a "ubiquitous assumption underlying nineteenth-century social literature was the belief that immoral habits and behavior patterns are communicable," and quotes Stallard to illustrate this: "no honest woman [claimed Stallard] can hear the language used in the wards, or associate with the characters who habitually live there, without contracting infamy" (1977, p. 68; below, p. 111). Stallard drew a clear distinction between the "two distinct classes" of casual ward inmate: the "old stagers" who were almost unreformable, and the "really destitute" class, which needed protection from "the degrading and contaminating influences" within the wards, which included the physical surroundings and the less reputable inmates themselves (below, pp. 110–112). Greenwood's account of his night in Lambeth workhouse contrasts the behavior of the respectable and the apparently unreformable, especially in their differing attitudes to the compulsory work task. His description of rural vagrancy in Hertfordshire also features disreputable activities among the vagrant population. In 1910, Edwards identified "two great classes of men" whom one met among vagrants: on the one hand, "professional mouchers, pickpockets, thieves, habitual beggars, and the hangers-on of the great cities," and on the other hand the "vile and outcast," dragged down by unemployment and "bad surroundings" (below, pp. 288–291). Widdup, whose socialist beliefs led him to lay more emphasis on environmental causes of immoral behavior, nevertheless contrasted two "fairly decent fellows" with another, "one of the worst types of ruffianism, which capitalism produces" (below, p. 201). Not all the sources drew this distinction—Wallace-Goodbody, for example, was concerned mainly to describe the squalor and cruelty of the casual ward, and had little to say about its inmates, except as victims of the behavior of the workhouse officials—but it was important, even in the versified account of Greenwood's exploits by the anonymous "M.A.," who remarked: "Of decent men there were but few,/Within this dreadful Workhouse" (below, p. 79).

The remedies proposed in most of these sources reflect the widespread punitive attitude towards the "undeserving," especially in the Edwardian period. This went hand in hand with sympathy for the respectable tramping class, and proposals to improve the accommodation that was provided for them. For example, Wyrall emphasized the need to improve casual ward accommodation, and praised the work of the Church Army "Labour Homes," but admitted that the latter were useless in dealing with the "habitual loafer," for whom "Detention Colonies" should be established (below, pp. 277–278). Edwards thought that the church should establish labor colonies, and although a program of improved education was needed to prevent the creation of a "criminal class," he also declared that "we must, by magistrates' order, clear the roads and streets of beggars, loafers and wastrels. We must classify them. We must clothe them and feed them and doctor and heal their poor bodies, and their poorer souls also, with the glad gospel of Hope" (below, pp. 312–313). Higgs hoped for the abolition of the casual ward and better regulation of lodging houses, but also hoped that the "tramp proper," "the man who would not work," would be removed to a labor colony, which was his "natural destination" (below, p. 229). Some of the earlier sources in the book also proposed some form of labor colony: Stallard's suggestion was a "House of Detention," with land attached, under the rule of a "labour-master." Although he disagreed with proposals to transfer responsibilty for vagrancy to the police, he advocated a poor law magistracy, which would certify the genuine vagrants and remove the non-certified to the "House of Detention" (below, p. 114). Even "M.A.," pleading for more humanity in the treatment of genuine poverty, was careful to outline the limits to what should be done:

"John Bull will now most plainly see
The want of Christian charity;
Or e'en of that philanthropy
That ought to rule the Workhouse!
Not that John Bull would wish to see
The Workhouse full of luxury…" (below, p. 80)

The distinction between the deserving and undeserving vagrant pervades the language, and shapes the policy proposals, in these texts, and unites them as a genre almost as much as the act of disguise itself. As such, they are an integral part of the history of social research and social policy in the late Victorian and Edwardian period. Historians may be sceptical about the extent to which the vicarious vagrants provide us with a window into the lives of the very poor in this period, and it is certainly possible to question the extent of their penetration of the "abyss." The impressionism of these descriptive accounts of vagrancy throws obvious doubts onto their veracity, and the incognito method itself raises questions of research ethics that have only been touched upon in this introduction. Yet whatever the limitations of their method, the information that they conveyed was taken seriously by many of their contemporaries, and it may also be of some value to us. Moreover, they can be seen as precursors in a longstanding tradition of undercover social research that remains influential and popular. Today, incognito social exploration is used in academic sociology and popular journalism, and has been used to investigate many different areas of modern life. Among many other groups and situations, extremist political groups, football hooligans and those in low-paid occupations have been investigated in this way.[66] One journalist has even gone undercover as a traffic warden, to experience at first hand the treatment of this much maligned group by members of the public.[67] The investigations of modern journalists reflect the concerns of the early twenty-first century, just as the focus on vagrancy by those writing a century and more ago reflected the widespread fears prompted by the growth of vagrant numbers and the resultant fears of social contamination and political revolution. This was a period when the gathering of information about all areas of working-class life, and in particular the problem of poverty, was prioritized by the government, and by social investigators of many kinds. Homelessness was much more difficult to investigate than many other social problems, hence the popularity and importance of the vicarious vagrancy that we showcase in this book. The vicarious vagrants produced social documents that both reflected and shaped the concerns of legislators and philanthropists in this key period of social and political change, and they therefore represent a significant strand in the history of British social policy.

---

66. *The Secret Agent*, BBC1, 15 July 2004, described Jason Gwynne's experiences as an undercover reporter investigating the British National Party; Donal MacIntyre secretly filmed football hooligans for the BBC programme *MacIntyre Undercover*, helping to secure convictions; "Football hooligan 'generals' jailed." *The Guardian*, 9 December 2000, p. 13. On low-paid occupations, see Toynbee 2003 and Ehrenreich 2002.

67. "The Thin Yellow Line; Who'd be a Traffic Warden…?" *The Independent*, 6 February 2006, p. 37.

MARK FREEMAN is a senior lecturer in the Department of Economic and Social History at the University of Glasgow. He is the author of *Social Investigation and Rural England 1870-1914* (Royal Historical Society Studies in History, 2003), and a number of other books and articles on modern British social history.

GILLIAN NELSON is completing a PhD at the University of Glasgow with a dissertation on the topic "Covert Ethnography in Britain since the 1880s."

Denis Crane (Walter Cranfield), the "Vicarious Vagabond."

NOTE ON THE TEXT

The works included here are presented in the same form as the originals, with the following exceptions: Typographical and other errors have been corrected in the text and such corrections are designated within [square brackets], with the original of the word or phrase given in a footnote. Punctuation has only been changed when necessary to support internal consistency. All foreign words and phrases, and all titles of books and periodicals, are *italicized*. In works which originally included tables of contents, these have been omitted as redundant.

All footnotes are those of the editors, unless otherwise stated.

ACKNOWLEDGEMENTS

The editors and publisher are grateful to the Royal Holloway, University of London and the Bridgeman Art Library for permission to use Sir Luke Fildes' painting *Applicants for Admission to a Casual Ward* (1874) as the cover image.

We are also grateful to the following institutions for allowing us to reprint from materials in their collections: the British Library, the Library of the City College of the City University of New York, the National Library of Scotland, and the New York Public Library.

The editors would also like to thank Tony Simpson for his assistance and encouragement throughout the process of producing the book

Chapter One

"A Night in a Workhouse"
by James Greenwood

Pall Mall Gazette 12 January 1866, pages 9-10;
13 January, page 10; 15 January, pages 9-10

January 12th.

At about nine o'clock on the evening of Monday, the 8th inst., a neat but unpretentious carriage might have been seen turning cautiously from the Kennington-road into Princes-road, Lambeth. The curtains were closely drawn, and the coachman wore an unusually responsible air. Approaching a public-house which retreated a little from the street, he pulled up; but not so close that the lights should fall upon the carriage door, nor so distant as to unsettle the mind of any one who chose to imagine that he had halted to drink beer before proceeding to call for the children at a juvenile party. He did not dismount, nor did any one alight in the usual way; but any keen observer who happened to watch his intelligent countenance might have seen a furtive glance directed to the wrong door: that is to say, to the door of the carriage which opened into the dark and muddy road. From that door emerged a sly and ruffianly figure, marked with every sign of squalor. He was dressed in what had once been a snuff-brown coat, but which had faded to the hue of bricks imperfectly baked. It was not strictly a ragged coat, though it had lost its cuffs—a bereavement which obliged the wearer's arms to project through the sleeves two long inelegant inches. The coat altogether was too small, and was only made to meet over the chest by means of a bit of twine. This wretched garment was surmounted by a "birdseye" pocket handkerchief[1] of cotton, wisped about the throat hangman fashion; above all was a battered billy-cock hat,[2] with a dissolute drooping brim. Between the neckerchief and the lowering brim of the hat appeared part of a face, unshaven, and not scrupulously clean. The man's hands were plunged into his pockets, and he shuffled hastily along in boots, which were the boots of a tramp indifferent to miry ways. In a moment he was [out][3] of sight; and the brougham,[4] after waiting a little while, turned about and comfortably departed.

The mysterious figure was that of the present writer. He was bound for Lambeth Workhouse, there to learn by actual experience how casual paupers are lodged and fed, and what the "casual" is like, and what the porter who admits him, and the master who rules over him; and how the night passes with the outcasts whom we have all seen crowding about workhouse doors on cold and rainy nights. Much has been said on the subject—on behalf of the paupers—on behalf of the officials; but nothing by any one who, with no motive but to learn and make known the truth, had ventured the experiment of passing a night in a workhouse, and trying what it actually is to be a "casual."

The day had been windy and chill—the night was cold; and therefore I fully expected to begin my experiences amongst a dozen of ragged wretches squatting about the steps and waiting for admission. But my only companion at the door was a decently dressed woman, who, as I afterwards learned, they declined to admit until she had recovered from a fit of intoxication from

---

1. A brightly spotted handkerchief, named after the flower.

2. A round hat, low-crowned and made of felt. In *On Tramp*, Greenwood encountered two vagrants wearing a similar kind of hat. See below, pp. 172, 175.

3. In the original: "ought."

4. A four-wheeled, fully enclosed carriage, used by the prosperous classes.

which she had the ill fortune to be still suffering. I lifted the big knocker, and knocked; the door was promptly opened, and I entered. Just within a comfortable-looking clerk sat at a comfortable desk, ledger before him. Indeed the spacious hall in every way was as comfortable as cleanliness and great mats and plenty of gaslight could make it.

"What do you want?" asked the man who opened the door.

"I want a lodging."

"Go and stand before the desk," said the porter; and I obeyed.

"You are late," said the clerk.

"Am I, sir?"

"Yes. If you come in you'll have a bath, and you'll have to sleep in the shed."

"Very well, sir."

"What's your name?"

"Joshua Mason, sir."

"What are you?"

"An engraver." (This taradiddle I invented to account for the look of my hands.)

"Where did you sleep last night?"

"Hammersmith," I answered—as I hope to be forgiven.

"How many times have you been here?"

"Never before, sir."

"Where do you mean to go to when you are turned out in the morning?"

"Back to Hammersmith, sir."

These humble answers being entered in a book, the clerk called the porter, saying, "Take him through. You may as well take this bread with you."

Near the clerk stood a basket containing some pieces of bread of equal size. Taking one of these, and unhitching a bunch of keys from the wall, the porter led me through some passages all so scrupulously clean that my most serious misgivings were laid to rest. Then we passed into a dismal yard. Crossing this, my guide led me to a door, calling out, "Hillo! Daddy, I've brought you another." Whereupon Daddy opened unto us, and let a little of his gaslight to stream into the yard where we stood.

"Come in," said Daddy very hospitably. "There's enough of you tonight anyhow! What made you so late?"

"I didn't like to come in earlier."

"Ah! That's a pity, now, because you missed your skilley

(gruel). It's the first night of skilley, don't you know under the new Act?"[5]

"Just like my luck!" I muttered dolefully.

The porter went his way, and I followed Daddy into another apartment, where were ranged three great baths, each one containing a liquid so disgustingly like weak mutton broth that my worst apprehensions crowded back. "Come on, there's a dry place to stand on up at this end," said Daddy, kindly. "Take off your clothes, tie 'em up in your hank'sher, and I'll lock 'em up till the morning." Accordingly I took off my coat and waistcoat, and was about to tie them together when Daddy cried, "That ain't enough, I mean everything." "Not my shirt, sir, I suppose?" "Yes, shirt and all; but there, I'll lend you a shirt," said Daddy. "Whatever you take in of your own will be nailed, you know. You might take in your boots though—they'd be handy if you happened to want to leave the shed for anything; but don't blame me if you lose 'em."

With a fortitude for which I hope someday to be rewarded, I made up my bundle (boots and all), and the moment Daddy's face was turned away shut my eyes and plunged desperately into the mutton broth. I wish from the bottom of heart my courage had been less hasty; for hearing the splash, Daddy looked round and said "Lor now! there was no occasion for that; you look a clean and decent sort of man. It's them filthy beggars" (only he used a word more specific than "filthy,") "that want washing. Don't use that towel—here's a clean one! That's the sort! and now here's your shirt" (handing me a blue striped one from a heap), "and here's your ticket. Number thirty-four, you are, and a ticket to match is tied to your bundle. Mind you don't lose it. They'll nail it from you if they get a chance. Put it under your head. This is your rug—take it with you."

---

5.   "Daddy" was referring to the Metropolitan Houseless Poor Act of 1865 (28&29 Vict., c.34). There had been another Act of the same name in the previous year (27&28 Vict., c.116). Koven has described the 1865 Act, which forced poor law guardians to give food and shelter to vagrants without regard to whether they were "deserving," as "a kind of bill of rights for vagrants, some of whom kept up with the latest enactments of the Poor Law and tenaciously invoked its clauses in their often brutal encounters with recalcitrant local officials." Koven, Seth. *Slumming: Sexual and Social Politics in Victorian London.* Princeton: Princeton University Press, 2004, p. 33. See above, pp. 15–16.

"Where am I to sleep, please sir?"

"I'll show you."

And so he did. With no other rag but the checked shirt to cover me, and with my rug over my shoulder, he accompanied me to the door at which I had entered, and, opening it, kept me standing with naked feet on the stone threshold, full in the draught of the frosty air, while he pointed out the way I should go. It was not a long way, but I would have given much not to have trodden it. It was open as the highway–with the flagstones below and the stars overhead; and, as I said before, and cannot help saying again, a frosty wind was blowing.

"Straight across," said Daddy, "to where you see the light shining through. Go in there and turn to the left, and you'll find the beds in a heap. Take one of 'em and make yourself comfortable." And straight across I went, my naked feet seeming to cling to the stones as though they were burning hot instead of icy cold (they had just stepped out of a bath, you should remember), till I reached the space through which the light was shining, and I entered in.

No language with which I am acquainted is capable of conveying an adequate conception of the spectacle I then encountered. Imagine a space of about thirty feet by thirty feet enclosed on three sides by a dingy whitewashed wall, and roofed with naked tiles which were furred with the damp and filth that reeked within. As for the fourth side of the shed, it was boarded in for (say) a third of its breadth; the remaining space being hung with flimsy canvas, in which was a gap two feet wide at top, widening to at least four feet at bottom. This far too airy shed was paved with stone, the flags so thickly encrusted with filth that I mistook it first for a floor of natural earth. Extending from one end of my bedroom to the other, in three rows, were certain iron "cranks" (of which I subsequently learnt the use), with their many arms raised in various attitudes, as the stiffened arms of men are on a battlefield. My bed-fellows lay among the cranks, distributed over the flagstones in a double row, on narrow bags scantily stuffed with hay. At one glance my appalled vision took in thirty of them— thirty men and boys stretched upon shallow pallets which put only six inches of comfortable hay between them and the stony floor. These beds were placed close together, every occupant being provided with a rug like that which I was fain to hug across my shoulders. In not a few cases two gentlemen had clubbed beds and rugs and slept together. In one case (to be further mentioned presently) four gentlemen had so clubbed together. Many of my fellow-casuals were awake—others asleep or pretending to sleep; and shocking as were the waking ones to look upon, they were quite pleasant when compared with the sleepers. For this reason: the practised and well-seasoned casual seems to have a peculiar way of putting himself to bed. He rolls himself in his rug, tucking himself in, head and feet, so that he is completely enveloped; and, lying quite still on his pallet, he looks precisely like a corpse covered because of its hideousness. Some were stretched out at full length; some lay nose and knees together; some with an arm or a leg showing crooked through the coverlet. It was like the result of a railway accident; these ghastly figures were awaiting the coroner.

From the moral point of view, however, the wakeful ones were more dreadful still. Towzled, dirty, villainous, they squatted up in their beds, and smoked foul pipes, and sang snatches of horrible songs, and bandied jokes so obscene as to be absolutely appalling. Eight or ten were so enjoying themselves—the majority with the check shirt on and the frowsy rug pulled about their legs; but two or three wore no shirts at all, squatting naked to the waist, their bodies fully exposed in the light of the single flaring jet of gas fixed high up on the wall.

My entrance excited very little attention. There was a horse-pail three parts full of water standing by a post in the middle of the shed, with a little tin pot beside it. Addressing me as "old pal," one of the naked ruffians begged me to "hand him a swig," as he was "werry nigh garspin." Such an appeal of course no "old pal" could withstand, and I gave him a pot full of water. He showed himself grateful for the attention. "I should lay over there if I was you," he said, pointing to the left side of the shed; "It's more out of the wind then this 'ere side is." I took the good-natured advice and (by this time shivering with cold) stepped over the stones to where the beds of straw bags were heaped, and dragged one of them to the spot suggested by my naked comrade. But I had no more idea of how to arrange it that of making an apple-pudding; and a certain little discovery added much to my embarrassment. In the middle of the bed I had selected was a stain of blood bigger than a man's hand! I did not know what to do now. To lie on such a horrid thing seemed impossible; yet to carry back the bed and exchange it for another might betray a degree of fastidiousness repugnant to the feelings of my fellow lodgers and possibly excite suspicions that I was not what I seemed. Just in the nick of time in came that good man Daddy.

"What! not pitched yet?" he exclaimed; "here, I'll show you. Hallo! somebody's been a bleedin'! Never mind; let's turn him over. There you are, you see! Now lay down, and cover your rug over you."

There was no help for it. It was too late to go back. Down I lay, and spread the rug over me. I should have mentioned that I brought in with me a cotton handkerchief, and this I tied round my head by way of a nightcap; but not daring to pull the rug as high as my face. Before I could in any way settle my mind to reflection, in came Daddy once more to do me a further kindness and point out a stupid blunder I had committed.

"Why, you *are* a rummy[6] chap!" said Daddy. "You forgot your bread! Lay hold. And look here, I've brought you another rug; it's perishing cold to-night." So saying, he spread the rug over my legs and went away. I was very thankful for the extra covering, but I was in a dilemma about the bread. I couldn't possibly eat it; what then was to be done with it? I broke it, however, and in view of such of the company as might happen to be looking, made a ferocious bite at a bit a large as a bean, and munched violently. By good luck, however, I presently got half way over my difficulty very neatly. Just behind me, so close indeed that their feet came within half a yard of my head, three lads were sleeping together.

"Did you 'ear that, Punch?" one of them asked.

"'Ear what?" answered Punch, sleepy and snappish.

"Why, a cove forgot his toke! Gordstruth! you wouldn't ketch me a forgettin mine."

"You may have half of it, old pal, if you're hungry," I observed, leaning up on my elbows.

"Chuck it here, good luck to yer!" replied my young friend, starting up with an eager clap of his dirty hands.

I "chucked it here," and, slipping the other half under the side of my bed, lay my head on my folded arms.

Here I must break my narrative. In doing so, permit me to assure your readers that it is true and faithful in every particular. I

---

6.   Cant: odd or unconventional.

am telling a story which cannot all be told—some parts of it are far too shocking; but what I may tell has not a single touch of false colour in it.

January 13th.

It was about half-past nine when, having made myself as comfortable as circumstances permitted, I closed my eyes in the desperate hope that I might fall asleep, and so escape from the horrors with which I was surrounded. "At seven to-morrow morning the bell will ring," Daddy had informed me, "and then you will give up your ticket and get back your bundle." Between that time and the present full nine long hours had to wear away.

But I was speedily convinced that, at least for the present, sleep was impossible. The young fellow (one of the three who lay in one bed, with their feet to my head) whom my bread had refreshed, presently swore with frightful imprecations that he was now going to have a smoke; and immediately put his threat into execution. Thereupon his bedfellows sat up and lit their pipes too. But oh! if they had only smoked—if they had not taken such an unfortunate fancy to spit at the leg of a crank distant a few inches from my head, how much misery and apprehension would have been spared me! To make matters worse, they united with this American practice an Eastern one; as they smoked they related little autobiographical anecdotes—so abominable, that three or four decent men who lay at the farther end of the shed were so provoked they threatened, unless the talk abated in filthiness, to get up and stop it by main force. Instantly, the voice of every blackguard in the room was raised against the decent ones. They were accused of loathsome afflictions, stigmatized as "fighting men out of work" (which must be something very humiliating, I suppose), and invited to a "round" by boys young enough to be their grandsons. For several minutes there was such a storm of oaths, threats, and taunts—such a deluge of foul words raged in the room—that I could not help thinking of the fate of Sodom; as, indeed, I did several times during the night. Little by little the riot died out, without any [of][7] the slightest interference on the part of the officers.

---

7.   Word omitted in the original.

Soon afterwards the ruffian majority was strengthened by the arrival of a lanky boy of about fifteen, who evidently recognized many acquaintances, and was recognized by them as "Kay," or perhaps I should write it "K." He was a very remarkable-looking lad, and his appearance pleased me much. Short as his hair was cropped, it still looked soft and silky; he had large blue eyes, set wide apart, and a mouth that would have been faultless but for its great width; and his voice was as soft and sweet as any woman's. Lightly as a woman, too, he picked his way over the stones towards the place where the beds lay, carefully hugging his cap beneath his arm.

"What cheer, Kay?" "Out again, then, old son!" "What yer got in yer cap, Kay?" cried his friends; to which the sweet voice replied, "Who'll give me part of his doss (bed)? --- my --- eyes and limbs if I ain't perishin'! Who'll let me turn in with him for half my toke" (bread)? I feared how it would be! The hungry young fellow who had so readily availed himself of half my "toke" snapped at Kay's offer, and after a little rearrangement and bed-making, four young fellows instead of three reposed upon the hay-bags at my head.

"You was too late for skilley, Kay. There's skilley, nights as well as mornins."

"Don't you tell no bleeding lies," Kay answered incredulously.

"Blind me, it's true. Ain't it Punch?"

"Right you are!" said Punch, "and spoons to eat it with, [what's][8] more. There used to be spoons at all the houses, one time. Poplar used to have 'em; but one at a time they was all nicked don't you know." ("Nicked" means "stolen," obviously.)

"Well I don't want no skilley, leastways not to-night," said Kay. "I've had some rum. Two glasses of it, and a blow out of puddin'— regler Christmas plum puddin'. You don't know the cove as give it me, but, thinks I this mornin' when I comes out, Blessed if I don't go and see my old chum. Lordstruth! he *was* struck! 'Come along,' he ses, 'I saved you some puddin' from Christmas.' 'Whereabouts is it?' I ses. 'In that box under my bed,' he ses, and he forks it out. That's the sort of pal to have! And he stood a quartern,[9] and a half

---

8. In the original: "that's."

9. A four-pound loaf of bread.

a ounce of hard-up (tobacco). That wasn't all neither; when I come away, ses he, 'How about your breakfus?' 'Oh, I shall do,' ses I. 'You take some of my bread and butter,' he ses, and he cuts me off four chunks buttered thick. I eat two on 'em comin' along,"

"What's in your cap, Kay?" repeated the devourer of "toke."

"Them two other slices," said Kay; generously adding, "There, share 'em amongst yer, and somebody give us a whiff of 'bacca."

Kay showed himself a pleasant companion; what in a higher grade of society is called "quite an acquisition." He told stories of thieves and thieving, and of a certain "silver cup" he had been "put up to," and that he meant to nick it 'afore the end of the week, if he got seven stretch (seven years) for it. The cup was worth ten quid (pounds),[10] and he knew where to melt it within ten minutes of nicking it. He made this statement without any moderation of his sweet voice, and the others received it as serious fact. Nor was there any affectation of [secrecy][11] in another gentleman, who announced, amid great applause that he had stolen a towel from the bath-room; "And s'help me, it's as [good][12] as new; never been washed more'n once!"

"Tell us a 'rummy' story, Kay," said somebody: and Kay did. He told stories of so "rummy" a character that the decent men at the further end of the room (some of whom had their own little boys sleeping with them) must have lain in a sweat of horror as they listened. Indeed, when Kay broke into a "rummy" song with a roaring chorus, one of the decent men rose in his bed and swore he would smash Kay's head if he didn't desist. But Kay sang on till he and his admirers were tired of the entertainment. "Now," said he, "let's have a swearing club! you'll all be in it?"

The principle of this game seemed to rest on the impossibility of either of the young gentlemen making half-a-dozen observations without introducing a blasphemous or obscene word; and

---

10. In the original: "(? pounds)."

11. In the original: "secresy."

12. In the original: "good;"

either the basis is a very sound one, or for the sake of keeping the "club" alive the members purposely made slips. The penalty for "swearing" was a punch on any part of the body, except a few which the club rules protected. The game was highly successful. Warming with the sport, and indifferent to punches, the members vied with each other in audacity, and in a few minutes Bedlam in its prime could scarcely have produced such a spectacle as was to be seen on the beds behind me. One rule of the club was that any word to be found in the Bible might be used with impunity, and if one member "punched" another for using such a word the error was to be visited upon him with a double punching all round. This naturally led to much argument; for in vindicating the Bible as his authority, a member became sometimes so much heated as to launch into a flood of "real swearing," which brought the fists of the club upon his naked carcase quick as hail.

These and other pastimes beguiled the time until, to my delight, the church chimes audibly tolled twelve. After this the noise gradually subsided, and it seemed as though everybody was going to sleep at last. I should have mentioned that during the story-telling and song-singing a few "casuals" had dropped in, but they were not habitués, and cuddled down with their rugs over their heads without a word to any one.

In a little while all was quiet—save for the flapping of the canvas curtain in the night breeze, the snoring, and the horrible, indescribable sound of impatient hands scratching skins that itched. There was another sound of very frequent occurrence, and that was the clanking of the tin pannikin[13] against the water pail. Whether it is in the nature of workhouse bread or skilley to provoke thirst is more than my limited experience entitles me to say, but it may be truthfully asserted that once at least in the course of five minutes might be heard a rustling of straw, a pattering of feet, and then the noise of water-dipping; and then was to be seen at the pail the figure of a man (sometimes stark naked), gulping down the icy water as he stood upon the icy stones.

And here I may remark that I can furnish no solution to this mystery of the shirt. I only know that some of my comrades were

---

13. A small drinking vessel.

provided with a shirt, and that to some the luxury was denied. I may say this, however, that *none* of the little boys were allowed one.

Nearly one o'clock. Still quiet, and no fresh arrival for an hour or more. Then suddenly a loud noise of hobnailed boots kicking at a wooden gate, and soon after a tramping of feet and a rapping at Daddy's door, which, it will be remembered, was only separated from our bedroom by an open paved court.

"Hallo!" cried Daddy.

"Here's some more of 'em for you—ten of 'em!" answered the porter, whose voice I recognized at once.

"They'll have to find beds, then," Daddy grumbled, as he opened his door. "I don't believe there are four beds empty. They must sleep double, or something."

This was terrible news for me. Bad enough, in all conscience, was it to lie as I was lying; but the prospect of sharing my straw with some dirty scoundrel of the Kay breed was altogether unendurable. Perhaps, however, they were *not* dirty scoundrels, but peaceable and decent men, like those in the farther corner.

Alas for my hopes! In the space of five minutes in they came at the rent in the canvas—great hulking ruffians, some with rugs and nothing else, and all madly swearing because coming in after eleven o'clock there was no "toke" for them. As soon as these wrathful men had advanced to the middle of the shed they made the discovery that there was an insufficient number of beds—only three, indeed, for ten competitors.

"Where's the beds? D'ye hear, Daddy? You blessed, truth-telling old person, where's the beds?"

"You'll find 'em. Some of 'em is lying on two, or got 'em as pillows. You'll find 'em."

With a sudden rush our new friends plunged amongst the sleepers, trampling over them, cursing their eyes and limbs, dragging away their rugs; and if by chance they found some poor wretch who had been tempted to take two beds (or bags) instead of one, they coolly hauled him out and took possession. There was no denying them, and no use in remonstrating. They evidently knew that they were at liberty to do just as they liked, and they took full advantage of the privilege.

One of them came up to me, and shouting, "I want that, you ---," snatched at my "birdseye" nightcap and carried it off. There was a bed close to mine, which contained only one occupant, and into this one of the new comers slipped without a word of warning, driving its lawful owner against the wall to make room. Then he sat up in bed for a moment, savagely venting his disappointment as to toke, and declaring that never before in his life had he felt the need of it so much. This was my opportunity. Slipping my hand under my bed, I withdrew that judiciously hoarded piece of bread and respect-fully offered it to him. He snapped at it with thanks.

By the time the churches were chiming, two matters had once more adjusted themselves, and silence reigned, to be disturbed only by the drinkers at the pail, or such as, otherwise prompted, stalked into the open yard. Kay, for one, visited it. I mention this unhappy young wretch particularly, because he went out without a single rag to his back. I looked out at the rent in the canvas, and saw the frosty moon shining on him. When he returned, and crept down between Punch and another, he muttered to himself, "Warm again! Oh, my G-d! warm again!"

I hope, Mr. Editor, that you will not think me too prodigal of these reminiscences; and that your readers will understand that, if I write rather boldly, it is not done as a matter of taste. To me it seems quite worth while to relate with *tolerable* accuracy every particular of an adventure which you persuaded me ("ah! woeful when!") to undertake for the public good. In another paper I shall conclude.

January 15th.

Whether there is a rule which closes the casual wards after a certain hour I do not know; but before one o'clock our number was made up, the last comer, signalizing his appearance with a grotesque *pas seul*.[14] His rug over his shoulders, he waltzed into the shed, waving his hands, and singing in an affected voice as he sidled along—

"I like to be a swell, a-roaming down Pall Mall,
Or anywhere—I don't much care, so I can be a swell—"[15]

a couplet which had an intensely comical effect. This gentle-man had just come from a pantomime (where he had learned his song, probably.) Too poor to pay for a lodging, he could only

---

14. A dance routine for a single performer.

15. Music hall song written by Gaston Murray in 1865.

muster means for a seat in the gallery of "the Vic.";[16] where he was well entertained, judging from the flattering manner in which he spoke of the clown. The columbine was less fortunate in his opinion. "She's werry dicky![17]—ain't got what I call 'move' about her." However, the wretched young woman was respited now from the scourge of his criticism; for the critic and his listeners were fast asleep; and yet I doubt whether anyone of the company slept very soundly. Every moment someone shifted uneasily; and as the night wore on the silence was more and more irritated by the sound of coughing. This was one of the most distressing things in the whole adventure. The conversation was horrible, the tales that were told more horrible still, and worse than either (though not *by any means* the most infamous things to be heard—I dare not even hint at them) was that song, with its bestial chorus shouted from a dozen throats; but at any rate they kept the blood warm with constant hot flushes of anger; while as for the coughing, to lie on the flagstones in what was nothing better than an open shed, and listen to that hour after hour, chilled one's very heart with pity. Every variety of cough that ever I heard was to be heard there: the hollow cough; the short cough; the hysterical cough; the bark that comes at regular intervals, like the quarter-chime of a clock, as if to mark off the progress of decay; coughing from vast hollow chests, coughing from little narrow ones—now one, now another, now two or three together, and then a minute's interval of silence in which to think of it all, and wonder who would begin next. One of the young reprobates above me coughed so grotesquely like the chopping of wood that I named him in my mind the Woodcutter. Now and then I found myself coughing too, which may have added just a little to the poignant distress these awfully constant and variable sounds occasioned me. They were good in one way: they made one forget what wretches they were, who, to all appearances were so rapidly "chopping" their way to a pauper's graveyard. I did not care about the more matured ruffians so much; but

---

16. This theater was founded in 1818 as the Royal Coburg, later known as the Royal Victoria. Now known as the Old Vic, it still produces pantomimes in season.

17. Cant: in sorry or poor condition.

though the youngest, the boys like Kay, were unquestionably amongst the most infamous of my comrades, to hear what cold and hunger and vice had done for them at fifteen was almost enough to make a man cry; and there were boys there even younger than these.

At half-past two everyone being asleep, or at least lying still, Daddy came in and counted us: one, two, three, four, and so on, in a whisper. Then, finding the pail empty (it was nearly full at half-past nine, when I entered) he considerately went and refilled it, and even took the trouble in searching for the tin pot which served as a drinking cup, and which the last comer had playfully thrown to the farther end of the shed. I ought to have mentioned that the pail stood close to my head; so that I had peculiar opportunities of study as one after another of my comrades came to the fountain to drink: just as the brutes do in those books of African travel. The pail refilled, Daddy returned, and was seen no more till morning.

It still wanted four hours and a half to seven o'clock—the hour of rising—and never before in my life did time appear to creep so slowly. I could hear the chimes of a parish church, and of the Parliament Houses, and well as those of a wretched tinkling Dutch clock somewhere on the premises. The parish church was the first to announce the hour (an act of kindness I feel bound to acknowledge), Westminster came next, the lazy Dutchman declining his consent to the time o'day till fully sixty seconds afterwards. And I declare I thought that difference of sixty seconds an injury—if the officers of the house took their time from the Dutchman. It may seem a trifle, but a minute is something when a man is lying on a cold flagstone, and the wind of a winter night is blowing in your hair. Three o'clock, four o'clock struck, and still there was nothing to beguile the time but observation, under the one flaring gaslight, of the little heaps of outcast humanity strewn about the floor; and after a while, I find, one may even become accustomed to the sight of one's fellow-creatures lying around you like covered corpses in a railway shed. For most of the company were now bundled under the rugs in the ghastly way I have already described—though here and there a cropped head appeared, surmounted by a billy-cock like my own or by a greasy cloth cap. Five o'clock, six o'clock chimed, and then I had news—most welcome—of the world without, and of the real beginning of day. Half a dozen factory bells announced that it was time for working men to go to labour; but my companions were not working men, and so snored on. Out through the gap in the canvas the stars were still to be seen shining on the black sky, but that did not alter the fact that it was six o'clock in the morning. I snapped my fingers at the Dutchman, with his sixty seconds slow, for in another hour I fondly hoped to be relieved from duty. A little while and doors were heard to open and shut; yet a little while, and the voice of Daddy was audible in conversation with another early bird; and then I distinctly caught the word "bundles." Blessed sound! I longed for my bundle—for my pleasing brown coat, for the warm if unsightly "jersey," which I adopted as a judicious substitute for a waistcoat—for my corduroys and liberty.

"Clang!" went the workhouse clock. "Now, then! wake 'em up!" cried Daddy. I was already up—sitting up, that is—being anxious to witness the resurrection of the ghastly figures rolled in their rugs. But nobody but myself rose at the summons. They knew what it meant well enough, and in sleepy voices cursed the bell, and wished it in several dreadful places; but they did not move until there came in at the hole in the canvas, two of the pauper inhabitants of the house, bearing bundles. "Thirty-two," "Twenty-eight!" they bawled, but not my number, which was thirty-four. Neither thirty-two nor twenty-eight, however, seemed eager to accept his good fortune in being first called. They were called upon three several times before they would answer. Then they replied with a savage "Chuck it here, can't you!" "Not before you chucks over your shirt and ticket," the bundle-holder answered, whereon "[twenty eight]"[18] sat up and, divesting himself of his borrowed shirt, flung it, with his wooden ticket; and his bundle was flung back in return.

It was some time before bundle No. 34 turned up, so that I had fair opportunity to observe my neighbours. The decent men slipped into their rags as soon as they got them, but the blackguards were in no hurry. Some indulged in a morning pipe to prepare themselves for the fatigue of dressing, while others, loosening their bundles as they squatted naked, commenced an investigation for certain little animals which shall be nameless.

At last my turn came, and "chucking over" my shirt and ticket, I quickly attired myself in clothes which, ragged as they were,

18. In the original: "thirty-eight."

were cleaner than they looked. In less than two minutes I was out of the shed, and in the yard; where a few of the more decent poor fellows were crowding round a pail of water, and scrambling after something that might pass for a "wash"—finding their own soap, as far as I could observe, and drying their faces on any bit of rag they might happen to have about them, or upon the canvas curtain of the shed.

By this time it was about half-past seven, and the majority of the casuals were up and dressed. I observed, however, that none of the younger ones were as yet up, and it presently appeared that there existed some rule against their dressing in the shed; for Daddy came out of the bath-room, where the bundles were deposited, and called out "Now four boys!" and instantly four little wretches, some with their rugs trailing about their shoulders and some quite bare, came shivering over the stones and across the bleak yard, and were admitted to the bath-room to dress. "Now four more boys," cried Daddy and so on.

When all were up and dressed, the boys carried the bed rugs into Daddy's room, and the pauper inmates made a heap of the "beds," stacking them against the wall. As before mentioned, the shed served the treble purpose of bed-chamber, workroom, and breakfast-room; it was impossible to get fairly at the cranks and set them going until the bedding was stowed away.

Breakfast before work, however; but it was a weary while to some of us before it made its appearance. For my own part I had little appetite, but about me were a dozen poor wretches who obviously had a very great one: they had come in overnight too late for bread, and perhaps may not have broken fast since the morning of the previous day. The decent ones suffered most. The blackguard majority were quite cheerful—smoking, swearing, and playing their pretty horse play, the prime end of which was pain or discomfiture for somebody else. One casual there was with only one leg. When he came in overnight he wore a black hat, which added a certain look of respectability to a worn suit of black. All together his clothes had been delivered up to him by Daddy; but now he was seen hopping disconsolately about the place on his crutch, for the hat was missing. He was a timid man, with a mild voice; and whenever he asked some ruffian "whether he had seen such a thing as a black hat," and got his answer, he invariably said "thank you," which was regarded as very amusing. At last one sidled up to him with a grin, and showing about three square inches of some fluffy substance, said—"Is *this* anything like wot you've lost, guv'ner?" The cripple inspected it. "That's the rim of it!" he said. "What a shame!" and hobbled off with tears in his eyes.

Full three-quarters of an hour of loitering and shivering, and then came the taskmaster: a soldierly-looking man, over six feet high, with quick, gray eyes, in which "No trifling" appeared as distinctly as a notice against trespassing on a wayside board. He came in amongst us, and the gray eyes made out our number in a moment. "Out into the yard, all of you," he cried, and we went out in a mob. There we shivered for some twenty minutes longer, and then a baker's man appeared with a great wooden tray piled up with such slices of bread as we had received overnight. The tray was consigned to an able-bodied casual, who took his place with the task master at the shed door; and then in single file we re-entered the shed, each man and boy receiving a slice as he passed in. Pitying, as I suppose, my unaccustomed look, Mr. Taskmaster gave me a slice and a large piece over.

The bread devoured, a clamour for "skilley" began. The rumour had got abroad that this morning, and on all future mornings, there would skilley for breakfast, and "Skilley, skilley!" resounded through the shed. No one had hinted that it was not forthcoming, but skilley seems to be thought an extraordinary concession, and after waiting only a few minutes for it, they attacked the taskmaster in the fiercest manner. They called him thief, sneak, and "crawler." Little boys blackguarded him in gutter language, and looking him in the face, consigned him to hell without flinching. He never uttered a word in reply, or showed a sign of impatience; and whenever he was obliged to speak it was quite without temper.

There was a loud "hooray!" when the longed-for skilley appeared in two pails, in one of which floated a small tin saucepan, with a stick thrust into its handle, by way of a ladle. Yellow pint basins were provided for our use, and large iron spoons. "Range round the walls!" the taskmaster shouted. We obeyed with the utmost alacrity; and then what I should judge to be about three-fourths of a pint of gruel was handed to each of us as we stood. I was glad to get mine, because the basin that contained it was warm and my hands were numb with cold. I tasted a spoonful, as in duty bound, and wondered more than ever at the esteem in which it was held by my *confrères*. It was a weak decoction of oatmeal and water, bitter, and without even a pinch of salt to flavour it—that I could discover. But it was hot; and on that account, perhaps, was so highly relished, that I had no difficulty persuading one of the decent men to accept my share.

It was now past eight o'clock, and, as I knew that a certain quantity of labour had to be performed by each man before he was allowed to go his way, I was anxious to begin. The labour was to be "crank" labour. The "cranks" are a series of iron bars extending across the width of the shed, penetrating through the wall, and working a flourmill on the other side. Turning the "crank" is like turning a windlass.[19] The task is not a severe one. Four measures of corn (bushels they were called—but that is doubtful) have to be ground every morning by the night's batch of casuals. Close up by the ceiling hangs a bell connected with the machinery; and as each measure is ground the bell rings, so that the grinders may know how they are going on. But the grinders are as lazy as obscene. We were no sooner set to work than the taskmaster left us to our own sweet will, with nothing to restrain its exercise but an occasional visit from the miller, a weakly expostulating man. Once or twice he came in and said mildly, "Now then, my men, why *don't* you stick to it?"—and so went out again.

The result of this laxity of overseeing would have disgusted me at any time, and was intensely disgusting then. At least one half the gang kept their hands from the crank whenever the miller was absent, and betook themselves to their private amusements and pursuits. Some sprawled upon the beds and smoked; some engaged themselves and their friends in tailoring, and one turned hair-cutter for the benefit of a gentleman who, unlike Kay, had *not* just come out of prison. There were three tailors: two of them on the beds mending their coats, and the other operating on a recumbent friend in the rearward part of his clothing. Where the needles came from I do not know; but for thread they used a strand of the oakum (evidently easy to deal with) which the boys were picking in the corners. Other loungers strolled about with their hands in their pockets, discussing the topics of the day, and playing practical jokes on the industrious few: a favourite joke being to take a

---

19. On a ship, a beam on which the anchor chain is wound.

bit of rag, anoint it with grease from the crank axles, and clap it unexpectedly over somebody's eye.

The consequence of all this was that the cranks went round at a very slow rate and now and then stopped altogether. Then the miller came in [and][20] the loungers rose from their couches, the tailors ceased stitching, the smokers dropped their pipes, and every fellow was at his post. The cranks spun round furiously again, the miller's expostulation being drowned amidst a shout of "Slap, bang, here we are again!"[21] or this extemporised chorus—

"We'll hang up the miller on a sour apple tree,
We'll hang up the miller on a sour apple tree,
We'll hang up the miller on a sour apple tree,
And then go grinding on.
Glory, glory, hallelujah, &c. &c."[22]

By such ditties the ruffians enlivened their short spell of work. Short indeed! The miller departed, and within a minute afterwards, beds were reoccupied, pipes lit, and tailoring resumed. So the game continued—the honest fellows sweating at the cranks, anxious to get the work done and go out to look for more profitable labour, and the paupers by profession taking matters quite easy. I am convinced that had the work been properly super-intended the four measures of corn might have been ground in the space of an hour and a half. As it was, when the little bell had tin-kled for the fourth time, and the yard gate was opened and we were free to depart, the clock had struck eleven.[23]

I had seen the show—gladly I escaped into the open streets. The sun shone brightly on my ragged, disreputable figure, and

---

20. Word omitted in the original.

21. Title and first line of a popular music hall song written by Harry Copeland about 1865. Also known as "The School of Jolly Dogs."

22. One of several variants of "John Brown's Body," the famous Union march-ing song of the American Civil War. Sung to the tune of a revivalist hymn attributed to William Steffe.

23. In other words, the task had taken almost three hours.

showed its squalor with startling distinctness; but within all was rejoicing. A few yards, and then I was blessed with the sight of that same vehicle—waiting for me in the spot where I had parted from it fourteen weary hours before. Did you observe, Mr. Editor, with what alacrity I jumped in? I have a vivid recollection of you, Sir,— sitting there with an easy patience, lounging though your *Times*, and oh! so detestably clean to look at! But, though I resented your collar, I was grateful for the sight of a familiar face, and for that draught of sherry which you considerately brought for me, a welcome refreshment after so many weary waking hours of fasting.

And now I have come to the end I remember many little anecdotes which escaped me in writing the previous articles. I ought to have told you of two quiet elderly gentlemen who, amidst all the blackguardism that went on around, held a discussion upon the merits of the English language—one of the disputants showing an especial admiration for the word "kindle," "fine old Saxon word as ever was coined." Then there were some childish games of "first and last letters," to vary such entertainments as that of the swearing club. I should also have mentioned that on the dissolution of the Swearing Club a game at "dumb motions" was started, which presently led to some talk concerning deaf and dumb people, and their method of conversing with each other by means of finger signs; as well as to a little story that sounded strangely enough coming from the mouth of the most efficient member of the club. A good memory for details enables me to repeat this story almost, if not quite, exactly. "They are a rummy lot, them deaf and dumb," said the story-teller. "I was at the workhouse at Stepney when I was a young un, don't you know; and when I got a holiday I used to go and see my old woman as lived in the Borough. Well, one day a woman as was in the house ses to me, ses she, 'Don't you go past the Deaf and Dumb School as you goes home?' So I ses, 'Yes.' So ses she, 'Would you mind callin' there and takin' a message to my little gal as is in there deaf and dumb?' So I ses, 'No.' Well, I goes, and they lets me in, and I tells the message, and they shows me the kid what it was for. Pooty little gal! So they tells her the message, and then she begins making orts and crosses like on her hands. 'What's she a doin' that for?' I ses. 'She's a talkin' to you,' ses they. 'Oh!' I ses, 'what's she talkin' about?' 'She says you're a good boy for comin' and tellin' her about her mother, and she loves you.' Blessed if I could help laughin'! So I ses, 'There ain't no call for her to say that.' Pooty little kid she was! I stayed there a goodish bit, and walked about the garden with her, and what d'ye think? Presently she takes a fancy for some of my jacket buttons—brass uns they was, with the name of the 'house' on 'em[24]—and I cuts four on 'em off and gives her. Well, when I give her them blow me if she didn't want one of the brass buckles off my shoes. Well, you mightn't think it, but I gave her that too." "Didn't yer get into a row when you got back?" some listener asked. "Rather! Got kep without dinner and walloped as well, as I wouldn't tell what I'd done with 'em. Then they was goin' to wallop me again, so I thought I'd cheek it out; so I up and told the master all about it." "And got it wuss?" "No, I didn't. The master give me new buttons and a buckle without saying another word, and my dinner along with my supper as well."

The moral of all this I leave to you. It seems necessary to say something about it, for the report which Mr. Farnall made after visiting Lambeth Workhouse on Saturday[25] seems meant to suggest an idea that what has been described here is merely an irregularity. So it may be; but an irregularity which consigned some *forty men* to such a den on the night when somebody happened to be there to see, is probably a frequent one; and it certainly is infamous. And then as to the other workhouses? Mr. Farnall was in ignorance of what was done at Lambeth in this way, and I select-

---

24. In the original: "e'm."

25. Greenwood was responding to a report which appeared in *The Daily News* that morning (the *Pall Mall Gazette* was an evening paper) giving a quite favorable evaluation of the Lambeth Workhouse. H.B. Farnall was the Poor Law inspector whose generally supportive comments were quoted in full in this article. An editorial in the *Pall Mall Gazette* the following day gave a detailed criticism of this report: "The Houseless Poor and the Workhouses." *The Daily News* 15 January 1866, p. 2; "Casual Wards." *Pall Mall Gazette* 16 January 1866, pp. 2-3. See also Koven, *Slumming*, pp. 45-6, 56, 66. References to Farnall were removed from the version of "A Night in a Workhouse" that was reprinted in Keating, *Into Unknown England*, pp. 33-54. The remainder of the penultimate paragraph (after "merely an irregularity") was removed from the one subsequent reprint of Greenwood's articles as a pamphlet; *A Night in a Workhouse. From the Pall Mall Gazette.* London: F. Bowering, 1866, p. 16.

ed it for a visit quite at random. Does he know what goes on in other workhouses? If he is inclined to inquire, I may, perhaps, be able to assist the investigation by this hint: my companions had a discussion during the night as to the respective merits of the various workhouses; and the general verdict was that those of Tottenham and Poplar were the worst in London. Is it true, as I heard it stated, that at any one of these workhouses the casual sleeps on bare boards, without a bed of any sort?

One word in conclusion. I have some horrors for Mr. Farnall's private ear (should he like to learn about them) infinitely more revolting than anything that appears in these papers.

Chapter Two

A Night in the Casual Ward of the Work-House, in Rhyme. Dedicated to the Million.
by 'M. A.'

London: News Agents' Publishing Co., 1866

I sallied forth the other night,
In a sad and piteous plight,
To do, as I considered right,
To sleep within a Workhouse.

I wished to set my mind at rest,
And be with anecdotes possessed,
From those, who do these homes infest,
So drove towards a Workhouse.

The night was windy, frosty, cold,
It shook the courage of the bold,
It tried the young, it nipped the old,
As I went to the Workhouse.

Though tedious, I would fain pursue,
The work, that night I planned to do,
And hoped for strength to take me through,
A night within a Workhouse.

I took the heavy knocker—knocked—
The door was speedily unlocked,
To which so many poor had flocked,
For shelter in the Workhouse.

"What do you want," the porter said;
"I want a lodging, sir—a bed."
"You'll have to sleep beneath the shed,"
If passed within the Workhouse.

I looked, of course, disconsolate;
And dreaded my approaching fate.
The clerk said bluffly, "You are late"
To pass within the Workhouse.

"Here, porter, you may take him through
And also take his bread with you;"
Which I was glad for him to do
The first time in a Workhouse.

The hall was spacious, clean, and light,
And all looked comfortably bright;
So my misgivings vanished quite
When first within the Workhouse.

"Daddy" spoke kindly unto me—
Yes, yes, indeed, most feelingly,
And treated me hospitably,
This night within the Workhouse.

"You're late for skilley," I was told,
While I was shivering with cold;
Not for myself I cared,—the old
I thought of in the Workhouse.

"Just like my luck," I made reply,
Dolefully, with a heavy sigh;
And scarcely can I tell you why,
Save being in a Workhouse.

My footsteps nothing would retard,
Although I felt it very hard,
From skilley thus to be debarred,
When once within the Workhouse.

Three baths were stationed in a row,
In one of which I had to go;
On no account could I say no,
Because within a Workhouse.

The water looked like mutton broth;
A nasty smell came issuing forth;
But luckily a cleanly cloth
They lent me in the Workhouse.

I wish I had less hasty been;
Though ragged, all my flesh was clean,
And that by daddy soon was seen
When stripped within the Workhouse.

The flagstones next I had to tread,
'Ere I could reach my filthy bed,
With [naught][1] upon my feet or head,
When I went through the Workhouse.

All my poor things were packed up then,
To save the grasp of thieving men,
Or boys within that dreadful den,
When passing through the Workhouse.

I went with an appalling dread,
Thither by daddy kindly led,
Into this almost open shed,
Just through that horrid Workhouse.

Unconsciously I did provoke
A little merriment and joke,

---

1. In the original: "nought."

For I forgot to take my "toke,"
As I passed through the Workhouse.

My feelings I can't well express,
But they were ones of bitterness;
And oh! the wretched loneliness,
I felt within a Workhouse.

How many anxious hearts there were,
Brim full of sorrow, hardening care,
I wished almost I'd not been there,
It tried me in the Workhouse.

My heart bled pity for each one,
The old, whose race was nearly run,
The young, whose life had scarce begun,
That slept within this Workhouse.

Not after eight is skilley given,
To those who want and care had driven,
To seek a shelter under Heaven
Provided by the Workhouse.

All, all combined within my view,
A sight revolting, yet so true,
Of decent men there were but few,
Within this dreadful Workhouse.

The varied coughs, the hectic hue,
The riot no one could subdue;
Compassion every moment drew
From me when in the Workhouse.

The "swearing club" was most profane,
While [naught]² but tumult seemed to reign,
And decent men complained in vain;
'Twas no use in a Workhouse.

---

2. In the original: "nought."

They smoked foul pipes, if only that,
At this I never wondered at,
They danced, they swore, they sang, and spat,
Just near me in the Workhouse.

The ribaldry, the impious song,
The thought of contemplated wrong,
Issued from that Satanic throng,
That breathed within the Workhouse.

No discipline, no one to guide,
No one to care for those inside;
The devil's jaws seemed open wide
For those within the Workhouse.

The constant dipping at the pail,
The canvass flapping like a sail,
Told but a melancholy tale
That night within the Workhouse.

(MORAL.)

John Bull will now most plainly see
The want of Christian charity;
Or e'en of that philanthropy
That ought to rule the Workhouse!

Not that John Bull would wish to see
The Workhouse full of luxury;
But certainly from danger free,
In England's parish Workhouse![3]

---

3.   The reference to "England's parish Workhouse" is intriguing. The Poor
Law Amendment Act of 1834 had grouped parishes into poor law unions, which built
larger and more forbidding workhouses than had existed under the "old poor law."
(See above, p. 15.) "M.A." invokes John Bull, the archetypal Englishman, and the ideal
of the parish, where there was no place for the administrative cruelties of the union
workhouse. The implication was that there was something un-English about the cruelties of the "new poor law." The word "parish" was also used by C. W. Craven, F. G.
Wallace-Goodbody and Mary Higgs: see below, pp. 186, 122, 132, 219.

Chapter Three

The Female Casual and Her Lodging
by J. H. Stallard
London: Saunders, Otley & Co., 1866, Pages 1-79[1]

CHAPTER I.
INTRODUCTORY.

Until the publication of "A Night in a Workhouse"[2] there was a very general ignorance both of the character of the vagrant poor and the treatment they receive in the casual wards. Inspection was indeed provided by the law, but it is surrounded by enormous difficulties, because the moment a visitor appears, the authorities are on the alert, and the poor themselves put on their best behaviour. Association on the footing of

---

1. Only the first 79 pages of Stallard's book are reproduced here. The remainder is a supplementary section—to all extents and purposes a separate text—on workhouse infirmaries.

2. James Greenwood's articles in the *Pall Mall Gazette*. See pp. 53–75 above.

equality is as necessary to secure the confidence of the vagrant as it is to disarm official caution; and considerable address is required to pass through the wards without arousing the suspicions of the police and the attendants, and without exciting the jealousy and anger of the paupers themselves.

Now, if the difficulties were great in ascertaining the character of the male casual and the treatment he receives, how much greater will they be when the females are in question! A gentleman, having dressed to the part, descended from his brougham[3] to the dirty gruel, and assuming the air and character of the casual himself, passed safely through the wards with little chance of insult; but no lady could be found to imitate the act, and if the attempt were made, no rags would disguise her character, no acting would conceal her disgust; discovery would be all but certain, and one can scarcely tell where the disagreeables [sic] would end.

Nor is it possible to appeal to the casuals themselves. They are suspicious; their confidence is not easily obtained by strangers of a different class, and the chances of ascertaining the truth would be still less if you were to attempt to bribe them. Nor are the officials and attendants to be relied upon. They naturally put down all tramp visitors in the same category, and will describe them all as utterly worthless, in order to justify the harsh manner they too commonly use towards them; besides, they are far too ready to make things agreeable to their auditor, in the hope of getting his good opinion or some other recompense.

One might look in vain, therefore, for a person qualified to visit the haunts of these female Bohemians; she must be accustomed to dirt and rags, and hardships must be no novelty to her. She should be one who has slept without a bed upon the floor, who has dined upon a crust of bread, and by a course of suffering has been prepared to endure misery of the very lowest kind without a murmur of complaint. Yet with all this she must be sufficiently familiar with cleanliness, honesty, and plenty, to be

---

3.   See above, p. 54, note 4.

able to contrast the condition of the vagrant with that of the industrious poor. Cleverness, courage, and tact will be required, moreover, to evade the scrutiny of the police and the sharp eyes of workhouse officials ever ready to pounce upon those whom they regard as impostors; and besides this, there must be a real good nature, which is the only passport to the hearts even of the most abandoned, and the only means of ascertaining the true character of these most degraded specimens of their sex.

Some of these qualifications are evidently possessed by the person who made the following narration. She is a pauper widow, who, having received some slight assistance in a period of great distress, volunteered, as an act of gratitude, to visit these wards for the express purpose of describing them. Not only has the character of this person been vouched for by persons who have known her many years, but every effort has been made to confirm the truthfulness of the descriptions by visits to the wards themselves and other means.

Whilst, therefore, it is impossible to rely implicitly upon every detail of statements made, as these are, at second-hand, there is nevertheless every reason to believe that they are substantially true, and that the picture may be regarded as practically correct. It was absolutely necessary to soften down much of the language, which was too gross for publication, and an apology for its character may still be thought necessary; but it was impossible to convey an idea of the misery necessarily endured by a respectable woman in real distress without giving the language of those into whose company she is forcibly thrown, in considerable detail; indeed, the same remark is applicable to the whole narration, which shows that we have legalized a demoralizing institution of the very worst class, from which we have taken every pains to exclude the very objects for whose shelter it was primarily designed. There is, in fact, an indiscriminate herding together of the hardiest and most impudent vagrants in the Metropolis, who night after night brave the police with impunity, and exist upon the liberality of the law, regardless of everything except their own idleness. Their dreadful language and disgusting habits drive away the decent poor even more effectually than the police; and we can scarcely wonder that in Bethnal Green an honest woman should prefer to spend a cold December night in the public water-closet rather than enter one of these dens of infamy and filth.

CHAPTER II.
NEWINGTON.

"⁴I SET out to visit the casual ward at Newington Workhouse on Friday evening, the 13th of July. I put on a blue velvet bonnet, very old and dirty; a grey skirt much torn, which I have been ashamed to wear in the streets for some time; and a cloth check shawl and worn-out boots. I purposely went out as dirty as I could; but I may mention it here that I was regarded by the officials in every case with great suspicion: they looked at me as though I were not a real casual, and only let me through when they had seen my boots, which appeared to satisfy their standard of distress.

Thus dressed, I went off to the workhouse at Walworth about half-past seven o'clock. I found the porter at the gate talking to a detective, and I asked him to give me a night's lodging. He inquired if I had an order, and I said "No." He said I must get one at the police-station, P division, in Kennington Lane. It took me three-quarters of an hour to find it, and I had to wait about a quarter of an hour until the inspector was disengaged. He then asked me my name. I told him, Ellen Stanley; that I was a tailoress out of work; that I had lived last at Deptford, but had been without any fixed residence for several days. He asked me where I worked, and I told him I was only a helper, and that my last employer worked for some one in the City. He scrutinized me very fiercely, and wanted to know why I came there; I told him I had been to see a friend at Norwood, but was too tired to get home. He then wrote out the order. Whilst this was going on several men of the force stood by, and one in particular stared very closely at me, and they laughed and jeered at me as if it was fine fun; one was different, and seemed to pity me, for he said he was sorry he had not a penny in his pocket for half a pint of beer.

It was after nine o'clock when I again reached the workhouse-door, and I was obliged to knock very gently because the knocker was fastened down with wire. A pauper opened the door, and shut

---

4.   Chapters II, III, IV and V begin and end with quotation marks. The text is Stallard's written version of his accomplice's accounts of nights in various casual wards, which were presumably given to him verbally.

it again as soon as he saw my order for admission. I waited ten minutes and a lot of people came out of the neighbouring cottages to stare at me, which they did until the porter let me in. He asked my age, and beckoned to a woman with some keys to take charge of me, and she conducted me to a building on the right-hand side of a small yard near the principal entrance to the workhouse. She gave me a piece of bread, and opening the door, told me to undress. She waited to take everything away from me but my boots, stockings, and chemise, and I made the rest into a bundle, which she took charge of. I was then left quite alone.

The place was about 13 feet long, and 7 or 8 feet wide, with a sloping roof, in which was a skylight of six panes. Over the door was a small opening for ventilation, but the place was dreadfully hot, and I tried in vain to open the skylight. There was a gaslight at one end, and only a narrow passage between the beds and the wall. There were nine beds arranged in wooden troughs, with sides a foot high, so that when you lie down it is impossible to see the person in the next bed. The beds are made of straw in canvas ticks, with a straw bolster, both being very hard. There were two thick rugs to each bed; they were like horsehair, and both doubled to the width of the bed. One was placed underneath, and the other was used to cover, and as the beds were so narrow the whole weight of the upper rug was thrown upon you if it was used at all; there was, in fact, no alternative but lying without any covering on so warm a night.

After a time I felt very lonely, and began to cry, for I feared my visit would be in vain, and very soon my trouble was increased by finding that the place was alive with vermin, and that scores of bugs were running about the bed. Feeling sick and faint, I got up and sat upon the end of the bed, and shortly afterwards two women came in and relieved my loneliness. They were after hours, and their clothes were not taken away. The first was an elderly woman of about fifty-four years of age, very strong, ruddy, and sunburnt; she had a basket with some scraps of food in it, and a blacking-box with Day and Martin's[5] name upon it, which was

5. Carr & Day & Martin is a company, founded in 1765 and flourishing today, specializing in products used for the care of saddlery and other leather articles.

filled with cottons, tapes, stay-laces, and other articles of a similar kind. She was literally clothed in filthy rags. Her dress consisted of an old body-lining, which scarcely reached her waist, and a black skirt—she had nothing on else but a bonnet and shawl. After taking these off she removed a series of rags which were pinned in pieces round about her, and as each was taken off she drew it briskly through her hand to knock off the vermin with which everything was covered. She then removed her boots, which were without a bit of sole and very old, and her stockings, which had no feet, a few rags being tied round the toes to protect them on the road. When she had reduced herself to complete nudity she commenced to destroy the vermin on her body, the skin being covered with sores and dirt, such as made me ill to look upon.

The other woman was somewhat younger; her outside clothes were rather more respectable, but underneath she was quite as bad, and was very soon as naked as the other, and actively engaged in the same way.

When they had finished with themselves they began to pick their clothes, shaking them over the beds generally, and turning over the gathers of the dresses to find out what they sought.

After a time I got a little tranquil, for no one can conceive my horror at the sight which presented itself, and which I could not help watching spite of all my fear. I asked them what time it was, and they said it was about eleven o'clock, and then I said, "I suppose you are friends." They said, "No, they had met accidentally at the police-station." Both were hawkers out of luck. The younger had no money, and nothing to sell. She said that she would like to wash her chemise, and the other said she could go to the public wash-house at three-halfpence an hour; but what, said the former, if you have not got the money? They remained in this way fully one hour and a half, and then they shook the rugs and the beds, making a great dust, and lay down talking to each other in low tones which I could not hear.

They soon went to sleep, but I was frightened to death. I found myself covered with vermin, and in a state of constant misery the whole night through. I could neither sit nor lie, and I went as near the door as I could get, in order to get a breath of air if one came in through the narrow opening I have already noticed.

About three o'clock I heard the bell ring, and the key turned in the door. Fearing to be found out of bed, I again forced myself to get in before the woman came, and I had scarcely done so when she brought in a woman of about thirty years of age, who was tall, strong, and almost as dark as a gipsy. She appeared under the influence of drink, but not intoxicated, and she sat down sullenly in the corner, and began to pick over her "dress" as the others had done. She wore a dark linsey skirt, very torn and dirty; the body was of striped calico, and she said she had bought it for twopence of a workhouse nurse, but she added that they chaffed her about getting it in gaol, which seemed more likely. She said, "D--- that fellow that made a bother about the vagrants; he has only given us extra trouble. I came here at two o'clock, and they made me go all the way to the police-station for an order; if I had known that, I could have got one easy enough on my way, for I have passed them twenty times." Her feet were also encased in rags, and she said "she had not had a wash for more than three weeks."

In my life I never saw a human being in such a dreadful state; there she sat, tearing her skin to pieces, and on her back were sores as large as your hand, which must have been intolerably painful. The stench was terrific; and dirty as she was, I was obliged to ask her for a little water to prevent my fainting. She fetched the tin and poured some water into it, and seeing me shiver at the dirty can, she put in her fingers to clean it out. I thought I must have died, for I could not touch the water, and when she saw the reason she said, "What a fool I am, I forgot what I had been doing;" and then she swilled the tin several times, and I took a little and was revived. She remained sitting in the corner until it was daylight and then lay down, and they were all fast asleep when the nurse arrived in the morning soon after six o'clock.

For myself, I never felt more thankful than to see the door open, and to breathe once more the fresh air. The heat and stench were indescribable; the whole place swarmed with vermin, and the restlessness even of those who were asleep was most painful to behold. The woman brought in my bundle, and I was soon dressed, but we had to wait for the others, who were a long time putting on their few rags.

When all were ready, we went through the workhouse to the oakum room, which is fitted up with benches and seats all round. It was clean and more airy than the dreadful hole in which we had passed the night. Here we were served with a pint of oatmeal porridge and a piece of bread. It was very good, but I could not touch it. The rest ate it greedily and asked for more, and as there was some left it was divided between them. Two men were also brought in to have their breakfast and do their work, and as soon as it was given out a great deal of slang chaff began. The tall woman especially joked with them, and I asked her how it was that she was always scratching herself. She replied, "All who come to these places have the itch, and are covered with vermin;" and when I said that I was clean, she replied, "You will not be so long, for the beds in these places are all infected."

I asked whether we could not have a little water to wash. "You may have as much as you like to drink," they said, "but none to wash." "Ah," said the woman, "I should so like a bath, for I am in a wretched state;" and the old hawker said it was a shame that they might not wash themselves, because their hands were dirtied by the oakum, and it was impossible to sell her bits of laces without soiling them.

The young woman advised me to stay as long as I could over my work, "for," she said, "it is the only chance of making yourself clean."

I asked her why, and she explained that in the fields men were often about and drove you away, and that "if you did it in the streets the police are down upon you, you are so well looked up."

When the rest left she had not done picking one quarter of her work, and even in the presence of the men she constantly turned up her dress to remove vermin. I came out with the youngest hawker, and we tried at several cottages to get some water to wash, but they all refused us. I asked her how it was there were so few, and she said that most of them were in the country, lying out in the fields.

When I got home I found scores of vermin on my clothes, and I was obliged to burn my chemise. I felt very ill from fright and loss of rest, and thought it was impossible that I could ever again enter a casual ward."

CHAPTER III.
LAMBETH.

"AFTER a few days' rest I again set out, and on the evening of Tuesday, July 17, 1866, I applied at the Lambeth Workhouse for a night's lodging, and was sent to the police-station in Kennington Lane for an order of admission. The inspector on duty was very abrupt; he did not seem to like his duty, and he asked me shortly what I wanted. I said, an order for a night's lodging. He continued:—

"What is your name?"

"Jane Wood," I answered.

"Your age?"

"Forty."

"Where did you sleep last?"

"Greenwich."

"What are you?"

"A hawker of embroidery."

"Where is your stock?"

"I have none."

"Where is your stock-money?"

"I have none."

"Then," said he, "you ought to have; here is your order; go along."

I then returned to the workhouse, and was admitted by two men, and the elder, having read the order, sent the other with me to the casual ward.

I was here taken charge of by a stout woman of about fifty years of age, who said, "Come along, this way to the bath."

The whole place is far superior to that at Newington; the bath-room is separated from the sleeping ward by a door and a curtain; there is a stove in it to dry the clothes if they are wet, and three zinc baths, well supplied with hot and cold water; the floor was very clean and covered with wood. I had a very clean and comfortable bath, with soap to wash with, and a clean towel to dry myself, and then I put on a blue gown which was given me to sleep in.

I then went into the sleeping ward, which was a large place, with twenty-four beds in it, each one made in a wooden trough, which turns up against the wall when not in use. The beds are of straw, in rough canvas ticks.[6] They were tolerably clean, but the rugs were very dirty; and I saw many vermin upon the one on my bed, so that I sat on the edge of the bed nearly all night, as I did before. There were eight women, all busily engaged in picking vermin from their clothes, and they began to chaff me as soon as I got in. I had put on a very old and brown chemise, yet they soon observed that it was better than their own, and they wondered how

---

6.   Covers, used for mattresses.

I had got it and why I wore it. In the next bed to me was a stoutish woman, of about thirty-seven years of age, with her face drawn to one side by a fit. She was well known to them all as Cranky Sal, and she took my part whenever she had a chance to do so.

One woman said she supposed I had bilked[7] some old fellow, as I was well up; and Sal told her to mind her own business, for it was nothing to her if I had. I said I must have clean linen if I washed it in the ditch.

They did not believe me, and said, "Ah, I dare say, but you have your own reasons for all that."

They then asked me if I was married, and how many children I had, or if I was an old maid. "Old maid be ---," said one.

"Ah," says another, "I suppose she is like the rest of us." "I suppose you are a bad one yourself," replied Cranky Sal, "or you would not ask."

They then made me show them my hair, at which they uttered expressions of the greatest admiration.

"So help me G---," says one, "if I had your head of hair, it would make my fortune."

"Yes," said another, "if you were hard up you could cut it off and sell it."

I then began to chaff them in return, to prevent a row. I told them I had been crossed in love; upon which a woman said, "She would be --- if she would take that in; she dared say I was no better than I should be, but that she'd find out what I was;" and another said, "I was --- modest, and that being crossed in love was all --- kid. She supposed that I had come like that --- fellow who had caused all the bother, and made them get orders from the police. What good had he done? They thought they were going to have meat every day all over London, so much stir as he had made."

"D--- him," said another, "I should like to give him twelve on his back;" but twelve what I could not tell.

At length the row became so great, that Cranky Sal told them to shut up, and if they would not be quiet that she would call the nurse; upon which they said, "You may call her and be ---, she will not come."

7.   Cheated.

Cranky Sal then related her luck. She had been in the country, and had got at one place bread-and-butter and meat, and twopence in money, but she met some others, and they "collared her can"—that is, divided it between them; she then met a navvy, who treated her with beer. After this she fell in with a woman named "Navvy Nell," who had been lucky, and had "nailed" one of her powerful friends for half-a-crown, and by this time, as it was night, they agreed together to look for a place to sleep in. They went into a field, and made a bed between two haystacks, but they were disturbed by a labouring man, who told them to be off. Their next attempt was more successful, and they had a good night's rest.

In the morning they met a man, who asked them if they wanted work, and said he could give them strawberry-picking for a fortnight, at which he said they could earn two shillings and sixpence per day. Sally, however, thought they would not like it, as the sun was so very hot, and they declined. Soon after that they met a man who paid their fare to London, where they arrived very late, and the beershops being all closed, he treated them to coffee instead.

Since then they had been to Wimbledon and Wandsworth, where Navvy Nell had made a good thing of it. A few weeks ago she had neither stockings nor clothes; but, said Cranky Sal, "she is now well togged up."

They then began to talk about workhouses and casual wards, to all of which Sal had paid a visit. She said the wards at Richmond were the best; there they had feather-beds to sleep upon, and everything was nice; they had also good fare at Marylebone, and a few other places were well spoken of. The nurse knew Sally well, and said, "What! are you here again?"

In the winter Sally prefers Marylebone or Richmond, and then she trades upon her reputation for crankiness to get into the imbecile ward, where, as she boasted, there is meat every day and nothing to do.

All this time the operation of picking her clothes was going on, and the appearance of the women, nearly all with short hair, was most extraordinary. About eleven o'clock another woman came in. She had been picking roses all day at one penny per bushel; and "Strike me dead," says she, "if it is not too bad, for I only earned fivepence all the day. Last year it was much better, and I got twopence a bushel."

The last arrival was at twelve o'clock, when a woman and three children were shown in. They were at the police-station when I was there, and she said they had been kept waiting for more than two hours for the order for admission. One child was put into bed with the mother, another in a bed by her side, and the eldest was sent over to the men's ward. They seemed very tired, but for a long time they never ceased getting up and tearing themselves to pieces; indeed, the constant scratching of every one in the ward went on until it was quite daylight. They all seem accustomed to vermin, and they look for nothing better.

One woman said, "She didn't care how many l--e she had, but that she couldn't abide them Pharaoh flights" (fleas); and she sat for twenty minutes catching them with great industry, and cracking them between her nails.

Another woman said, "She would be d---d if she would ever pay for a night's lodging, even if she had a pound in her pocket;" but another said, "She would; for see," said she, "what a time they keep you in to pick the oakum."

"Ah," replied the first, "if it wasn't for that I would come here every night; but I do not care while the weather is fine, I would as [lief]⁸ sleep out of doors as in."

"Ah," said a third, who suffered greatly, "we have more peace in winter, there are fewer vermin."

They all seemed to know that sleep was out of the question until the feeding-time was fairly over, and daylight had arrived; then a common repose gradually took possession of the casuals and their voracious companions, and I was the only person awake when the bell rang for us to get up.

Shortly afterwards the woman came in and expressed surprise that they were not yet dressed, and hurried them on. The beds were then turned up, and a deaf-and-dumb girl brought in a pint of good skilly and a piece of bread for each. After breakfast the oakum was brought in, and we were set to work, superintended by the female already described.

The operation of picking their clothes went on even whilst they were eating their breakfast, and seems the only habitual method of cleanliness; it was continued whilst they were at work, and there was a woman named Shipton, of middle age, the wife of

---

8.   In the original: "lieve."

a vagrant in the male ward, who could not sit still one moment without turning up her clothes to relieve the violent irritation of her skin. After sitting at her work for an hour and doing very little, this woman became suddenly frantic; she jumped, and rushed about the ward, as if she were insane, crying piteously, "I cannot bear it—I cannot bear it."

Roaring with madness, she stripped herself entirely naked, retaining only her bonnet and a small shawl. The clothes she took off scarcely held together, and she tore them into rags. At this moment the woman came in and began to blow her up.

"What have you done that for?" she said; "you ought to be ashamed of yourself. This is the twelfth case of tearing up, and you will have three days for it on bread and water. If you wanted to tear up, why did you not do it outside, and not keep me here two or three hours waiting on such as you?"

"I could not bear it any longer," answered the woman, "and I cannot help it."

The attendant then went out for the assistant matron, who was a sour-looking woman in spectacles. When she came in she turned over the torn rags with her keys, and said that they were clean and free from vermin; that she had seen much worse; and that it was not through dirt she did it, but devilment. She went away, but turned back again to tell the superintendent to take care that the woman did her oakum before she left. Neither the nurse nor the other person seemed to have a grain of pity for this poor creature, but I believe her sufferings to have been genuine. She appears to have had the fever, which made them less easily borne; even the nurse was frightened, and in my whole life I never saw so pitiable an object. For myself, I cried at her distress, and I wished to help her. They brought her an old petticoat to put on; it was of blue and white calico behind, and dark damask in front; it was clean, but patched all over, and reached scarcely to her knees; a jacket of workhouse cotton, and a checked chemise, and in this shameful costume, without stockings etc., she was made to finish her work. I heard afterwards that the master of the workhouse forbade her being sent out in this shameful way, and gave her better clothing. We left her behind, and as soon as we were ready a tall stout man came in and took us to the door.

Cranky Sal went out with me, and was extremely anxious that I should go to Wimbledon with her. She said we should be sure to do well whilst the camp was there, and then we could go to

Richmond, which was as good as your own home. She said she enjoyed herself finely in the summer-time, and that she could always pick up a navvy. In the winter it was not so easy and pleasant, and then she went in. I came to the conclusion that she was more rogue than fool, and indeed she boasted that she was so. I had a great difficulty in shaking her off, but in Lambeth Walk she complained of thirst, and I offered her a pint of porter, which she drank with great gusto, whilst I gave her the slip and returned home."

CHAPTER IV.
WHITECHAPEL.

"ON the evening of Friday I again set out for a visit to the female casuals, and having ascertained that the police are not employed either at Whitechapel or St. George's-in-the-East, I selected the former, being glad enough to escape the ordeal of the station, which is enough to deter any one who is respectable from seeking a night's lodging in the places provided for the destitute. I again dressed myself in my worn-out and dirty clothes, and after a long and fatiguing walk I arrived at the gate of the Whitechapel workhouse about half-past nine. Having asked for a night's lodging, I was told to go to the stone-yard, which is at the back of the Pavilion Theatre, in the Whitechapel Road. Passing up a wide entry the gates are on the left-hand, and near it there are many stables and a number of empty carts, which seemed to be employed by contractors who mend the roads.

I had great difficulty in finding the place, and when I had found it could not make known my wants, because the knocker was tied down, and could not be raised so as to make any noise. After kicking at the door I succeeded in bringing out a little grey-headed old man, clad in the workhouse clothes, who had a kindly expression, which he tried to disguise by a very stern manner. He asked me shortly what I wanted. I told him a night's lodging. He replied, "You cannot have it; we are full."

I said, "I must have a night's shelter somewhere;" and looking through the gate at a wooden lodge which appeared to be his room, I added, "I can sit down there, if you please."

"Oh, no, indeed," said he, "you will get me into fine trouble if you go there; you had better go somewhere else, for we cannot take you in here."

I pretended to be greatly distressed, but he said, "You must be off, I have no room," and he slammed the gate, taking good care however to leave it a little open, that he might see what I did.

I said, "I shall go and sleep in one of those carts, and then the police will come, and lock me up, for I cannot go any further; and if they find me there, you will catch it."

All this time he watched me through the nick of the door, which he held ajar, and seeing that I still remained, he said, "Well, there, come along; I got one bed left, and you seem a decent sort of woman. I don't think you were ever here before;" and looking at me very hard, but very kindly, he added, "Poor soul, I hope you will not want to come again, for there is a rough lot here;" and, thinking that I was still crying, he said, "There, come along in, and you shall have a bed."

I was then shown into a little square office, just inside the gate, and was asked my name, which was on this occasion Ellen Smith. He asked me where I slept last. I told him Dockhead. My trade? I told him, a tailoress, but not a regular hand. My age? I said forty-two; and he then dismissed me with a ticket, upon which my name was written, and with a man's blue and white calico shirt to sleep in.

I asked him if I was to undress and give him all my clothes, and he said, "Yes, everything I had, as there was a very rum lot."

Looking at the shirt, I said, "But this is not clean, and if I put it on and get disease what would become of me?"

He then whispered in my ear, and said, "Well, you don't look like one of the roughs, and if I was you, I wouldn't put it on; I can't answer for it, they are a dirty lot. But mind what you are about, and put it under your pillow, and don't let the nurse see you in your own shift in the morning, or I shall catch it; and now put your clothes together, and pin them in a bundle, and put the ticket on them, that they may be safe."

He then led me across the yard to a wooden building; which seemed to have been built for a waggon-shed, the sides [having][9] been boarded up to make it habitable. He unlocked the door, and showed me in. The place was already well filled; it was nearly square, two sides being occupied by shallow trough beds inclined

---

9. In the original: "shaving."

from the wall. It was about eighteen feet long, and there were nine beds on the one side and seven on the other. There was a tap of water on the right-hand side of the door, and a gaslight hanging from the ceiling. At one corner there was an opening into a second ward, which was about eight feet wide, and held also nine beds, similar to the rest. In the first compartment all the beds were occupied except two, and I took one of those vacant next the door. They were altogether eleven women and five children, and they all lay without speaking whilst the old man went into the other ward, and brought out a bundle of clothes. He told me to undress, and when he came out I was obliged to screen myself with the shirt he gave me.

As soon as he was gone three of the women rose up in their beds and began to talk. It was fearfully hot, and there was not a breath of air. "Oh dear," said one, "what a dreadful night, and what a dreadful place!" "It is enough to kill us," said another; and the third observed "that she would be eaten alive." Indeed the place was swarming with vermin. The walls were all of wood, white-washed, but very old, and the vermin ran in and out of the cracks like bees at the entrance of their hive on a summer's morning. It is no exaggeration to say that there were myriads; indeed, it is difficult to conceive so many in so small a place.

A woman now said, "Have you got your pannum, old girl?" I did not understand, and another said, "Don't you know, your toke?"[10] and a third then put in, "Why the --- don't you speak plain? Don't you see the woman ain't up to your flash talk?"

"No," said I, "I've got nothing."

"Then, why," said she, "don't you ask him?"

Presently the old man came in and asked me for my clothes. I was sitting up on the bed, with a cotton apron over my shoulders, which I had taken on purpose to put over me. Fearing to betray myself I said, "I could eat a piece of bread, for I am very hungry."

---

10. "Pannum" was another cant (or "flash talk") word for "toke." James Greenwood and Everard Wyrall encountered the latter, while C. W. Craven was given "Tommy:" see above, pp. 59, 61, and below, p. 183. Greenwood also encountered "Tommy" in *On Tramp*: see below, p. 170. The word "pannum" does not occur in any of the other texts in this volume.

He went and got it for me, and said, "There, there! I am sure I forgot you, but here it is." I put it under my head, for it was impossible to eat; and very soon afterwards I saw it absolutely covered with black vermin. At the same time one of the women asked for some water, and he went for a can and drew some from the tap. He then took away my clothes, and after some time he brought in another woman, and passed her through into the other ward. About two o'clock he again came in, smoking his pipe. He went into both compartments to see that all was quiet, and at four he brought in a ladder and turned the gas off.

It was utterly impossible to lie down: the beds were alive with vermin, and the rugs with lice. The walls and woodwork were all spotted over with marks where they had been killed. On the opposite side of the ward the women lay quiet for some time, but on my side they were up and down the whole night. Here, as elsewhere, there was no rest until daylight. The principal subject of conversation was the filthiness of the place, which they all agreed to be the worst in London. One asked me from what part of the world I came, and I said, Dockhead. She asked me what I worked at, and I told her my needle. "That is hard lines," said she; "you had better do anything than that, it is so --- badly paid for." She recommended me to try the road, where I might do much better; and she wanted me to join her, as she was herself getting too well known. She was evidently a cadger and beggar, and she seemed to think that I might do well under her guidance.

At this time the night was indescribably dreadful. There lay the women, naked and restless, tossing about in the dim gaslight, and getting up from time to time in order to shake off their disgusting tormentors, which speckled their naked limbs with huge black spots. When the old man came in, he motioned to me to lie down and go to sleep, but I told him I dared not, for the vermin were so bad. "Ah," said he, "you are not used to it." About twelve o'clock the closeness and heat of the room became intolerable, and every one began to feel ill and to suffer from diarrhoea. Several were drawn double with cramp, and I felt sick and ill myself. The children began to cry constantly, and seemed extremely ill. From this time the closet was constantly occupied by one or another, and the stench became dreadful. "So help me God," said one, "I will never come here again. I would rather go to prison a hundred times." Another said, "Hold your tongue, you --- fool, or he will hear you." Another groaned for a little brandy, with language too dreadful to repeat; and some one else added, "If you were dying, you would get none here." For myself, I suffered more than I can say, and as long as I live I shall never forget the horrors of that dreadful night. No wonder there is cholera at the East of London,[11] for it is generated every night in the Whitechapel casual ward.

About seven o'clock in the morning a big, stout woman came in and said "All up!" and she was followed by a man who brought the clothes. "Here," said she, throwing them towards us, "make haste." She stood by watching us dress, and urging them to get on and be quick. If any one lingered for a moment to pick vermin from her clothes, she immediately stopped them, saying "that she would not have it done there," and she seemed determined to get over her disagreeable duty with the utmost speed. She stared particularly at me, and seemed to wonder what business I had there, and appeared to be only satisfied when she saw my boots. Outside the door there was a pail of water, but neither soap nor towels. Several attempted to wash, and particularly a woman with three children, who was more decent than the rest. The majority never washed at all, for they had no time, the big, fat woman continually driving them on by saying "be quick," "be off," "get on," etc. etc. Those who succeeded in wetting their faces dried them on their own rags.

When all were ready, we were conducted across the yard to the office before mentioned, and skilly and bread were there served out. The former was horrible stuff; it was black, and totally unfit to eat. At the former places I ate some of it, but I could not touch it here, and many others also left the greater part. It was served partly in tin cans, and partly in white earthenware mugs. We had to carry it across the stone-yard to the oakum-room, which is also a filthy place. It is a wooden building covered with tar, and whitewashed inside, the walls being covered with slang writing and

---

11. Epidemics of cholera—a potentially fatal diarrheal disease spread primarily by contaminated water—occurred regularly in cities in England, and elsewhere in Europe, during the first half of the 19th century. The last of these occurred in London in 1866, just as construction of sewage and water treatment systems was being completed. The East End was the last part of the metropolis to be served by these systems.

directions for the road. Some now began to undress, and three of them stripped naked to look over their clothes to destroy the vermin. Two of them commenced smoking. Altogether there were sixteen women and five children. One child asked a woman for a block to sit upon, and she refused it. The mother said, "You know it is not allowed to sit on the oakum-block," and a row commenced, in which the language used cannot be repeated; it ended in a fight, which was interrupted by the entrance of the old man. The woman again sat down on the block, and the other appealed to him, saying, "You know me before to-day;" and he said, "Yes, you are always kicking up a row," and he then ordered the woman to get off the block; but as she did not move he pulled her off, and he said, "I won't have this talk, and if you are not quiet I'll turn you out." She said, "I wish you would." He replied, "If you do, it will not be at the door you want to go out of."

When the breakfast was over, the pots were put on the floor, and we had to go again to the lodge to fetch the oakum. Every one had a pound. It was very old and hard, and quite unfit for women to pick. I was nearly four hours doing mine, although I worked very hard, and my hands were quite sore when I had finished. There were four women who, after doing a little bit, refused to go on. I observed that none of them troubled themselves to do it; and when I had nearly finished mine I said to a woman, "Why don't you get on? you will never be let out to-day." "Oh no," said she, "they cannot keep you in after twelve o'clock." I said if I had known that I would not have done mine. She said, "Ah! I thought you were a --- fool, but we don't hurt ourselves with work." In the meantime there was a general conversation, chiefly about the road and the workhouse, conducted in flash language.

There were now four smoking, and some appeared very contented and happy. One asked another when she tore up last. She said, "it was a long time since, for she got seven days for it;" and another said, "she would tear up every day rather than go lousy, as she had done." Nevertheless, tearing up did not seem so popular as it had been, for they said the magistrates now gave it so --- stiff. "Such places as this," said another, "ought to be set fire to, and a woman had better do anything than come to it."

One poor old woman, who had evidently been more respectable, sat in silence, but in great agony; she was sixty years of age, and quite grey. She said to me, "I feel very faint; I could not touch that muck of stuff, and it is a shame to make a woman do such work as this." She worked very hard, and got done ten minutes before me.

The woman and her boy continued quarrelling with some one or other the whole time, and one of the women told her that "she ought to be ashamed of herself coming there, the money she made on the road." All her clothes had the workhouse marks upon them, and she was evidently a regular beggar. She said, "How do I get more than you?" and the other replied, "Because you are so --- impudent, and can go where we dare not." There appeared to be a great difference amongst the women, a few being more cleanly and respectable. Twelve out of the sixteen had a yellow look, as if they had been jaundiced, and six or eight had short hair, either from having had the fever or from having been in prison. There was none except the old widow who was not able to do a good day's work.

When I had finished I was in no hurry to leave, wishing to observe what was going on, and to read the writing upon the walls, but I was immediately taken to task. "What the --- are you waiting for?" said one. "You seem --- modest over it," said another; and a third thought that I would be glad to get out of it. It was half-past eleven when I had done, and I left five women amusing themselves, and making no attempt to finish their task. I asked them what the man would say. They said they did not care; they supposed they would get a good blowing up, but they did not mind that.

Bad as the night was at Newington, it was a palace compared with this, which was enough to kill any one, and ought to be at once closed."

CHAPTER V.
ST. GEORGE'S-IN-THE-EAST.
JULY 23RD, 1866.

"THE Workhouse of St. George-in-the-East is near the Docks. I had the greatest difficulty in finding it, and was very tired when I arrived. The doors were open, and in the gateway I saw a stout man with a cap on, who was leaning over the half-door of the office, smoking a cigar. Puffing the smoke in my face, and taking it very easily, he questioned me as follows:—

"What do you want?"

"A night's lodging."

"What brought you this way? What are you?"

"I am a shirt-maker."

"Where have you been living all your life, and what are you now?"

"I have been a widow three years, and have lived at Deptford."

"Why not make your claim to the proper authorities at Deptford?"

I answered "that I only wanted a night's lodging to get over this bother, and that I hoped soon to get some work."

"Where did you sleep last night?"

I replied, "Holborn."

"How old are you?"

"Forty-two."

I was very confused, his manner was more searching than that of the police, and he said, "I cannot make it out, what you want here. Do you know what a casual ward is? It is a great pity that you cannot manage better than to come here. What is your name?"

"I told him 'Ellen Taylor.'"

Again he looked me over from head to foot; he clearly suspected that I was not a vagrant, and was surprised that any other person should venture into a casual ward, nor do I believe that he would have admitted me had my boots been better than they were; here, as at Whitechapel, they saved me from detection.

This conversation took place in the large gateway of the workhouse, and it was so clean and airy that I hoped the wards would be the same, and I fully anticipated a better and more comfortable lodging than I had as yet had. After a few minutes a woman appeared, and ordered me to follow her. She brought three pieces of stale and mouldy bread, pinned together with a wooden skewer. They were evidently the leavings of the sick ward, and if I had been really hungry I could not have touched them. We went outside the workhouse, and descending a flight of stone steps, she unlocked the door of an underground cellar.

It was now ten o'clock and quite dark, so that on entering I could not see my conductor, and I shivered on perceiving the stifling closeness of the air, and a stench which was much worse than anything I had yet experienced.

I said, "What a dungeon! Surely I am not to sleep here! I cannot do so. I really dare not."

But my conductor passed carelessly across the dark cellar, and opening the door of a second place where there was a gaslight and some rugs, she brought one out for me and said, "That is your bed."

I said, "Where?" for I could see nothing; but I put my hand upon a cold bench, which I afterwards found to be covered with a kind of [tarpaulin].[12] I said, "I cannot undress and lie on that place; must I do so? Will you want my clothes?"

She replied, "You may please yourself about that, and either take them off or not."

I said, "I must keep them on, for if I lie there without I shall catch my death."

Dreading to be left, as I then thought, quite alone, I tried to detain the woman, and asked her what time we rose in the morning.

She replied, "A quarter to six o'clock;" and locking all the doors she went away.

I had now become accustomed to the light. I saw that I was in a square apartment, lighted by a gaslight, opposite to an opening about one foot square, leading to the place where the rugs came from, and where the light really was.

Groping about, I came in contact first with a black mass in the corner, which I found to consist of women's clothes, and, satisfied that other persons were near, I turned towards the bench and aroused a young girl, who said, "This is your bed, next to mine." I took off my bonnet and folded up my cloak, and said to the girl, "What a dreadful place!" She replied, "Yes, indeed it is; you can't see me, but feel my arms, I am bitten all over." I felt, and found her arms covered with wheals.

"God help you, poor girl!" said I; "you seem young."

"Yes," said she, "and I do not feel very well; do you perceive this dreadful smell?"

I replied, "I do, and I feel faint myself." Indeed I became greatly alarmed. The idea of having cholera haunted me, and I sat down trembling with fear.

The nurse now unlocked the door and came in. She placed three pint-tins full of water upon the window-sill, and went away. I spoke to her, but she did not hear me. I was then seized with faintness, sickness, and diarrhoea. A cold perspiration came over

---

12. In the original: "tarpauling."

me, and I said to the girl, "Where is the closet?" I opened the door in the corner and found it, and whilst I live I can never forget it. I thought it must be the dead-house, and that I had made a mistake; and when I lifted the seat-lid I flew back, for there was no pan, and the soil reached nearly to the top. I felt too ill to remain, for even the floor was saturated and wet with the filth which oozed up out of it. I returned to the ward and vomited, which relieved me of the pain. I then rested against a bed, and the occupant asked me what was the matter.

I replied, "I am very ill." She said, "It is enough to kill us all; it is not fit for human beings."

I was very much alarmed and tried the door, and sought for the means of making my illness known, but there was neither bell nor knocker nor any means of getting out; and having heard that walking about was the best remedy, I never ceased doing so until it was nearly daylight. I then tried to lie down, but the rugs were alive, and the vermin so bad, that I could not even sit.

The girl in the next bed lay upon the bare tarpaulin, with nothing on but her chemise. I said, "Are you not afraid to lie in this way?" But she said, "What is the use of making a bother about it? They do not care for us."

For an hour I watched, thinking only of the horrors of this stinking dungeon. How I longed that some one interested in the treatment of the poor could look in! I thought of the kind interest which that dear lady, Miss Burdett Coutts,[13] had taken in the laying out of the live child at St. Pancras, and I thought if she could see the way in which her sisters suffer she would stir to help them. Often and often I hoped you would look in, and I prayed that you might hear the groans of the women and the wailing of the children, one of whom was at the mother's breast, and was

---

13. Angela Burdett-Coutts, 1st Baroness Burdett-Coutts (1814-1906). On inheriting her fortune in 1837, she came to be regarded as the wealthiest woman in Britain. She used most of her wealth to support a variety of social causes, including the establishment of soup kitchens and housing for the working classes, and was known as "the Queen of the Poor." At the time of her death, she had reportedly given away some £3,000,000. Healy, Edna. *Lady Unknown: The Life of Angela Burdett-Coutts*. London: Sidgwick and Jackson, 1975.

crying at intervals the whole night long. Far better that the vagrants be put in an open shed upon the bare stones, or that they should be permitted to sleep in the gutter itself.

There were in all six women and three children lying half-exposed in the glimmering daylight,—all of them restless, their sleep broken by exclamations of "Oh dear!" "God help us!" "What shall we do?" I then got very cold, and vomiting incessantly I was forced to cover myself with the rug to preserve my life; and from that moment my torture was beyond the power of any tongue to tell. It was impossible to see anything, but I felt stung and irritated until I tore my flesh till it bled in every part of my body.

About six o'clock the door was opened, and the woman exclaimed, "Oh dear! What a horrid smell! It is enough to kill you;" and then she tried to pull the window down, but could not. Most of us were half-dressed when she came, and before they had all finished two men came down the stairs, and brought the skilly and the bread, and then, turning round to see who had been my fellow-sufferers, I saw with astonishment my old friend Cranky Sal.

One of the men said, looking at her, "We have some fine women here to-night." Sally laughed, and taking the compliment entirely to herself, said "that she had been told that before."

The man remained whilst Sally was dressing. She was a long time, and took great pains with her toilet, being very proud of her good looks. One of the women was still asleep, and Sally roused her up to tell her of the compliments she had received. "You d---d fool," said the woman, "it was not you that he said it to, but that woman yonder," pointing to me; but Sally observed that she knew better, and had been told it many a time; and then another woman came up, and said, "Hold your d---d row," and struck her a most violent blow in the face.

This person was short, about sixty years of age, and with white cropped hair. She wore no cap, and was literally clothed with dirty rags, which, if once taken off, could not possibly be put on again. She had a thoroughly brutish expression, and the savage manner of her blow not only frightened Sally but all the rest. I threatened to call for help, for the row was great and the language dreadful. Sally behaved very well, and only said that she would have them locked up if they did not give over. She told the woman that she had no business there, but ought to have been lodged in the station-house, for that she was drunk when she came in. Sally winked at me not to speak, and, as at Lambeth, she became my protector until they got again quiet.

One of the women now came and sat down on the bed beside me. She looked at me very hard, and said, "What a respectable woman you seem to be, and what a pity it is to see you here!" and then leaving for a moment, Sally jumped up and took her place, saying, "I think I have seen you before;" but I pretended not to know her, for I was anxious to see how far her memory went, and what she would say.

The other woman then returned, and demanded her seat next to me, but Sally refused it, saying that she would not get up. The other replied, "It was my place before it was yours;" but Sally answered, "I slept nearer to her last night than you did and I sha'n't get up, and that ends it." She appealed to me for protection, and said again, "I think I have seen you before; I cannot make you out;" but I again pretended to have no recollection of her.

"Sally," said I, "you have got a black eye; how did you get that?"

She replied, "because I would not let a man do as he liked with me;" upon which all the rest set up a loud laugh. They began to tease her, and one said, "Did I not tell you what she was?" Sally answered with great spirit, and indignantly said "she was not that which they suspected." "Shut up!" said she, and the old woman with the grey head again came up and said, with a threatened blow, "I will shut you up if you are not quiet."

The skilly and bread was now consumed, and Sally and I began to talk about the casual wards.

She said, "Lambeth is the best place out."

I asked when she slept there last.

She replied, correctly, "Tuesday night and Friday night."

I asked her if she recollected a women tearing up her clothes? and giving me a look full of inquiry and astonishment, she said, "she saw her do it."

"Do you think she was really dirty?" said I.

"Yes," she replied, "I am sure she was. Some of them thought her mad, but I did not."

I asked her if she remembered what she had on, and she described it all accurately, and said it was a shame to turn her out in that way.

I told her that I had heard she had better things given her before she left, and Sally thought it was very lucky that she had.

I asked her if she had seen her since, and she said yes, and that she had herself left Lambeth with a woman, through whom she had got her black eye. Coming close to me she whispered in my ear, that the woman had promised to be her "pal" to Wimbledon; that they went into a field together to lie down and have a sleep, and that when she awoke the other had bolted clean away.

I said, "Was that the woman you went strawberry-picking with?" and she said, "How do you know about that? If you are hard of hearing you have got a good memory; and now I will tell you how I got my black eye. Does it look bad?"

I said, "Rather."

"Well, I will tell you. I met a man on Saturday night in the New Cut, and he asked me if I would have a pennyworth of whelks. He seemed decently dressed, and I told him I didn't mind."

"What time was that, Sally?" said I; and she replied, "It was getting late. He then asked me if I would have a pie, so I said I didn't mind, and I had a twopenny pie, for I thought I might as well have a twopenny one as a penny one. Then we strolled along, and stopping at a doorway he offered me a shilling. He said that would get a lodging for the night, and by this time we reached St. George's in the Borough, and he asked me if I was going to take his money, and I said 'Oh no! I don't do business like that,' and he gave me a violent blow. I screamed out, and he ran away. I began to cry, and a policeman came up, to whom I complained; but he only laughed at me and said that the man must have a strong stomach to fancy such as me. He asked me for my photograph; and at last he told me to go along, and that he had known me for five years, which was not true, for I had never been out of the workhouse or seen life for more than two." She then met another policeman and complained to him, be he also refused to listen, and pushed her from the pavement into the middle of the street, and then the two laughed at her together. A little further on she met a third, who spoke to her more kindly. He looked at her eye and saw that it was swollen; and he said that the other police ought to be ashamed of themselves, and that he would have been glad to have thrashed a rascal who could strike a woman in that way.

I then asked Sally how she lived, and what she meant by seeing life.

Then said she, "It is hard to tell you. I do not do anything really bad. You know what I mean; I beg and pick up what I can, and go about anywhere for a bit of food or a night's lodging. Sometimes I make do on what they give me at these places here; sometimes I get a few pence given me. For months I have not tasted meat until last Saturday, when I met a crippled old woman, who gave me a piece of bread-and-meat and three-quarters of a pint of beer. I thought she was going to be kind to me and be my pal, but whilst I was eating and drinking she ran away, just as the other did. I am very badly off now. I have applied several times for an order to go into the workhouse, but they refuse to give me one whilst the weather is fine. I belong to Lambeth, and they send me out when the summer comes. I mean to go and ask the guardians for five shillings, and if they give it to me, I want to buy a clean gown, a pair of shoes, and a few pipe-lights to sell. I am so dirty now that I do not know what to do; and I want some soap to wash me and my clothes, more than food."

Poor Sally! I am convinced she is not vicious, and is to be greatly pitied. I promised her a penny for some soap, and she scarcely believed me in earnest, "For," said she, "you know I never get much kindness, especially from women, they hate each other so much."

When we had finished breakfast, they gave us two pounds of oakum to pick, and they expect you to do it all. A notice is put up that "Every person who receives relief in this ward will be expected to pick two pounds of oakum."

About half-past ten the nurse came in and helped me to pick mine. I asked if we were expected to do it all, and she said in a whisper, "Do all you can, and they will not be hard with you. Say you are a needlewoman and cannot do it, and at eleven o'clock they will let you out whether you have done it or not;" and at that hour a man came and took away our work without remark.

Whilst we were at work one of the girls asked for some water to wash. The woman replied that there was none, and no place for a bath. She said the bath-rooms and other wards were given up to the cholera cases; and another remarked "that she thought they were going a good way to have it there, as the stench was so bad, and they were all ill. Can't we have a drop of water in a pail just to swill our faces?" "No," said the woman, "we have no orders."

We were then turned out. Sally kept very close to me and asked me where I was going. I was sorry indeed to leave her, and I told her so, but I was obliged to say she could not join me. I offered her a glass of beer, and whilst she was drinking I started home. I had gone a good step, when I found her again at my elbow, and I only pacified her by a promise to see her again at some future time. I felt truly sorry, and left her with regret, wishing that I could do more for her.

I can only hope, in conclusion, that these experiences will not have been in vain, for since my visit to Whitechapel I have felt how necessary it was that the dreadful character of these places should be better known, and that better regulations should be made for these unfortunate women, many of whom are not altogether bad."[14]

CHAPTER VI.

SINCE these visits have been made, the author has inspected the places described.

At Newington the ward was already in course of demolition, but enough remained to show the truthfulness of the description and the unfitness of the accommodation then in use.

At Lambeth the general arrangements appear excellent. The female ward is large and airy, and the bath-room clean and well appointed. The floors are washed daily, but less care seems to be taken that the beds and rugs are maintained in a cleanly state; no doubt this is almost impossible, but nevertheless it seems hard that a woman of cleanly habits should be forced to lie upon infected beds, and cover herself with rugs alive with vermin, for the convenience and accommodation of a class which, if treated according to law, would be most of them in prison. The policy of employing the police as assistant relieving officers will be discussed presently; it will be sufficient to notice now that the number of vagrants at Lambeth has greatly diminished since their employment there, and that a portion of the female casual ward has been permanently converted to another purpose.

The wards at Whitechapel are utterly unfit for human occupation. We hear that others are in course of erection, but, in the interests of humanity, those now in use ought to be instantly

---

14. At this point the vicarious vagrant's narrative ends, and Stallard's voice returns in chapters VI and VII.

closed. The boarded floors and whitewashed walls fail to conceal the real filthiness of the place, the full horrors of which come forth at night. The want of ventilation and the crowding together of half destitute and dirty people constitutes a focus from which diarrhoea and cholera is liable to be carried into the whole district. No one can read the harrowing account of the night spent there without feeling that illness is almost a necessity of the place,—if not in the ward itself, soon afterwards. Let the Guardians set up a tent in the yard, and lay fresh straw daily upon the very stones, and let water be abundantly supplied, and the sanitary conditions will be more successfully observed than they are now.

These remarks apply with tenfold force to the dangerous cellars in St-George's-in-the-East, condemned long ago by Mr. Farnall.[15] These wards are now reoccupied, because the new ones have been appropriated to cholera cases; but surely this course cannot have been sanctioned by the Poor-Law Board. It is a curious anomaly of the law that the sanitary officer of the district has no power to inspect the workhouse, although it is part of his duty to superintend the ventilation and sanitary state of churches, chapels, and other public buildings. This is unfortunate, for the health standard of the Poor-Law authorities has hitherto been extremely low, and the introduction of a little medical inspection from without must have had a beneficial effect. For many years the Poor-Law Board had no adviser of its own, and it ought to have welcomed persons able and willing to expose evils which it was unable or unwilling to recognise itself. Half the evils of the workhouse infirmaries might have been remedied long ago if the local health officer had been permitted to inspect them; and even now, if he could visit the casual wards of St. George's-in-the-East, he might rightly insist upon their instant closure. At the time of our visit, there was everywhere a copious sprinkling of chloride of lime, which masked but did not destroy the stench of the closet, where the filth was openly exposed, as already described. The attendant informed us that it was cleaned out daily,—a statement which was manifestly untrue; and even had it been otherwise, it only palliates an evil which is beyond defence. We were also

---

15. On Farnall, see above, p. 74 note 25.

shown the bath-room, and the same attendant assured us repeatedly that the bath was used and the people washed. This is distinctly denied by our visitor, and the general appearance of the place justified her report. Not only are the baths not used, but the unfortunate women were refused a pail of water in which to wash their faces. The whole management of the place reflects the highest discredit upon the Guardians, and inculpates those who are appointed to supervise it.

CHAPTER VII.
CONCLUSION.

THE evidence derived from the foregoing narrative shows that two distinct classes are admitted to the casual wards. The one consists of old stagers,[16] who are accustomed to the life, are satisfied with the treatment they receive, no matter what it is, and tramp from place to place, living as they can and doing anything but work. To reform such characters is almost beyond our hope: no ordinary machinery has the least effect upon them; they refuse to work, they care but little what they eat, they wallow in filth, and look upon vermin as their natural companions; they set the Guardians, the relieving officers, and even the police, at complete defiance, and, with extraordinary ingenuity, they avoid the prison, only to prey upon society in a more contemptible way. To such as these the Houseless Poor Act has given legal position, and privileges of lodging and food at the public expense, which are not in the least deserved.[17] What right have such idle vagabonds, whether male or female, to our sympathy and relief? and is it not shameful that the heavily-burdened ratepayer should be taxed for their support? Are they not the very persons who have heretofore been sent to gaol as the violators of public morals, and as examples of idleness which could not be tolerated amongst an industrious people? A vast amount of misplaced sympathy has been thrown around the

---

16. Old hands, or those long accustomed to a particular situation or way of life.

17. Stallard refers to the Metropolitan Houseless Poor Acts of 1864 and 1865. See above, p. 15, 27, and p. 56 note 5.

class, and we have legislated in direct antagonism to our ancient law. Instead of vagrancy being treated as a crime, we have offered it direct encouragement; and having diverted the workhouse from its original purpose, which was a test of destitution and not a refuge for infirmity and disease, we have invented a new system of outdoor relief which practically precludes the possibility of discrimination, and gives such assistance to the idle and degraded pauper as enables him to live without work, and to pursue his wandering habits entirely without control.

But there is also a second class, which consists of the distressed poor who are really destitute. In the Metropolis they form a small proportion of those who seek lodging in the casual ward; but as they manifestly have the highest claim to the assistance they require, the arrangements ought to be sufficient for their accommodation, and such as will protect them from the degrading and contaminating influences which inevitably surround them in the wards we have described. What right have we to keep a destitute but honest wayfarer, whether man or woman, standing at the door of a police office, mixed up with a score of foul-mouthed vagabonds, and exposed to the inclemency of the weather, the mockery of passersby, and the jeers of the police, who reluctantly perform their hateful duty? What right have we to insult those who are already in despair, by a treatment which infers the possibility of crime and wrong, simply because they do not form a majority of the class to be relieved, and because we do not attempt to reach the real vagabond, except through the outraged feelings of the deserving poor. Under the old law, happily not yet repealed, we isolated the vagrant as completely as we could, and if we failed to reform his habits, either in the workhouse or the gaol, we at least circumscribed his influence, and reduced his sphere of operations to the very smallest limits. No greater mistake was ever made by the Legislature than when it placed the professional vagrant on the same footing as the deserving but destitute traveller. To put them together under the same roof, to make them sleep in the same bed, destroys the innocent, and reduces all to a common level. No honest woman can hear the language used in the wards, or associate with the characters who habitually live there, without contracting infamy; and the wonder is that poor Cranky Sally has not long ago succumbed to the immorality and vice which now surrounds her, especially as we have seen how anxious the old tramps are to gain companions and recruits. The casual ward is a school of vagrancy and petty crime, in which those who enter by compulsion are taught to prefer a wandering life, and to acquire the means for indulging in their preference; but happily the pupils are comparatively few, because the genuine wayfarer shuns the horrors of the accommodation, and feels that he cannot associate with the vagrant without losing caste and self-respect. Every night respectable but destitute persons prefer to walk the streets, or, as in Bethnal Green, to sit in the public water-closet, rather than remain in such debasing company.

Now the real question is, which of the two classes are we called upon to relieve in this particular way? and the answer is, the destitute wayfarer, and not the tramp. How, then, are we to distinguish them? How admit the one and treat him kindly, and discard the other without incurring the scandal of their starving in the streets? We have seen, from the narration given, that there is practically no discrimination under the existing system. The only check to vagrancy now in force is the employment of the police as assistant relieving-officers, to distribute the tickets of admission to the wards; and we saw at Lambeth that the numbers have been greatly diminished since the period of introducing this repellent practice. But the question is, does it work effectually? Does it really diminish the facilities for a wandering life? And does it secure for the honest but destitute traveller the relief to which he is entitled? Most decidedly not. The criminal at large may be deterred by the ordeal of the police-station, because he cannot face the inspector who has him on his list; but, at the same time, the process will deter those who have a right to our sympathy, and will exclude the most deserving persons whom we desire to relieve. None, therefore, but the most callous and undeserving will brave the police, and then, as we have seen, they will do so night after night, and week after week, with impunity, because they know that the police themselves have no special power of discrimination, and are not authorized to refuse them, so long as they do not positively belong to the criminal class. We therefore dissent entirely from the proposal to transfer the administration of vagrant relief into the hands of the police. It is open to the gravest objections, and those who advocate the transfer must feel that there are insuperable difficulties in the way. Before imposing upon them a duty so foreign to their ordinary occupation as is the relief of destitution, we ought, at least, to be sure that they have the power to carry out that which we require, and it is clear they fail. What is really wanted is a certificate of temporary destitution, which shall distinguish those who are entitled to relief from the worthless vagrant, and this certificate ought to be given by the relieving officer, and not by police.

A Poor-law magistracy can alone deal with this vast disease. We conceive that every *bona fide* traveller, destitute of means, should be provided with a bed and breakfast at the public cost, and be permitted to depart as early as he pleases, either to pursue his journey or to seek for work. This privilege should be surrounded with certain guarantees for honesty, not difficult to obtain. Thus, a route signed by a master in the presence of a police inspector, a clergyman, or a magistrate, should be held good for a certain reasonable time; and in London a certificate of destitution might be granted after due inquiry by the magistrate we have alluded to, which should entitle the bearer to bed and breakfast for a week, the right to be renewed at discretion, until work is found. If a return of such certificates were made to a central office, the cases of professional vagrancy would soon be known, and all persons without a certificate found wandering and homeless in the street would be taken before the Poor-law magistrate, and either supplied with the necessary certificate or remitted to the house of detention, which we will presently describe. The fear of detention is the greatest bugbear of the incorrigible casual. You may wash him, and he will bear it; you may put him in a shed to sleep, and he will not complain,—herd him with fever and disease, and he does not care,—make him work, and he sullenly picks his oakum, saws his wood, or breaks his stone, but nothing cures him of his wandering and idle habits but detention in one place. Before the institution of casual wards there were no vagrant visitors at the Paddington Workhouse, and how were they deterred? Not by refusal, not by harsh treatment, not by scanty food, not by work, but simply by detaining them in the workhouse until the Board of Guardians met. One would have supposed that a week of rest and good food would have been gratefully received by these hungry wanderers; but no, once fairly away they never returned; and if a plan something like this were universally adopted, the wandering habits of the class would soon be checked.

A somewhat similar plan prevails in Leeds, and works extremely well, even without the intervention of the police. Mr. Corbet, in his recent report,[18] describes it in the following terms; and if only detention for a few days were added at the discretion of the master, the result would be the same as it was at Paddington:—

"At Leeds the supervision by a Vagrant master and mistress is excellent; the work,—grinding corn by men, and washing clothes and cleaning the wards by women,—strictly exacted; and not only is each person required to go through a warm bath, which to the professional tramp is no less distasteful than work, but his clothes are taken from him for the night, which he dislikes, if possible, still more, when he is furnished with the unwonted and unappreciated luxury of bed-linen. In spite therefore of a good bed to sleep on, and a sufficiency of plain food, fewer of the true vagabond class frequent the wards of this workhouse than could have been expected in a manufacturing town of such magnitude; and during the recent distress in the cotton district a proportionately greater number of *bona fide* wayfarers in search of work sought and obtained the shelter of these wards."

This is as it should be; but in discarding the professional vagrant from the regular casual ward, we must take care that he is detained elsewhere. The "House of Detention" should be a real workhouse, under the direction of a labour-master, assisted, if necessary, by the police; and to this all persons wandering without a certificate should be sent, if they are not able satisfactorily to account for their destitution. Several such establishments would probably be required; they should have land attached; vegetables and other necessaries should be cultivated for the supply of the Metropolitan Pauper Hospitals, whilst the females should be made to wash for the sick, as well as make the linen and other useful articles for the same class. No inmate should be allowed to leave without having behaved well for at least one month. If he is industrious, some reward might be

---

18. *Reports on Vagrancy to President of Poor Law Board by Poor Law Inspectors.* Parliamentary Papers 1866. [3698] xxxv.631, p. 129. These remarks are from the report of U. Corbet, M.P. Jr., Poor Law Inspector. The first sentence should begin: "Nothing, it is true, can work much better than the system does at Leeds (even without the intervention of the police), but there the supervision…"

offered for his work, and a certificate to travel may then be given him that he may seek for employment. The superintendent should have a register of persons wanting labourers, and he should recommend the inmates when he can properly do so. None but the able-bodied should be sent here. The fare should be as good as a convict's, and the work somewhat less severe. An institution of this kind, in which the inmates might be classed in two or three divisions, would afford to every one a reasonable chance of reform, if any habits of industry should still survive. At the present moment, not only is the classification of the vagrant totally impossible, but his treatment is anything but uniform. In some Unions he is petted, but in most despised. At one place food and accommodation are good, at another execrable; the general management must therefore be conducted by a central board, in which the Government should be fairly represented. In the meantime, we would recommend the Poor-Law Board to adopt a system of registration and certificates, in order to fix the crime of vagrancy on the able-bodied vagabonds who systematically occupy the casual wards, and then let orders be given for their prosecution under the Vagrant Act.[19] A little wholesome energy would go further to diminish the evil, than a powerless interference of the police or the institution of a labour-test, which we discover to be so easily escaped.

In conclusion, let us urge upon the Government the necessity of attacking vagrancy at its true foundation. The Guardians of whole districts in the Metropolis avow themselves "unable to relieve the rising generation so that they may be eventually independent of the rates." Let us think for a moment what a statement like this involves. It tells us that the 30,000 children now imperfectly relieved are taught from their earliest years to become familiar with want in all its forms,—want of food, want of clothes, want of education, and want of occupation, such as

---

19. The Vagrancy Act of 1824 (5 Geo. IV, c.83): see above, p. 14–15. The Act enabled magistrates to sentence vagrants to a term of imprisonment, ranging from a month to a year. Harsher sentences were reserved for "incorrigible rogues." See Humphreys, Robert. *No Fixed Abode: A History of the Responses to the Roofless and the Rootless in Britain.* Basingstoke: Macmillan, 1999, p. 82.

may give them a chance of gaining an honest living; and in the train of these wants are dirt, dishonesty, and crime; and irreligion, disease, and death; and, worst of all, there is education to habitual pauperism and vagrancy, from which generation after generation is unable to escape. Only a few days ago, a man entered the casual wards of a West-end Workhouse in company with his son, now seventeen years of age. The master remembers this youth carried into the same wards as an infant in his father's arms, and has observed them from time to time ever since. In no other country in Europe professing to have a Christian Government would such an education be permitted, nay, even encouraged by the law, as it is here.

It is impossible to destroy hereditary pauperism, vagrancy, and crime, whilst the law gives a parent the uncontrollable right over the treatment of his own children, the right being in no case subordinate to his social duties. We boast as Englishmen of our personal, political, and religious freedom; but it is impossible to feel proud of that which permits a parent to indulge his own appetite at the cost of starvation to his offspring,—to put his children to work at the very tenderest age that he himself may live at ease,—and to bring them up, should it suit his selfish and wicked purpose, in idleness, misery, and crime. If a parent keeps out of the workhouse or the gaol, he may use his children as he pleases, and may starve and abuse them without control; and is it not time to check the licence to bring up children in ignorance—to make them hereditary paupers, habitual beggars, and at last expensive convicts, and to call upon parents to perform their duty under peril of the law, and of having their children taken away and put under the education of the State.[20] In the Metropolis the number of juvenile thieves increases rapidly, and the inspector of reformatory schools states, that "nothing short of a law which shall compel a father to have his children fairly educated, and which shall send the children to a school appropriate to their condition if the parents can or will not so send them, making the parents pay some trifling quota towards the expense of their education,—nothing but this, I say, can meet the evil; without this, the gaol will be crowded as

---

20. Stallard does not use a question mark here.

well as the reformatory—filled by children whom mere neglect and idleness have first made mischievous, then criminal."[21]

And lastly, the insufficient nourishment of the young destroys the stamina of the people, unfits them for anything like hard work, and reduces the labouring classes to puerile occupations and low wages, which, after a few generations, will impair the productive power of the country, and make us even more dependent than we are now upon the importation of foreign labour. It is a dreadful fact that honest labour was never so scarce as it is now; and the day has arrived when Belgians have been required to complete an English railway.[22] A man can only perform the duty for which he is physically fit, and his power will depend upon the food he has received in youth, and the general conditions of health in which he has been brought up.

On the 1st of January last there were 34,092 children in the receipt of out-door relief in the Metropolitan Unions, more than half of these being dependent upon poor widows, and all deriving their chief means of existence from the public rates. The allowance varies from fourpence-halfpenny to two shillings per head per week, and the average is not one shilling each. On this they exist indeed, but do not live and grow; and so they arrive at a feeble but precocious maturity, and are driven by necessity to those casual occupations which indeed children of ordinary vigour and intelligence are as capable of carrying on as these puny men. You cannot obtain

---

21. Inspector of Reformatory Schools of Great Britain. *Ninth Report*. 1866. Parliamentary Papers [3686] xxxviii.305, p. 11. These comments were made in the context of a report documenting the recent and dramatic increase in the numbers of juvenile offenders in urban areas.

22. "In 1866 the building of the railway near Tunbridge Wells was delayed following skirmishes between English labourers and foreign workers from France and Belgium who were believed to be employed to under cut [*sic*] English wage rates. Houses where foreigners stayed were attacked by mobs and local shops were closed and premises boarded up until order could be restored by hastily sworn in Special Constables, and the threat of one thousand infantrymen who were placed on alert at nearby barracks." Gordon, Kevin. "A History of Policing the Railway." http://www.btp.police.uk/ [accessed 19 December 2007].

labour from an exhausted population any more than you can obtain crops from an exhausted farm, and the profitable return in both cases will depend upon the liberality of the preparatory treatment. When, therefore, thousands of children are thus brought up, their stock-in-trade consists of debility, sharp wits, and chicanery. They scarcely know what good food is; they have learned to live on bread, tea, and offal, and they care for nothing else; and so, not having the stamina and the pluck of men, they live upon a low cunning, exercised principally in the streets. From the class described is derived our stock of costermongers, cadgers, street-finders, low porters, crossing-sweepers, and vagrants,—and in fact every form of occupation which does not involve continuous and healthy effort. And then, because of the very nature of the employments, we have in their train gambling, drunkenness, vice, and crime, which amply retaliate upon society for the wicked neglect with which it has treated those who have been thrown upon its care; and the disgrace is, that we then turn round and tax our unhappy victims with being the cause of their own misery, and punish them as if they were responsible for the state in which they live. Our present system of public relief rears vagabonds and thieves by thousands; and if we desire to diminish vagrancy and crime, we must pay more attention to the physical and moral education of the rising generation, so many thousands of whom become dependent upon the public charity by the many causes which destroy health and life in this large and struggling place.

We must equalize the rates, and organize a responsible executive of the Poor Law; and we must consolidate the system of public relief, that the poor may be uniformly and fairly dealt with in every part of the Metropolis, whether it be rich or poor.

Chapter Four

"The Tramp's Haven" by F. G. Wallace-Goodbody

The Gentleman's Magazine, 254, (January–June 1883), pp. 176–192.

THE TRAMP'S HAVEN.
"Homely, ragged, and tanned,
Under the changeful sky, &c."—*The Vagabond*.[1]

Misfortunes greatly open the mind and mentally enlighten us, and are so far to be hailed as our deliverers, inasmuch as, when once plunged by them into the depths of misery, we appreciate the more any slight benefit that may accrue to us, and, once raised from the abyss, experience a feeling of contentment with circumstances and surroundings, however modest, that in the days of our former prosperity we should have looked upon almost as hardships. To a mind capable of undergoing such impressions I cannot recommend a more salutary cure for extravagant ideas, and consequent production of contentment, than my experience of the Casual Ward in Sinai

---

1.   Written in 1871 by Charles Lamb Kenny. Note that the first two lines should read: "Homeless, ragged, and tanned,/Under the open sky…."

Avenue,[2] where I discovered that I had capped all my former fol-
lies and evil doings by a crime that, until that night, I had not
been aware of having committed—the most heinous of all—
poverty. The victim to this criminal malady can, in its advanced
stages, hardly be reckoned as a human being; he is to be classed
with unclean beasts and venomous reptiles, with this difference,
that whereas the latter are killed instantly when once under the
heel of their lord and master—Man, the pauper, on the other
hand, is made to die, or rather live as it were, a slow and linger-
ing death—a mortal life—so ignominious, so shameful, that the
most exquisite tortures of Torquemada's[3] tribunal would be a
mere *bagatelle* in comparison with the sufferings that he must
undergo. For at least around the victims of the Inquisition there
was shed the lustre and halo of martyrdom, that to some degree,
in the eyes of the fervent, atoned for the horror of the death; but
the unfortunate creature, termed, when an inmate of the workhouse—a pauper, and when at large penniless, friendless, and
starving—a vagabond, what is he? This is what he is: a creature
utterly lost to the possession of all individual rights; he has merely the outward semblance of man. He has, it is true, the same
number of veins and arteries as the most adored of modern society; but his very breath, his limbs, his sinews are not his own; the
wretched rags, swarming with vermin, that barely cover his own
nakedness, are not so much intended for their original purpose
as that his superiors may wipe their feet upon them.[4]

Worn-out, footsore, famished, travel-stained, the tramp
arrives in London, after many nights passed on the bare roadside
under a hedge or a hay-stack, and, perhaps, as a dishonoured guest
in one of those dens similar to the one that he now hails as a haven,

---

2.   There was, and is, no Sinai Avenue in London (it does not appear in the
Post Office London Directory for 1882 or 1895).

3.   Tomás de Torquemada (1420-98), Grand Inquisitor during the Spanish
Inquisition.

4.   Author's footnote: "This last expression was actually made use of by a
tramp with whom I was once conversing."

and which are a standing disgrace and shame to this our enlightened country. There, at least, he will obtain a crust of bread and a
straw-pallet, grudgingly bestowed it is true, and to be paid for by
hours of labour on the morrow.

I have been led into this somewhat lugubrious train of
thought by the memory of the experience vouchsafed to me upon
a previous occasion, when I, for a period extending something
over twenty hours, became an inmate of the Casual Ward in Sinai
Avenue. One eventful evening—and I shall not easily forget it—I
found myself fairly at a loss where to obtain shelter for the night.
During the few weeks previous, since the horrors and sufferings
of poverty had come upon me, I had succeeded in extricating
myself (or, more properly speaking, Providence had extricated
me) from my temporary dilemmas; but this night I was fairly driv-
en to bay, and I pondered within me what course I should pursue.
Should I walk the streets during the whole of the night, miserably
clad as I was, and famished? But then, on the other hand, why go
through so much martyrdom? On the morrow, my position by
this act of deprivation would be unimproved, and my sufferings
would have become intensified. At length my mind was made up.
I would take advantage of the charity provided by my wealthier
fellow-creatures; and, dismissing some wandering, yet not entirely evanescent, ideas of suicide, I directed my faltering steps
towards my destination.

Sinai Avenue is *not* situated in a quarter of the capital by any
means in keeping with the character of this charitable and hospitable institution, nor (may it be added on the other hand) is the
entertainment there to be met with administered at all in the manner in which it is lavished in mansions situated but a few yards off.
Sinai Avenue is *not* surrounded on all sides by a labyrinth of filthy
alleys and lanes teeming and seething with vagabond turbidity;
but, on the contrary, reposes at a stone's throw from one of
London's best-known squares. It was dusk when I attained these
environs of contrarieties, and paused, animated by no agreeable
thoughts—by such thoughts, in fact, as were most likely to occur
to one upon such an eventful occasion; at length eight o'clock
sounded from a neighbouring church and I started from my
painful reverie. To my surprise, the vicinity of the entrance where-
at I had taken my stand, and which but a few moments before had
been almost deserted (the habitual frequenters having shrunk
shudderingly by, in deadly fear doubtless of the fate that overtook

birds when fluttering over the entrance to Avernus[5]), was now occupied by a long line of vitality of a most motley description, their abject feelings prompting them to shrink as closely as possible to the railings; at the sign of the wicket being opened, they sidled into the interior, myself among them, the burly janitor who acted as porter counting each individual by inflicting upon his shoulders something partaking of the nature of a blow and a "shove" combined, and, his number completed, peremptorily closing the door to the remainder. Men and women alike were ushered into a room or hall of considerable size, presenting that mixed appearance of plainness, cleanliness, and deal boards characteristic of workhouses. With the women I have nothing to do; after certain formalities had been fulfilled they were led away by the matron (a harsh-visaged virago) to some secret portion of the building that it was not permitted to my gaze to fathom, and I saw no more of them; consequently, I shall confine my remarks entirely to my immediate associates—the men. It occurred to my mind as I gazed around the bare apartment, so devoid of ornamentation of any description, that the arms of the parish[6] might well have been displayed upon some part of the wall in a conspicuous situation, so that some of the occupants of the rows of bare benches might have been thoroughly convinced as to their whereabouts, should they have any doubt upon the subject. The seal of the Guardians, by-the-by, is a pretty and appropriate device (as all the world knows), comprising a sheaf of wheat, with "fiddle"[7] pendant, surmounted by two swords inclining cross-ways, the whole

---

5.   Portrayed in Virgil's *Aeneid* as the entrance to the Underworld.

6.   Wallace-Goodbody refers to the "parish," although this was a union workhouse. The poet "M.A." also did this in the versified account of James Greenwood's workhouse exploits: see above, p. 80. Wallace-Goodbody also refers to the "parish authorities" (below, p. 132) and twice to "parochial authorities" (below, pp. 127 and 131).

7.   Author's footnote: "This is not a musical instrument, but an elegant and ingenious contrivance made use of in workhouses for the purpose of facilitating the operation of picking oakum."

inclosed within what I at first poetically imagined to be a St. Catherine's Wheel, but which is in fact a less romantic and more modern symbol of martyrdom, viz. the wheel of a corn mill. Returning, however, to thoughts less visionary and more appropriate to the occasion, I turned my regard upon my companions for the night, and never in my life did I—and most fervently do I hope never shall I again—gaze upon a scene that even in the midst of my own troubles typically revealed to me all the harrowing idiosyncrasies of poverty. One and all were clothed in rags that exposed rather than covered their nakedness, and upon the countenances of most was pictured that look of abject penury that stamped the being accustomed to perpetual misery. By this time the porter, or more strictly speaking the tramp-master, had imposingly taken his seat at a table situated at the head of the apartment (I have seen the Lord High Chancellor of England assume his seat upon the Woolsack with far less ceremonial); and as I eventually came into contact with this functionary, in a manner somewhat humiliating to my dignity, I will devote a few lines to the description of this Nebuchadnezzar,[8] before whom all stood in awe.

He was a tall, stoutly built, burly man, provided with a stomach that denoted by proof ocular that if the paupers themselves are half-starved in a workhouse, the same remark need not be applied to the officials of those institutions. His countenance was heavy, sensual, and brutal, indicating self-indulgence and a propensity to cruelty; but was not wanting in a certain kind of intelligence withal, which, however, is at best a species of cunning that, in the facility it affords to its owner to take advantage of circumstance, is productive of the epithet of "fly."[9] He himself gave this quality another term, as will be eventually seen. This agreeable physiognomy was illuminated at the upper extremities by a pair of greenish-hued, baleful optics, whilst the lower was decorated by a full dark beard—the whole thing being surmounted by

---

8.   Of the several kings of Babylon with this name, Nebuchadnezzar II (630-562 B.C.) is best known as the builder of the Hanging Gardens and the conquerer of Judea and Jerusalem.

9.   Knowing, sharp.

a greasy threadbare skull-cap that had once been velvet. This magnate having settled himself firmly in his chair, and having opened a huge volume placed upon the table before him, assumed a pair of spectacles, dipped the pen in the inkstand, and took a look round with the eye of a slaughterman running his gaze over a bevy of sheep, and mentally calculating which he shall first select for the knife.

No one stirring, the tramp-master grew impatient, and cried out in a loud, surly voice; "Now then, No. 1, come on, if you're coming."

The man crouching on the extremity of the first row of seats, nearest to the chairman, considering that this amiable invitation was addressed to him, rose, and shuffled towards the table, when, at the peremptory order of the dictator, having removed his head-gear, he stood, the veriest picture of sordid humility, and responded to the following interrogations, dictatorial enough in themselves, but furthermore couched in the most contemptuous language, and rendered still more intolerable by every look, act, and gesture that place it in the power of trumpery authority to trample upon the unfortunate victim of circumstance.

"What's yer name, if you've got one?"

"Samuel Smith," was the rejoinder.

"How old are yer?"

"Thirty-two."

"*What* are yer?" (with the most contemptuous emphasis on the word *what*.)

"Nothing!" was the demure reply.

The castigator was evidently accustomed to this mode of indicating a pursuit in life, for he inserted a word in the book without comment.

The fourth question was answered still more characteristically.

"Where did you sleep last night?"

"Nowhere," was the answer.

"Nowhere?" repeated the scribe, with ever so little evidence of astonishment and slightly elevating his eyebrows; then added, after a pause, "Are yer going back to the same place?" At this sally there was an attempt at a very slight titter on the part of the assembled congregation, and one old vagabond, evidently irresistibly tickled by the cheerful nature of the comic scene, indulged in a hoarse chuckle, and nudged his neighbour with his elbow.

The gesture did not escape the prowling eye of the Cerberus,[10] who apparently this evening was in one of his playful moods: "Look here, old chap," roared he, "you ought to have something else to think about besides laughing when you come here. If you were a young man, I'd pitch yer out."

The poor old *misérable* completely collapsed at this energetic reproof, and shrank within himself, whilst the tramp-master, having relieved his feelings by this unmistakable assertion of authority, continued his cross-examination.

"Where are you going to?" was the next question.

"Anywhere!" answered the vagrant.

"Anywhere," repeated the catechiser; "you must say where you're going to, if it's only to the nearest pump." The poor wretch murmured something unintelligible, which was duly inserted.

Question No. 6—"Have yer got any money?"—I at first thought somewhat superfluous, but, as the individual to whom the question was addressed was actually in possession of one halfpenny and a farthing, I altered my opinion, and mentally acknowledged the surpassing wisdom of the interrogation.

"Take everything out of your pockets and pitch them into that basket," said the master, indicating the *pot-á-salade*[11] in question that was placed upon the floor next to the table. The man produced a few miserable penates[12] enveloped in a dirty piece of newspaper. "Shall I put the three fardens in with them?" said he, bending down earnestly and inquiringly.

"No, give me your money," said the task-master with an air of sleek pomposity, "and p'r'aps I'll give it yer back in the morning."

At this juncture a loud knocking was distinguishable from the exterior, to which, however, the president paid not the slightest attention.

---

10. In Greek mythology, the fearsome three-headed dog guarding the entrance to Hades.

11. Author's footnote: "*Pot-á-salade* was the name given to the basket into which the head fell after having been severed from the trunk by the guillotine."

12. Literally, the Roman gods watching over a household. In this context, the possessions defining and embodying the owner.

"There's some one knocking at the door, sir," squeaked a shrill tenor from the benches.

"Well, let them knock," answered he contemptuously; "they won't get in to-night unless they break the door down, and I'll take care they don't do that."

"Number one" then returned to his seat, and was succeeded by number two. It would be wearisome to recapitulate the answers delivered to the same series of questions, which, to be brief, were repeated to all, and of which the answers of number one were fair-ly typical with slight variations. In fact, one and all seemed to be starving; had no idea when or how they would obtain their next meal; appeared hardly to know where they had been, whither they were going, and except in the case of the most hardened vagabonds seemed hardly cognisant of where they actually were.

One old misery, who had evidently served his time of three-score and ten, greatly excited the ire of the task-master by being in possession of threepence, and by endeavouring to conceal the same by a subterfuge. Upon its discovery the latter indulged in a powerful classical address appropriate to the occasion, and, insert-ing the guilty coppers in his fob, concluded with a remark more sensibly humane than I could have expected from his former evi-dence of brutality, which was to the effect than an old man like the culprit need not feel ashamed at having a few "a'pence" in his pocket, nor need he tell a lie to conceal it.

At length my own turn came, which, with a nervous timidity, easily conceivable upon such an occasion, I had hesitatingly post-poned until almost the last. The functionary whose duties are osten-sibly to afford relief to the poor, being as I have already observed in a sweet and playful mood, had not hitherto discovered in the com-monplace nature of the cases passed in review before him a strictly appropriate subject for the exhibition of his peculiar banter, nor, as it appeared, had the spring been touched that gave full play to his amiable wit and humour and propensity to repartee. As ill-luck would have it, I, by my total ignorance of the forms observable in such places as the present, where I was now an unwilling applicant, and the blundering manner in which I answered his surly interroga-tories, furnished him with the missing key-note.

It will be here necessary to state that, being in ill-health from recent exposure in tropical climate, I had obtained a certificate from my friend Dr. Coupons, to the effect that I desired treatment in a Workhouse Infirmary, and this certificate I had presented according to instructions received from the doctor at the work-house itself the preceding evening, and, having been informed that the infirmary was *au complet*,[13] I had been recommended by the porter, who favoured me with this information, to apply for admittance at the Casual Ward at the opening hour, and to present myself before the doctor of that establishment in the morning.

It so happened that, upon this particular evening, an ugly rush unexpectedly took place when the door was opened, and I failed to gain admittance. I, however, applied to the Cerberus, stating the urgency of my case, and referring to the order that I had received in the morning from Dr. Coupons; but he answered that he was unable to admit me, and declined to examine the order in question. Upon leaving, I was so irritated by my want of success and the dogged manner in which the refusal was framed to what I, in my innocence (ignorant of the position that parochial authorities through their satellites take up *vis-á-vis* of applicants to their bounty), considered to be a most harmless and reasonable request, somewhat impatiently and imprudently, as it afterwards transpired, exclaimed "that rather than enter one of those dens I would throw myself into the river." Utterly ignorant of the forms in use for obtaining admittance to Union Infirmaries, on the following day it occurred to me that I could do nothing better than present myself again at the same hour, taking care this time to gain admittance, and eventually see the doctor in the morning.

This, it is unnecessary to say, I had consequently done. I now found myself in a most awkward predicament, being under the necessity of accepting hospitality (such as it was) that I had barely twenty-four hours before contemptuously repudiated; join to this my state of mental anxiety, the physical disabilities under which I was labouring, and the precarious nature of my prospects—the reader, if endowed with but a drop of the milk of human kindness, will easily imagine the unenviable nature of my feelings. In fact, the sentiments that predominated within me at this moment were simply indescribable; I desired, moreover, to propitiate the animal before me by the modesty of my demeanour, and to maintain at the same time something of the bearing of a man who had once

---

13. Full up.

been possessed of considerable advantages in a mundane sense—
wilfully discarded; a bearing that sometimes disarms brutality and
puts a curb upon insolence.

Strange to say, it never occurred to me not to allude to the verbal *fracas* of the preceding evening, as this man had nothing whatever to do with the workhouse itself, far less with the infirmary,
being simply the master of the Casual Ward. Of all this, I repeat,
I was in entire ignorance.

I approached the table with a slow and hesitating step, and by no
means with the matchless dignity mingled with grace attributed by
the Northern Minstrel to Bois-Guilbert, as when, benighted (in his
turn) by the storm, he advanced up the Hall of Rotherwood to take
advantage of the half-unwilling hospitality of Cedric the Saxon,[14] nor
did my appearance correspond externally with the flowing robes of
the warlike crusader. My attire was in fact unique. The upper portion
of my body was shrouded in a coat, that evidently to the most obtuse
observer did not belong to its original, if legitimate, owner, whilst my
nether limbs were encased in a pair of trousers presented to me some
time before by a benign friend who had accidentally upset upon
them some description of acid; the natural shabbiness of my
appearance was thus enhanced by the corrosive matter absolutely in
various places eating the garment off my limbs. I bore, moreover, an
expression on my miserable countenance that would have excited the
commiseration of all but those who, by long intercourse with the
poor, are hardened to the wretchedness in all its aspects. But in this
case the effect was quite the reverse; the tramp-master saw nothing
before him but a fresh object for his banter. He took a slow,
deliberate look at me as I approached the table, and being an acute
man took in the whole situation at a glance.

"What's yer name?" began he, eyeing me curiously.

"Downatheel," answered I, meekly.

"Lord Downatheel, Earl Downatheel?" inquired he insolently,
with a look at the nether garment before alluded to.

---

14. These are characters in Sir Walter Scott's *Ivanhoe* (1819). Brian de Bois-
Guilbert is the would-be lover of Rebecca of York and is killed by Ivanhoe in trial by
combat. Cedric the Saxon is father of Ivanhoe, guardian of the aristocratic Lady
Rowena, and enemy of Norman supremacy.

"No," answered I, "nor Duke Downatheel either. Slitcoat is my Christian name." And down went into the omniscient volume my patronymic of Slitcoat Downatheel.

Now, as I have said before, had I simply confined myself to answering his questions, all would have been as well as could have been expected under such circumstance; I should have obtained my night's lodging, and should have been allowed to go about my business on the following morning. But no sooner had I launched into my story, and hardly had the name of Dr. Coupons issued from my lips, when a gleam of gratified malice shot from the monster's eyes, and settling himself more firmly in his chair, he said to me, weighing with great deliberation each word—

"Didn't you come here last night?"

"I did," I answered calmly.

"And didn't you," continued he in the same tone, "tell me a cock-and-a-bull story about Dr. Coupons recommending you for admittance to the infirmary?"

"It is perfectly true," I replied. "I was told by the porter at the principal entrance to apply here at eight o'clock for the purpose of seeing the doctor in the morning, as it was too late to see him then."

"And so," continued he in the same ironical tone, "you came here this evening to be too late again, just because you were too lazy, too cursed lazy, to come at a proper time."

I immediately entered into an explanation, but he would not allow me to continue; I offered at the same time to show him the passport form Dr. Coupons, but he answered impatiently, "I don't want to see it." Finding myself totally incapable of making the slightest impression on my amiable host, I then asked him with great simplicity, "What do you advise me to do, then, sir?"

"You can stand on your head, if you like," was the sympathetic answer.

This piece of advice, the very last that I should have suspected of being of any practical utility to me in my present distress, left me completely dumbfounded. After a pause he added, "I can give you a night's lodging." He then proceeded to the second interrogatory.

"How old are yer?"

"Thirty," I answered.

"*What* are yer?"

"Lately discharged," I replied, "from the 'Austral Brigands'[15] on account of ill-heath."

"I don't want to know what you've been," he rejoined. "What are yer now?"

"I have no occupation at present," I answered, "or should I not be here."

"Well, you are a *tramp*, then," and down went the word "tramp," after my hereditary appellative of Slitcoat Downatheel.

"Where were you discharged?" he continues.

"At Georgetown," I replied.

"How did you get back? Did they send you over?"

"Yes."

"Well," he continued, "I'm not surprised at their discharging you from the 'Brigands'; they want people with what is called 'nous'[16] out in the Colonies—at least, they did in my time—a thing that you don't seem to have got. Are you a good hand at picking oakum?"

"No," I answered, with a hectic attempt at a smile.

"Well," said he, "you'll have a good spell of it to-morrow, if that's any consolation to you."

With the consolatory reflections induced by this last remark, I returned to my seat.

It would be hard indeed if the poor-law authorities inflicted all these humiliations upon candidates for their bounty without a reward in some shape or another beaming in the immediate future; and doubtless, under the presumption that hunger is one of the principal motives that drive people to accept this species of hospitality, means are provided for the refreshment of the inner man.

The grand inquisitor now rose from his chair and approached the benches, bearing a wooden tray containing a quantity of pieces of brown bread corresponding to the number of guests assembled,

---

15. Possibly a sarcastic reference to imaginary involvement with Ben Hall, Ned Kelly, or other real-life bushrangers of the Australian Outback.

16. A Greek word implying intuitive and heartfelt understanding. Now, and apparently then, in occasional English usage.

gruffly ordering each individual to "take one"; each, in response to this cordial invitation, plunged his hand into the receptacle and withdrew it, containing a portion of the bread in question. The principal ingredient in the composition of this *panacea* seemed to me, to judge by the flavour, to be sawdust; and if it did not serve the purpose of appeasing hunger, it possessed at least the somewhat doubtful advantage of being singularly provocative of thirst.

The insertion of the names and descriptions, interlarded as it had been by the appropriate jocosity of the tramp-master, had occupied some considerable time, but the ceremonial, as will be ultimately seen, was far from being concluded.

The bread having been distributed, we proceeded to devour it, but not before we had been thoroughly searched; and no dynamite or other explosive material being discovered upon our miserable persons, we were ushered in great state—that is to say, we were driven like so many wolves—into another portion of what Bucklaw, in the "Bride of Lammermoor," would have termed this "beggarly castle of starvation,"[17] preparatory to benefiting by our much-needed repose.

I must now touch upon a subject that I approach with extreme diffidence, but which it would be impossible to omit, constituting as it does one of the most important features of the hospitality accorded by the parochial authorities; and in fear that ears polite may be offended, I will extricate myself from the temporary difficulty by addressing my remarks, bearing upon this particular subject, to devout students of the Koran. These latter then, knowing the importance attributed to cleanliness by the votaries of Mahomet, will not be surprised to find that one of the most salient points in the night's entertainment provided in the Casual Ward is the Oriental ceremony of the bath.

The religious element to be observed to so marked a degree in the Mussulman custom is in its Protestant prototype conspicuous by its absence, nor is the vernacular generally in use upon the

---

17. Bucklaw, a character in Scott's 1819 novel, is referring to Wolf's Crag, the dismal tower occupied by his enemies, the Ravenswoods, after the bulk of their property had been lost during the political upheavals preceding Scotland's union with England in 1707 (see chapter 21 of *The Bride of Lammermoor*).

occasion, or, indeed, the whole machinery of the institution, productive of divine ideas or inductive of religious inspirations—unless the much-cherished axiom be borne in mind of cleanliness being next to godliness. Be this as it may, the object of this institution is strictly corporeal and sanitary rather than religious, and if becomingly carried out would be in accordance with necessity, although the same brutality is observable in its infliction that characterises every phase of the hospitality granted to the unfortunate devotees—guilty of that most heinous crime of all, poverty.

To resume, after this slight digression, we now found ourselves in a species of shed or outhouse, situated at the back of the building, where we were ordered to remain whilst the "bath" was being prepared for our reception; and, judging by the appearance of some of my companions that more than one of them would soon be able to walk without the exercise of his limbs, I mentally resolved to be, if possible, one of the first. In the course of a few minutes a voice was heard from the exterior, exclaiming, "Now then, come on four of you!" and the requisite number immediately issued forth, myself among them, where a few paces led us to the foot of a rickety flight of wooden steps, which we duly ascended, and attaining the summit found our further progress, I was about to say barred by a door, but, the bight being extremely cold, the door was upon this occasion hospitably thrown open, so that we should not lack ventilation during the process of disrobing and immersion.

The interior presented that of a small room, in one corner of which, but in a separate compartment, stood the famous "bath." My companions in misfortune I should say, speaking roughly, number about thirty souls, and the whole of us, each in our turn, were to be immersed in this single receptacle. This, to the innocent reader, would appear to be somewhat of a lengthy operation, but the parish authorities possess in the master of the ceremonies, who now performed the function of entertaining Her Majesty's brigade of vagabonds, a master-spirit equal to any emergency, however insurmountable the obstacles might appear; and it was a source of no small wonder to me, and has been ever since, why such a *bel esprit*[18]

---

18. A wit or genius: the tone is sarcastic, as in the rest of this part of Wallace-Goodbody's account.

occupied so lowly a station. He now proceeded to expedite matters, and to be brief, instead of thirty *coups*,[19] the tramp-master, with the power of calculation of a chancellor of the exchequer or the keenness of vision of the most astute Monte Carlian, made fifteen by the simple mathematical process of ordering two individuals to plunge into the bath at the same time; the operation being repeated until the whole thirty had performed their ablutions by absolutely bathing in one another's filth. Not once was the water changed; as soon as two were out another two were in, and so on to the end of the chapter.

I marvelled at the time what reasons, sanitary or other, could possibly justify such an act of wholesale bestiality, and what were the mysterious economical precepts (secreted probably in the brain of some inscrutable Guardian) that failed to acknowledge the necessity for more than one bath and one supply of tepid water for thirty human beings to be plunged in two at a time, several of whom I noticed were suffering from various descriptions of skin diseases. In a similar establishment that I once had occasion to visit in the City I was informed that there were three baths provided, one of which was particularly reserved for diseases of the skin; but in this pandemonium no such precaution was considered necessary. Each man entered the bath dirty, and issued therefrom dirtier still, and perhaps in addition had the good fortune to contract some contagious malady. By the provision of two or three baths cleanliness would have been observed, or at least something in the shape of it, and undue humiliation would not have been inflicted—not upon a collection of hyaenas and jackals escaped from the gardens of the Zoological Society—but upon a score of two of human beings whose only crime was poverty.

*   *   *   *   *

---

19. Wallace-Goodbody's meaning is not entirely clear here. He may be using the word "coup" in its Scottish sense, defined in the Oxford English Dictionary as "The act of tilting or shooting rubbish from a cart, wheelbarrow, etc." In his representation, the tramp-master seems to have treated the inmates of the casual ward in just this way.

"Put yer head under!" said the tramp-master, who was presiding over the whole of the arrangements, to me, when my turn came to step into the bowl of ditch-water. I may here observe, parenthetically, that upon a former occasion, which among the tramps has attained the dignity of being historical, one of the guests entertained in this same hospitable mansion happened to be a gigantic negro, who, either misunderstanding the order to plunge his head into the greasy mixture, or, what is more probable, being unwilling to do so, the tramp-master, losing patience (and not possessing the necessary amount of *nous*, notwithstanding his colonial experience, to be aware that there are certain occasions when negroes are not always philosophers), violently pushed the man's head beneath the surface. The black immediately sprang out, seized his burly persecutor in his arms, and fairly hurled him into the bath, clothed as he was—whence he extricated himself with something less than his usual dignity. From that time the tramp-master confined his operations when superintending the ablutions to a verbal order.

The ceremonial was now concluded for the evening, and we all passed from the bath-room into the dormitory, or whatever name would be most appropriate to describe an apartment resembling the interior of a barn, provided with a somewhat steep and lofty roof, and along the sides of which were ranged two rows of what I, in my ignorance, at first imagined to be paupers' coffins. I must confess that I was startled for the moment, and the thought occurred to my mind that our sufferings were about to be terminated by a holocaust, and that it was intended to immolate us and subsequently bury us all on the premises; and that, in addition, we were on the point of being elevated from our present degradation to the dignity of the Castilian monarchs, who, by a visit to the subterranean chapel beneath the Escurial,[20] can behold, whenever the fancy seizes them, their sepulchral urns.

There was no ground for alarm, however, for on closer inspection what I imagined to be paupers' coffins turned out to be

---

20. El Real Monasterio de El Escorial is a complex of buildings erected in Castile in the late 16th century and was long the center of both religious and secular power in Spain. Wallace-Goodbody uses the spelling "Escurial."

straw-mattresses spread upon the ground, and separated from one another by a deal board. Upon each of these luxurious couches was what by a stretch of imagination might in parochial language be termed—a blanket, but which in reality was a threadbare quilt of the most meagre description, which, whatever might be its ostensible object, utterly failed to guarantee the shivering caitiff[21] shrinking beneath it from the frigidity of the atmosphere.

Over the summit of our bed, or rather *dosses*, as they are termed in Bohemian parlance, and extending the whole length of the wall, was a shelf, upon which we were ordered to place our rags formed into a bundle—a night-garment in the shape of a cotton shirt being lent to us for the occasion by the institution. We were not permitted to place our clothes upon our beds to further an increase of warmth, and, it being cold for the period of the year, my sufferings were intense, and were greatly enhanced by the peculiar nature of my situation, by my doubts as to the treatment I should meet with on the morrow, and by my harrowing anxieties. At length, at a late hour, I forgot my cares in a troubled slumber.

*   *   *   *   *

I had been awake but a few minutes when, at the matutinal hour of six, as I should judge, the door was thrown open and the tormentor of the preceding evening made his appearance in his shirt-sleeves. I had enjoyed a banquet composed of brown bread and water, had partaken of the luxury of the bath, and had profited by a night's lodging—now was to come the hour of reckoning.

"Now then," roared he, at the top of his voice; "out of it, all of you; tumble out! tumble out! Roll up your mattresses," continued he, with the commanding air and gesture of a Roman general giving the order to his legionaries, "and put your shirts on the top of them." This operation being soon performed, and our toilet completed with equal rapidity, we all passed out of the dormitory into the bath-room, and thence by the flight of rickety stairs we emerged into the chill morning air.

---

21. The word characterizes a miserable wretch, but has connotations of villainy.

The master having selected some half-dozen as cleaners, served out to each of the remainder, after duly weighing it in the scales, a bundle of short pieces of tarred rope to be unravelled and picked, by means of the fingers, into a fibre as fine as the production of the silkworm, and we all entered the shed or outhouse, the *salle d'attente*[22] where we had waited the night before, previous to the arrival of our turn for taking part in that ceremony that I most cordially hope I shall never more have occasion to refer to.

A more miserable aspect than that presented by this den would be difficult to describe, and as I gazed upon the blackened walls, and upon my companions ragged and forlorn *accroupis*[23] upon the two rows of benches, engaged in their hideous and ignoble employment, I fairly owned to myself that never until this moment had I known what misery was. And here I was to remain the whole of the day, for it would be a moral impossibility to my inexperience to complete my task within the prescribed limits, eleven o'clock being the hour of deliverance. An allowance of bread, of the same magnitude as that issued the preceding evening, was now distributed to us by the task-master, and, should it be necessary to detain any of us until eight o'clock at night, this was all that we had to depend upon to support nature.

An incident now occurred that it would be well to place before the public eye—an incident that I beheld with mingled disgust and rage, and after being a spectator of which I unhesitatingly affirm, and shall always maintain, that given a task-master possessing the necessary amount of brutality, and a pauper in the last stage of destitution, the position of the latter is as downtrodden as that of the serfs before they were emancipated by the late Emperor of Russia.[24] The victim upon this occasion was not a colossal negro, but a discharged soldier of emaciated aspect, slightly made and considerably under the middle height, and, as it afterwards transpired, in an advanced state of consumption, possessing only one

---

22. Waiting room.

23. Crouched.

24. Serfdom persisted in Russia until 1861.

lung—a worthy object for the barbarity of this transplantation from Siberia to the banks of the Thames.

Like myself, he had presented himself for the purpose of seeing the doctor, and being ill and infirm stated his inability to perform the task allocated to him when ordered to do so by the master. No sooner had the refusal passed his lips than the gaoler seized him by the shoulders and pushed him outside the door with great violence, inflicting at the same time more than one blow on the ears of the unhappy wretch with the flat of his hand.

"You are a cowardly man," shrieked the object of this atrocious act of cruelty.

"You humbug," roared his assailant, "you shall see the doctor at ten, and if he says you are fit for work, woe betide you!"

He then stalked off, and the sick man resumed his seat in the shed.

With the exception of myself I noticed that all the spectators beheld this scene with the most stolid indifference. One old tramp did so far express his feelings as to observe that, should he who had just submitted to this castigation have the courage to make his complaint before a magistrate, "no one in such a crowd as this," looking round the shed, "would back him up; and they wouldn't be believed if they did." Now that I am upon this subject, I may as well terminate it at once. At ten o'clock the poor soldier was summoned to the presence of the doctor; he did not return, and I was for a time ignorant of his fate. A few weeks after, having occasion to visit a Union Infirmary, I recognised in the wearer of one of the workhouse suits my companion of the eventful evening that I am describing. He informed me that he had been duly examined by the doctor, who immediately granted him admittance to the infirmary. Battered and trampled upon, he was unable to summon up the necessary amount of courage to form a complaint against the tramp-master, and was moreover but too delighted to escape from his talons; but this worthy, with the cowardice of low minds, said to him apologetically, as he escorted him to the infirmary: "You mustn't pay any attention to what I *SAID* to you this morning. I didn't know you were as bad as you are."

I forbear all comment.

But to resume. If my immediate surroundings were miserable and forlorn, the view presented to my gaze from without was mournful in the extreme; the shed, the scene of our present confinement, opened upon a small paved court, bounded by a row of iron railings, that served to separate the precincts of the work-house from what struck me as being perfectly in consonance with my situation, namely, a graveyard, over which protruded the irregular backs of the houses of a London street. Downpours of rain fell during the day, brightening the hues of the emerald green that carpeted the surface, upon which rested the tomb-stones indicating the last dwelling-place of the departed. Fine old tombs some of them, composed of solid blocks of masonry that in their time had had other spectators interested or disinterested than a bevy of wretched paupers. Rare gleams of sunshine—how rare!—occasionally broke forth, casting slanting shadows from the tombstones, the effect of which, either from the state of my mind or other causes, was to produce the very ecstasy of mourn-fulness and sorrowing. At that moment the silvery chime of a chapel bell fell upon my drowsy ears and recalled me for a moment, but for a moment, to the things of this world. "That's for the morning service of a Roman Catholic chapel," remarked an old tramp next to me, observing my look of mental interrogation, "and it's generally very fashionably attended."

The little chapel bell continued to tinkle summoning its votaries to morning prayer, conjuring up thoughts in my watchful mind that led me far away from the oakum-shed: I saw in my mind's eye the mysterious obscurity of the interior of the building, the variegated reflections from the stained-glass windows, the high altar with its lighted tapers, the urbane and priestly officiant administering to his wealthy communicants; the breviaries, and the incense. I beheld the beautiful young mother as she stepped from her carriage into the sacred build-ing, holding by the hand her daughter with the golden locks clustering over the velvet jacket, and could even distinguish the earnest devotion perceptible in the violet eyes of the child as she knelt before the altar.

*   *   *   *   *

Pathos and comedy, for some reason undefined, advance hand in hand in this world, and I was summoned from my too luxurious and inappropriate reveries by the gruff voice of the tramp-master, who at that moment made his appearance at the entrance of the shed, completely darkening it and bearing the *pot-á-salade* before alluded to, containing, to use the language of Gil Blas, the *hardes* and the *nippes* of the assembled company.[25] Never had such a motley collection of novelties found a home in a conjuror's basket: knives with several blades and every one of them broken; halves, nay, quarters, of old combs in an advanced state of decay, with nearly all the teeth out; broken old clay pipes black with use, dilapidated old newspapers, &c. &c. "Whose is this?" said the humourist, with an agreeable smile, holding up one of the latter objects; "to whom belongs the *Tramp's Journal?*" continued he, inflicting a name upon the periodical in question. Roars of hilarity. "He's not a bad sort of a chap," said the old beggar, my neighbour, "when he's let the steam off."

The various objects having been returned to their legitimate owners, and it being moreover eleven o'clock, those who had completed their task were at liberty to depart, among which number, it is needless to say, I was not included.

"Some of you will be pretty hungry before you've done," said the tramp-master, grimly eyeing in particular my performance, which I must own presented a most contemptible appearance; "you're only wasting your time now," added he: "all that will have to be picked over again."

The long hours succeeded one another, the rain fell, the gleams of sunshine ceased to appear—but enough of this! My back is nearly broken with the crouching, stooping posture I am compelled to adopt in the performance of my humiliating employment. At length, at half past five, I was liberated and emerged by a back entrance into the miserable streets. On finding myself once more upon the world's pavement and at liberty, I murmured involuntarily, as I stood half-clad in the drizzling, clinging rain that was gradually saturating me to the skin, "*Post tenebras lux*";[26] is it possible that I have been but twenty hours a resident in that hateful place?"—weeks, months, in fact, had seemed to have flown

---

25. Alain-René Lesage uses these slang terms in his black comedy *L'Histoire de Gil Blas de Santillane* (1715-35). The words usually mean "rags" or "garments," but in Lesage's context are usually translated as "goods and chattels" (see Book 3, chapter 8).

26. "After darkness, light." Attributed to the Vulgate, a 5th century version of the Bible in Latin. The second word is properly spelled *tenebris.*

over my head with the bitter experience and sombre thought crowded into a few hours.

Who says that London is not a beautiful city? asked I, as, starved, wet, and miserable, I gazed upon the brick buildings looming through the dank, murky atmosphere, with feelings of pleasure that had never visited me when gazing at sunrise over the Bay of Naples.

Chapter Five

On Tramp
by James Greenwood
London: Diprose & Bateman, 1883

CHAPTER I.

AN UNGENTEEL EXPEDITION—LIFE WITH THE TRAMP TRIBE—VAGABONDS BORN AND BRED—THE TRAMP PROPER—ADOPTING THE GARB—THE START—THE FIRST CONVERSATION WITH A TRAMP—THE POOR WAYFARING WIDOW AND HER SON BARNEY.

My reasons for undertaking the ungenteel expedition, the nature of which the above title indicates, may be stated in a few words. It is tolerably well known that our fields of human industry are curiously prolific of weeds, pictur-esque at times, perhaps, but always unprofitable.

About the hives where bees cheerfully toil, idle drones loaf idly all their lives, contributing to the commonwealth neither wax nor honey, but ever alert to obtain by hook or crook as much of both as serves to keep them fat and comfortable in their laziness.

These are of the Tramp tribe.

Vagabonds born and bred for the most part; free rovers, who resent and despise the trammels of civilization and the

responsibilities thereto pertaining, and willingly endure the hardships of highway journey-work, and take their chance of fair or
foul weather, food good or bad, plentiful or scanty; taking, just as
it may happen, the lodging under a house-roof and in a bed, or
beneath a hedge, with the dewy grass for a cold counterpane, and
all for the pleasure of indulging in unlimited liberty of much the
same kind as falls to the lot of an able-bodied homeless dog.

Official statistics reveal the unpleasant fact that, exclusive of
children, and in England alone, more than forty thousand adult
idlers are constantly wandering from place to place, not only without any visible means of existence, but, as is well known, with a
vicious habit of shutting their eyes wilfully when the said means
are exhibited to them.

Whence arises this incurable propensity for "tramping?" and
what are the peculiar delights of tramp life, that in the face of odds
so formidable—taking a decent view of the matter, that is to say,—
serve to allure so many of one's fellow mortals to adopt and stur-
dily abide by it?

This was what I wished to discover, and recognizing the truth of
"Poor Richard's" proverb, "If you want an errand done to your
satisfaction, do it yourself; if not, send someone else,"[1] I resolved,
that as soon as the haymaking season had fairly set in—that being
the time when the tramping fraternity are at their briskest,—to take
the road myself day by day, and for fifty miles or so,—meanwhile
doing in Rome as Romans do, and taking notes by the way. It need
not be mentioned that to give my design any chance of success it
was necessary for me to adopt a garb such as would preclude the
possibility of being regarded as a gentleman taking his walks abroad,
and as such a fair object for imposition and victimizing.

At the same time it was not necessary that the disguise
should be of the scarecrow kind. The tramp proper is not
invariably a tatterdemalion. The stick and bundle were of
course indispensable.

---

1. *Poor Richard's Almanack*, written and published serially by Benjamin
Franklin between 1733 and 1758, does not include this exact maxim, although it does
include several with a similar meaning. For example, "If you'd have a servant that you
like, serve yourself" (1737).

It was on Monday, the 18th of June, that I started on the road that was due north. I was induced to take this way because, as I was informed, the hay in Hertfordshire and Bedfordshire was earlier than in other parts, and that it was the custom for tramps to commence somewhere near Barnet, and to leisurely work their way through Northampton, Rutland, Leicester, Nottingham and Derby, to Yorkshire, occupying about six weeks on the journey,— indeed, timing their progress to the gradual ripening of the grass crop, which is at least a month later in Yorkshire than in Bedfordshire. This being so, it seemed to me that it would do well enough to begin at Barnet.

I must confess that, after all, my mind was not quite at ease as regards the correctness of my costume, but my apprehensions on that score were speedily set at rest before I had trudged half a mile. Happening, in a moment of forgetfulness, as well of my stick and bundle as of the part I was essaying, to approach the palings of a garden surrounding a gentleman's house, for the sake of contemplating the beautiful flowers there growing, I was greeted with such undisguised hostility on the part of a watchful creature of the canine species, with such a spiteful show of his teeth, and such an upraised ridge of angry hair along the whole length of the faithful animal's back, that there could be no doubt what he took me for. On such authority I could no longer doubt that my "get up" was all that could be desired.

For some miles my success could not be fairly spoken of as dazzlingly brilliant.

Near to the venerable obelisk outside Barnet, and on which is recorded the brief particulars of the battle which, four hundred years ago, took place at that spot, between the Earl of Warwick and Edward IV.,[2] I came on a young man of the kind I was in search of, but the encounter was disheartening rather than otherwise.

He was making his toilet at the brink of a horse-pond; drying his face on the legs of his cotton stockings (which he afterwards washed and hung round his neck, that they might dry in the sun as he walked), and combing his hair with his outstretched fingers.

---

2.   During the War of the Roses, the Battle of Barnet in 1471 was a decisive victory for the Yorkist king, Edward IV, over his Lancastrian opponents.

We got into conversation, and he informed me, with savage emphasis, that all the jobs I was likely to fall in with on the road I was taking, I might stand on my head and do.

He had tried it for more than a week, his trade being that of a French polisher; "and when I started," said he, in warning accents, "I had quite as big a bundle as yours, let me tell you."

"What have you done with it?" I asked him.

"What? Why, what you'll do with yours, mark me!" returned the young fellow, with a malicious relish. "I eat it—I eat it a bit at a time, and I sold the hankycher it was tied up in, coming through Hatfield, to get me a bit of victuals and pay my lodgings. It is my first time and my last. I've tried it and had enough of it, and I'm now making myself a bit respectable, so that when I get to London, they won't see what a fool I've been."

I should like to have questioned him further concerning his experiences, but he was so fiercely set against tramping and tramps, that he would having nothing further to say to me, but slipped his wrecked old shoes on his naked feet and took his way, leaving me to pursue mine.

I found very little between Barnet and Potters Bar to encourage the hope that my campaign would be a satisfactory one.

Tramps I met, and tramps overtook me, singly and in pairs, but they carried their character plainly written on their face, and were not of the sort I was in search of.

Within a mile of Bell Bar I fared better. The day was a hot one, and with the noonday sun blazing down on my head and shoulders, and my feet baking in my whitened boots, I gladly spied a resting place—a shady nook at the narrow entrance to a leafy lane,—where, on a sloping bank grew, knee-high grass, dark green, by reason of the sheltering boughs of an ancient beech. Nor was the retreat rendered less enticing by the circumstance of the said bank being topped by a tall ragged hedge, gay with fragrant honeysuckle and wild roses. There being, just now, no visible sign of tramp company, whither up or down the road, I was presently coolly couched with a soothing pipe, lazily listening to a blackbird that, unsuspicious of the near neighbourhood of a human enemy, was freely holding forth on the boughs overhead.

Presently, however, I was made aware of notes which were not those of a blackbird, but of a fellow-creature—a human Irish creature, and a woman, unmistakably.

—An irritating, drawling, droning voice. And raising myself on my elbows to discover who the owner of it might be, a queer kind of puzzle presented itself.

There, coming along the white road at a distance of a hundred yards or so, was a woman wearing her battered old bonnet uncomfortably perched on the top of a flaming red head, and with a small bundle slung over her shoulder. This was not all her burden, however.

With her broad good-natured face reeking with perspiration, she carried "pick-a'-back" a male fellow-creature, the disarrangement of her bonnet being occasioned by his big head resting on her shoulder, and his ragged arms clasping her neck. His feet appeared to be cased in boots much too large for the thin shanks; which owing to his trouser-legs having rucked up as high as his knees, were naked, and stuck out straight like the shafts of a cart.

It was such a goblin kind of spectacle that one could not but feel curious as to what it could mean. My first idea was, that it might be the strapping middle-aged Irishwoman's husband, who, despite his insignificant size, had somehow obtained inexorable influence over her, and insisted on this [pleasant][3] mode of travelling whenever he and his good lady took a country excursion together.

As she came closer, however, I could make out that the "pick-a'-backed" one was not a man at all, but a boy—a lanky lad of fourteen or so. Not a prepossessing youth, but blunt-nosed and bullet-headed, and with a thankless brooding scowl, making his black brows seem the heavier.

He looked languid and ill, and his complexion was yellowish, sickly. I have no doubt that, nearly hidden as I was in the tall grass and weeds, the strange pair would have passed on without observing me had I not purposely attracted their attention.

The effect was startling as unexpected.

With a malevolent glance in my direction, the pale-faced, bullet-headed boy flung himself away from the woman with an angry exclamation, and snatching himself from the expostulating hand she laid on his jacket, went slouching away alone. Nor did the woman show herself less angry—but it was with me, not with him.

---

3.   In the original: "pleasent."

"Bad luck to ye!" she exclaimed fiercely, "and could you find no better to do than go putting your shpoke in, and shpiling me when I was getting along so aisily wid him?" With more politeness than was, I am afraid, under the circumstances, allowable, I hastened to assure her that I intended no offence, and immediately tendered, what was much more to the purpose, a peace offering from my tobacco box.

"Barney, jewel!" she called after her sulking offspring, who continued to slouch along sullenly and without looking back, "stay a minnit, or come back while I light me pipe."

"What's the matter with him," I remarked; "he's rather a large size to carry."

"He's ill, poor sowl!" she replied, with a tear trickling down her coarse freckled face. "He's got no strinth! He's a-wasting, like his poor father and his two brothers that's dead. That's why I've got him with me. It's the wasting that gives him his sharp timper, and makes him shy like, and angry for anyone to see me carrying him."

"He must be a heavy load," said I.

"I wish it was heavier," replied the poor Irishwoman sadly, shaking her head.

"Why don't you leave him at home, since he can't walk," I suggested; on which she informed me that it was just because her son was so weak and unable to do much in the way of walking that she was on the road with him.

She lived in Middlesex Street, Whitechapel, she told me; and she could not bear this dreadful hot weather, which was so bad for his rest, in a close little room of nights, to see him lying there growing weaker and weaker—especially after what the doctor had said about the chance of a few weeks in the country doing him good; "and so," continued the kind soul, "it came into my head to sell a few bits of furniture to buy him some boots, poor boy and give us a start."

"And where are you going? How do you intend to live on the road?"

"Shure I'm looking out for a job of haymaking;" she replied respectfully, "and when I get one, he will do no harm sitting under the hedge amongst the sweet hay, while I work and earn a little for the bit of food and the lodging: and so we'll push on; and when he can't walk I'll carry him, and he'll be gettin' his strenth up again, plase God."

As a tramp-fellow, a hard-up out-o'-work, the best I dare do was to press on her acceptance another pipe of tobacco, which she thankfully took, and, wishing me luck, started at a half-run to overtake poor ill-tempered, consumptive Barney. I dare say he finely abused her before she could coax him to ride "pick-a'-back" again.

Little as I had bestowed on her, she had provided me with so much to think about that I was still reclining meditatively, in the odour of wild roses and honeysuckle, when it occurred to me that if I wished to make sure of a lodging that night, I had best push on.

CHAPTER II.

THE CROCKERY MENDER—MAD LUCAS THE FRIEND OF TRAMPS—THE SHOULDER OF MUTTON LODGING-HOUSE—HABITS OF LODGERS—PULLING THE RIGHT STRING AT THE "WHITE SWAN"—HOW TO RAISE THE WIND—THE WAY TO DRAIN 'EM—A TRAVELLER'S LODGING HOUSE—&c.

I HAD no idea, when I halted for the night at Stevenage, that I was within a mile of the spot held in affectionate remembrance by habitual tramps, beggars and outcasts of every degree who make the "Northern Circuit"[4] their familiar hunting ground.

I obtained the information from an umbrella mender and riveter of fractured crockery, whom I met on the road next morning. I told him I was going to Hitchin.

"Through Wimley?"

I had got the name of the place in my note book as Wymondly, but it was all the same.

"Yes."

"Lord! what a difference there is," said the crockery mender, "between the number as takes that way now to when Mad Lucas was alive and did the proper thing by 'em."

---

4.   At this time there were six assize circuits (plus the Central Criminal Court covering Metropolitan London). All the counties mentioned in Chapter I as on the tramp's itinerary were in the Northern Circuit. Stevenage, however, like the rest of Hertfordshire, lay in the Home Circuit.

I was ignominiously compelled to confess my ignorance on the subject, explaining that it was the first time that I had tramped that part of the country.[5]

"Why, heart alive!" cried he, in amazement; "I should have thought that Mad Lucas and his goings on were known to chaps of your kidney from Johnny Groats to the Land's End. Mad Lucas of Redcoats Green, I mean. Him that kept—well, I was going to say, like the old song says, 'open house to all;' but, if he didn't do that, he kept an open window to all,—leastways, when I say a open 'un, so it was, all but the iron bars—thick 'uns, too, before it. Don't you make any mistake," continued the china mender, with an admiring shake of the head. "There's many a man got a moniment put up for him that wasn't such a God-send to poor people on the road as Mad Lucas was. Tuppence was his money—tuppence in or'nary, 'cept your religion was the Irish religion, like his was, and you could patter a 'noster to him, and then you got fourpence and sometimes a glass of gin as well."

"He is dead now, you say?"

"He died three years ago last April,"[6] replied my informant readily, "and, believe me, or believe me not, ever since I was a boy so high, and worked this road with my father and mother, I never once met a tramp who had so much as 'arf a bad word to say against him."

He had the matter so at heart as to require but little egging on to volunteer to go a bit out of his way on purpose to show me the

---

5. It is remarkable that Greenwood was unaware of the reputation of James "Mad" Lucas. Lucas, who according to the definitions of modern medicine was a paranoid schizophrenic, achieved national fame after he was used by Charles Dickens as the model for "Mr. Mopes the Hermit" in the story "Tom Tiddler's Ground" (1861). After this sightseekers came in their thousands to gawp at the hermit and the police were often called out to control the crowds. See Whitmore, Richard. *Mad Lucas: The Strange Story of Victorian England's Most Famous Hermit*. Hitchin: North Hertfordshire District Council, 1983.

6. As Lucas died in 1874, this would date Greenwood's "tramp" to 1877, although the date of publication was 1883. On p. 151 below, Greenwood dates Lucas's death to "thirty odd months ago."

house which this kindly remembered benefactor of the tramp tribe occupied during his lifetime.

As we walked the china mender told me so many wonderful things concerning "Mad Lucas," that, I confess, I should have doubted many of them had I not afterwards found them so amply corroborated by the inhabitants of the nearest villages, Wimley and Ippolitts. Mad Lucas, it seems, came of a good family, and at one time was engaged in the West India trade, and, before the Emancipation Act, was a slave owner.[7] For several years he was chairman of the Imperial Gas Company, which may be taken as strong evidence that he was not always mad. His mother died at Redcoats in 1849, when his eccentricity first manifested itself in his refusing, for the space of thirteen weeks, to part with the oaken coffin in which the old lady's body was encased.

From the hour when the sanitary authorities deprived him of his treasure, Mr. Lucas renounced the world and its vanities, including the use of clothing and of soap to wash himself.

He discharged all his servants, and, hating all his kith and kin, barricaded his premises against them, locked all the inner doors, and with no other covering than part of a blanket, and no other companion besides a cat, took up his abode in the back kitchen.

He had a chair to sit on and a table to sit at, and that was the whole of the kitchen furniture. He slept there, but had no bedding; but he never let the fire out, and as the dustman's services were never put in requisition, he had, in the dingy hole that served him as kitchen and parlour and all, plenty of ashes to repose on.

He had plenty of money (over £50,000 which his brother inherited), but the only worldly comforts he allowed himself consisted of bread and milk. The latter was sent in a locked can for fear his wicked relations should tamper with it, and the former he would, for the same reason, select from a full basket of loaves brought by the baker to the grated kitchen window. There was only one other creature comfort he laid out money on, and that

---

7. The slave trade was outlawed in 1807, too early for Lucas (who lived between 1813 and 1874) to have participated in it. Slavery itself was not, however, abolished in the British Empire until the Abolition Act of 1833, which did not take full effect until 1838.

was gin. Whether he gave it all away to tramps, or whether he consumed a portion of it to cheer his solitude is not known, but it is a fact that after his untimely demise a large number of still full bottles and a still larger of broken ones were found heaped in the corners of his sooty lair. He was fond of little children, and bought "sweets" wholesale for them, and delighted to tempt the youngsters of the neighbourhood to his cell bars and scatter out "drops" and lozenges to them, like barley to chickens. He gave sweets to the children of tramps. He was kinder even than this at times, for seated in his sackcloth and ashes he read medical books, and gave to sick beggars who came to him the benefit of his reading in the shape of prescriptions, with money to have them made up at the druggist's.

"If there was anything poor old Lucas hated, it was a lawyer," remarked the friendly umbrella maker; "for I never shall forget the game we once had with a soft young fellow that me and two more met one time 'twixt this and Wimley. He was a decent-dressed young chap of his sort, and like you, he had never heard or read of Lucas,—so we pitched him a yarn about him: told him that he was being done out of his property because he couldn't get a lawyer to take his case up, and that was the reason why he barricaded himself in and had the bars put up at his windows. 'I know a little about the law,' the young fellow says, 'I was a matter of two years in a lawyer's office when I was a boy.' 'That's the sort for me. You know enough, anyhow, to gammon him into the belief that you know somebody who will take up his case, and you're as sure of five shillings as though you had it now in your hand.' Lord! You should have seen him when he come back!" And he laughed at the pleasant remembrance until he swallowed a mouthful from his stumpy-headed pipe, and stood holding on to the gate-post, and coughing for a minute or more.

"Did he come back with the five shillings?" I asked.

"He come back," replied the tickled china mender, still gasping for breath, "he come back while we was waiting for him round the corner,—with his eyes starting out of his head, and with half of his neckhanksher gone, and—ho, ho! with a lump at the back of his head as big as a braz-heel nut.—'How did you get on?' we asked him without a smile on our faces. And he told us. He made his way past the watch-box, and found the grated window, and there was the old boy in the blanket, as usual. 'Can I speak to you on a matter of business, sir?' he says to Mr. Lucas. 'You can please yourself as to that,'

Mr. Lucas says. 'Well, then, sir,' says the young fellow, 'I'm give to understand that your affairs are in a bit of a muddle, and that you are being imposed on by certain incourteous persons. Now, I am connected with the law—!' He didn't get no further than that. Making a dart at him through the bars, Mad Lucas caught him by the neckhanksher, and would have throttled him on the spot if it hadn't give way, and followed it up as the young fellow was running for his life by shying a half-quartern loaf after him, which caused the lump on his head I told you about. Ho, ho! I'd lay a farden cake that that young fellow never called on Mad Lucas again."

My friend the old umbrella man was in the midst of his rigmarole from which I was enabled to gather the above curious facts, when Mad Lucas's dwelling came in view. It required some such unmistakable evidence that the strange things I had heard were not ill-patched and pieced reminiscences of some wellnigh forgotten legend, but facts as it were of yesterday.

There was the dilapidated abode, and in pretty much the same state as when some thirty odd months ago[8] its preposterous proprietor was discovered, death-stricken in apoplexy, on his bed of soot and cinders, and carried out.

The *Hertfordshire Express* gives the following account of his last moments:-

"He was discovered in a fit on the morning of Friday the 17th of April, 1874. Some ladies and gentlemen, who had been visiting in the neighbourhood of Wymondley close by, moved by curiosity, had walked up to Redcoats Green in the early morning, in order to see the recluse, whose fame had reached the distant county where they resided.

Arrived at his house, they found the watchman somewhat alarmed because his employer, the hermit, had not answered to his call. After repeated knockings it was determined to force an entrance, and the door of his den was accordingly broken open. What a sight then presented itself!

There he lay upon the ashes, cold and naked, speechless and unable to move. The handkerchief of a lady who chanced to be at hand was used for bathing his face, and some of the grimy coating

---

8.   See p. 148 note 6 above.

of his features was removed even before he was taken to a more decent habitation.

The whole of his body was black with soot and the incrustation of years. His hair was long and matted, and full of soot and dirt. He was carefully wrapped in blankets and conveyed to the house of his tenant Mr. Chapman, who occupies the farm which forms part of the estate. After his removal it was at times thought that he had some return of consciousness, for on the following Saturday morning he appeared to be trying to speak, and it is certain he followed the motions of those who attended him with his eyes. He was, however, unable to utter a word to those who were anxious to minister to his dying wants. Frequent applications of a handkerchief to his face and neck had in a great measure altered his appearance even before his death. His last moments were full of pain. His breathing was laboured, and beads of perspiration stood on his face. When life was extinct, and the last duties had been performed, the deceased was restored to a semblance of humanity. The medical examination showed that he was a well-built and muscular man, and that the body was well nourished. When clothed in the habiliments of the grave those whose curiosity prompted them to visit the chamber where his remains were described him as looking calm and beautiful in death. Indeed, it seemed that the sooty covering that time had fixed on the whole of his body, and which had for years given him the appearance of some strange animal rather than of a man, had preserved his skin from the influence of the sun and climate.

He looked like alabaster or ivory, and his hands were small and delicate as a lady's. His hair, washed and freed from all the impurities it had contained, was brushed back from his forehead, and the brow of an intelligent man was revealed. He always wore a beard, and this, with his whiskers combed out and the ends just tipped with the wintry snow of age, gave him quite a handsome look."

Yes, this was the house, and my companion had not exaggerated when he likened it to a private madhouse, for the safe keeping of furious lunatics. It is hedge-carpenter's[9] sort of work, but

---

9.   A hedge-carpenter was a rural craftsman who worked with locally sourced wood, possibly unsuited to the job. The term was often used to denote rough work done by untrained hands.

tremendously strong. The trunks of young trees, just split in two, and left with the rough bark on, and bound about from end to end with stout hoop iron, and firmly secured to the outer brickwork to guard every approachable window, while heavy baulks of timber crutch up the outer walls, which are fast decaying. It is a house containing, perhaps, a dozen rooms, and it stands in a garden only a few yards from the road. One room appears to be at present occupied, but nobody was at home; so the china mender and I made bold to climb over the palings.

If Mad Mr. Lucas's ghost hovers there sometimes, it must be delighted to find what an able successor Chancery has proved itself in keeping the old place in much the same state of wreck and desolation as when it—the ghost—was so shabbily shuffled off by its grimy proprietor.

There were the tall fir trees rotting where they had fallen. There was the back kitchen, with its stout iron bars rusty red, and its tiled roof sinking through the mouldering rafters. My companion told me that he had seen as many as ten or a dozen clamorous tramps there at one time, with Mad Lucas at the bars, shrewdly questioning them.

There stood the coach-house, where was lodged the family carriage, and which was discovered, after a quarter of a century of idleness, a mere skeleton of rusty iron and worm-eaten wood, thickly shrouded in cobwebs. There, in a corner, by the crazy water-butt, was an old iron saucepan, but whether it was the same one that was found in the kitchen, under the window, and containing a quantity of pence and half-pence all ready for distribution (side by side with a large brown paper of sweets), my friend could not say. There, however, surrounding the root of a tree, were the identical ashes the recluse had lived amongst and slept on. The china mender was sure of that, because he chanced to be on this road when they were clearing out the kitchen, and the man who had the job told him there were nineteen barrow-loads, and that, before it was touched, it made such a heap that one couldn't stand upright without brushing the muck off the ceiling with his hair. I pointed to a weatherbeaten lumbering hut, on wheels. That was his watchman's box, with little bits of glass let into the roughly cut holes all about it, to afford an unlimited look-out. One time Mad Lucas did not employ a watchman, but would engage any tramp he took a fancy to to do odd jobs for him. But one of this sort got up in the night and tried to murder him for his money; after which he had a night-watchman and a day-watchman as well, and no tramp could approach the back kitchen window without passing the watch-box.

Our curiosity satisfied, the friendly crockery mender and myself walked on to the village of Ippolitts, about a mile distant, and there, amongst ale-house company, Mad Lucas was brought on the board again, and from what could be gathered on all sides, there could be no doubt that all I had heard concerning the eccentric individual in question was quite true.

On the road, late again in the afternoon, I fell in with an elderly gentleman, tramping Hitchin-ward, and who, for economy of shoe leather, wore his boots about his neck, pendant by the laces, while he forged along the stony road barefoot. He seemed to be a decent sort of man, and, for a wonder, was not an Irishman. He lived and worked, all the winter, at the Potteries at Shepherd's Bush,[10] he told me, and every June set out on tramp, working his way at any kind of field labour, and winding up with the Northern late corn harvest, when he returned home with a pound or so in his pocket, besides what he was able to send, from time to time, to keep his old woman. I gleaned from him that, about three-and-sixpence a day might be earned in the hayfield, and as much as six shillings a day, working from four in the morning until as long as you could see at night, at harvesting. He reckoned that about two days in six might be set down as "waste," *i.e.*, tramping from job to job, and that his average earnings through four months would be about sixteen shillings a week. Out of this he calculated to spend seven shillings a week in his own maintenance—fourpence for beer and tobacco, and eightpence for food. "And what for lodging and washing?" To which he replied that "a penno'th of soap would last him a month," and that he did his own washing, and that as regarded lodging, the sweetest and best bed in the world was a green clover field. "I thought," said I, "that you might be able to tell me where to get a lodging in Hitchin."

---

10. Shepherd's Bush, in West London, had a large area known as the Potteries, centered on Pottery Lane, which was known as a haunt of gypsies. See Borrow, George. *Romano Lavo-Lil: Word-Book of the Romany or English Gypsy Language.* London: John Murray, 1874, pp. 276-84.

"So I can," said he; "at odd times I've put up at the 'Shoulder of Mutton,' in Back Street,[11] and always found the charges reasonable and the ways civil."

In due time I found my way to Back Street. I was, of course, aware that Hitchin was a market town, and that, necessarily, it contained a mixed population. It was within my knowledge too, that the plaiting of straw was the staple employment of the women and children of the lower class thereabout;[12] but I must confess that I was altogether unprepared for the spectacle that greeted me as I turned into the unfashionable thoroughfare the old man had recommended. It is a long street, and a narrow, and evidently the head-quarters of the tramping fraternity. Deprived of its main feature, it is like a slice from the backslums of Whitechapel, or Kent Street in the Borough. As, in the delectable localities named, at least one house in a half-dozen throughout its length is a lodging-house for travelers—travellers, however, who are not so wornout and leg-weary but they prefer, on a sultry night in June, to sprawl in the house passages and on the steps, and all over the common footway, until an advanced hour, to commencing early enjoyment of the fourpenny pallet provided them. They clustered at the open windows, those ragged knights of the road; they smoked their pipes on the selvage of the pavement, and cooled their toes in the kennel.[13] But the one feature hinted at once quite redeemed the scene from the ruffianly and cockney commonplace, and made of it a picture fit for a storybook.

---

11. Back Street in Hitchin is now known as Queen Street.

12. In the eighteenth and nineteenth centuries straw-plaiting was the main employment for women and children in the south midland counties of Hertfordshire, Bedfordshire and Buckinghamshire. The towns in the region had many hat factories which used the plaited straw. By the late nineteenth century, straw-plaiting was in decline, as cheap imported plait was used in the factories. Hitchin was the site of a plait market. Grof, Laszlo. *Children of Straw: The Story of Straw Plait, a Vanished Craft and Industry*. Buckingham: Baron, 2002.

13. The "selvage" is the edge of the pavement and the "kennel" the gutter adjoining it.

Mixing with the herd of males were about as many of the other sex,—natives of Hitchin, and with a local habitation. Dozens and dozens of them, little girls and big girls, buxom matrons and dames bent and grey, spick-and-span-looking as the cotton print dresses, and natty shoulder shawl, and twinkling earrings, and smoothed hair could make them; plaiting away, every one of them, as though their very lives depended on it, with hanks and loops of the manufactured outside festooning their neck, or worn sash-wise across their shoulders, and with a sheaf of raw material pinned at their side. They moved amongst the slipshod and tattered men and lads, laughing and larking, but never for a moment staying the movement of their nimble figures. Made gamesome by syren bantering, merry hobble-de-hoy tramps pursued them up the lanes and sideways,—but as they ran, they plaited. There were two young women quarrelling, red with rage, and seemingly ready to fall on each other, tooth and nail, but they contented themselves by shrill and wicked words, and by weaving spitefully, as though the growing lengths in their hands were spells of witchcraft and mischief, against each other.

I discovered the "Shoulder of Mutton," but, out of respect for the feelings of the landlord, will simply remark that the sigh that escaped me when, in answer to my application, he replied that he was chockfull, and couldn't take one more, was not a sigh of regret. There was an odour wafted down the stairs that led, I suppose, to the bedrooms, scarcely suggestive of white dimity and lavender. This much must be allowed, however, that with the best possible intentions, as regards rigid police supervision and the most strict enforcing of the Common Lodging-house Registration Act,[14] it is simply impossible to keep these places in a satisfactory

---

14. The Common Lodging Houses Acts of 1851 and 1853 (14 & 15 Vict., c.28 and 16 & 17 Vict., c.41) required these houses to register and empowered local authorities to enforce rules relating to sanitation, cleanliness, and morality. The Acts were extended by later legislation, including the Public Health Act of 1875 (38 & 39 Vict., c.55). See Rose, Lionel. 'Rogues and Vagabonds': Vagrant Underworld in Britain, 1815-1985. London: Routledge, 1988, pp. 56-57; Humphreys, Robert. No Fixed Abode: A History of Responses to the Roofless and the Rootless in Britain. Basingstoke: Macmillan, 1999, pp. 93-94.

condition for any length of time. The reckless and unclean habits of the lodgers put it out of the question. For the sum of fourpence, and in some cases even threepence, the proprietor is expected to find a kitchen for his guests to sit in, a fire for them to cook by, cooking utensils, a safe locker in which a man may bestow any article of portable property that may tempt the cupidity of his comrades, and a bed. There was no reason why I should not lodge in Back Street because the "Shoulder of Mutton" could not accommodate me. I discovered nearly a score of such places to pick from. Without particularizing the sanctuary of my choice, I may express a hope that the landlady was not strictly speaking the truth when she declared that there was not another house in the street that was a patch on hers for all that made a lodging comfortable. It may have been so—but, Never again! I don't know how many times I mentally registered that resolve during that awful six hours—through the whole of which the eleven rhinoceros-hided villains shared the dormitory with me contentedly snoring as so many pigs in a sty. With the sun yet young in the heavens, I repeated the words yet once more, as I joyfully stepped across the threshold,—"Never again! A clover field, the lee of a haystack,—anything rather!"

With the accumulated dust of several hot miles thick on my shoes, I looked in at the "White Swan," the last wayside house of entertainment for man and beast before the town of Hatfield is reached, and while gratefully imbibing a pint of small ale, there presently came in a woman, sunburnt and brown as a berry, and with the black stuff jacket that should have covered the upper part of her body in her hand.

Would the landlady, for the love of Heaven, and as she was a mother herself, and had a wife's feelings, buy a jacket?

The poor creature's voice was husky with emotion as she made the beseeching inquiry, and a tear stood in her eye. I write "in her eye" advisedly, for only one of her distressed optics was visible, the other being concealed beneath a bandage of rag, in consequence, as she hastened to make known, of its being pretty nigh scorched out by a stroke of the sun. "It was nearly a new jacket," she solemnly averred (which it certainly was not, the button-holes being frayed, and some of the buttons missing), "and had originally cost nine shillings—and she would sell it for two."

With subdued and tearful manner, she explained that she was on the road with her poor husband, who was by trade a journeyman tailor, and had worked for many eminent firms at the West End, until a shopmate, in a stupid joke, pricked him in the leg with a rusty needle, causing him to be paralysed on that side, and the poor fellow had broke down altogether the day before, and was now lying in the workhouse infirmary, from whence she wanted to remove him by rail to Bethnal Green, so that she might nurse him herself.

The landlady was visibly moved by the pitiful story, but not so the landlord. Bluntly, even brutally, as at the time I confess it seemed to me, he declared that he had been bit so many times that he was shy of believing any story told by a tramp, however likely it seemed. "They are made up of lies and artfulness—the whole kit of 'em," said he, addressing himself to the local stonemason, who was taking a pint at the bar. "It was only last Saturday night that I was done as clean as a whistle out of sixpence. It was just as we was shutting up, and he—the vagabond that did me, came in—quite respectably dressed he was,—with a crushed and broken-hearted kind o'manner about him that might have moved a stoat (a Stoic I think he must have meant). He had just been, he said, up to Squire Barclay's place—the great brewers,[15]—in hopes of seeing the squire, who he used to go to school with, and whom he had not met since he had sat on the same form with him. But the footman would not take his name up, and he wouldn't even deliver a letter, but shut the door in his face. 'In the face of a gentleman bred and born!' says he; and he laid his head on the counter here, and sobbed and cried like a child. Well, as I tell you, I give him sixpence, to get him a lodging, so that he might try and see the squire in the morning; and, as I might have expected, I never see him again; it was all a hum, they're all alike, I tell you"—and he cast a sweeping glare around the bar, purposely including me.

I was humbly submissive: it was no affair of mine. I was not in a position even to resent the unkind way in which the landlord looked at me, as he gave as his opinion "that tramps were a bad lot,

---

15. Mr. Barclay was indeed a man of substance. In 1781, Messrs. Barclay and Perkins bought the Anchor Brewery, founded in Southwark in 1616. By 1815, it was reportedly the largest brewery in the world. It survived until 1955, when it was bought out by Courage. The Anchor Tavern, first outlet of the original brewery, survives.

and that there was not a pin to choose betwixt 'em," or even the suspicious manner in which he rubbed and applied his teeth to the obviously good sixpence I tendered him in payment of my liquor. I emptied the earthenware vessel, and pocketing my fourpence change, went my way, leaving the tailor's wife still endeavouring to prevail on the landlady. Trudging up the road, I discovered, lounging lazily against the 18th milestone, a stout and hearty grizzly bearded ruffian, smoking a filthy short pipe.

"Didn't you look in at the 'White Swan' just now matey?" he called to me. I replied in the affirmative, and inquired why he wished to know.

"I thought you might be able to tell whether my old woman is pulling the right string there," said he, with an oath; "not that there's much doubt about it."

I guessed the state of affairs at once. It was the paralysed tailor!

"Your old woman has got a jacket to sell, hasn't she?"

"My old woman has got a jacket to bounce with, if that's what you mean," replied the ruffian, with a grin. "D'ye mean to tell me that she took *you* in, and that you thought she wanted to sell it?"

I confessed that such was the case, on which he broke into such a guffaw, that those at the "White Swan" might have heard him.

"She's a woman as any man might be proud of," said he; "I wish you and every cove on the road had one as clever. Dashed if I don't think she and me could make a woyage round the world on that there jacket. It's beer—beer and bacca and wittles for us, since we left St. Nowts (St. Neots), and it will last us through the summer, if it ain't wore out with handling."

"You seem pretty strong on the leg that was pricked with a rusty needle," I remarked; and this served to send him into a great horselaugh again. "So you heerd her, did you?" he exclaimed, when his glee had subsided. "Isn't she a star at it? Don't she know how to draw 'em?"

"You should have that bad eye of hers seen to," I suggested.

"What about her eye?" he responded—his own twinkling.

"The one that the sun injured."

He laughed so heartily this time that he fairly rolled off the milestone. "And did you swallow that too?" he cried; "why, it's a black un; I blacked it. Fact! Here she comes herself, and she'll tell you so, if you don't believe me."

I preferred, however, to take his work for it, and nodding to the merry ruffian, "Good evening," went on my way, repenting in

my mind of the injustice I had done the sorely tried landlord of the
"White Swan."

I trudged on, reflecting how exceedingly unpleasant it would
be to share the dormitory of a travellers' lodging-house with ten
or a dozen sturdy vagrants of the paralysed tailor breed. For one
night, however, I was spared such delectable companionship. I
could discover, at Hatfield, no wholesale establishment of the
kind in question; the chief of the lodging business being done by
the owners of back street little houses, with a room or two to
spare. For the sum of fourpence, paid in advance, I secured, for
the night, a bed that, at all events, possessed the merit of cleanliness. It was no advantage, perhaps, that another bed in the same
room was occupied by a gentleman who came in very drunk
about midnight; and who, forgetting to take off one boot, somewhat disturbed my repose by frequently lunging out with it
against the footboard of his bedstead; nor could it be considered
a mitigation of the offence that each time he did so he woke himself up, and taking the sound to be a knock at the door, bawled
out, "Come in!" and eliciting no response, growled himself to
sleep again.

CHAPTER III

A SPECIAL CORRESPONDENT—WORKING THE
TICKET—A MEMBER OF THE "LOYAL UNITED
BROTHERHOOD"—A GENUINE TRAMP—LAZY, IDLE,
PROWLING VAGABONDS—THE CHANCE OF EARN-
ING AN HONEST SHILLING—A MODEST
QUENCHER—A NIGHT'S SOUND SLEEP—&c.

MY fellow lodger was still asleep when I turned out for an
early walk. When I returned, about an hour afterwards, I discovered him downstairs in his braces, and busy at the table with pen,
ink and paper, while the old woman of the house was employed at
the frying-pan, cooking the fine rasher of bacon and the eggs he
had sent her out to purchase for his breakfast.

He was so absorbed with his calligraphy that I had an opportunity of observing him without seeming rude.

It needed no second glance to be aware that though of the
tramp fraternity, as testified by his stick and bundle, he was not
one of the tag-rag and cadging order.

On the contrary, judging from his dress, he was or might be regarded as one of the skilled workman class.

Ready at hand were his seedy but still decent-looking black coat and waistcoat, and a tall black hat, and a starched collar to wear with his once white shirt—a well-fed man, with a blotchy and dissipated face.

Evidently he was not an apt penman.

He had already spoilt two sheets of paper, and was scowlingly scratching his head over a third, when, observing that I was watching him, he looked up with a laugh.

"Dashed if I don't think that my fingers are full of the gin I drank last-night. What sort of a fist are you at it?"

I modestly acknowledged my ability to write, on which he handsomely offered to stand a second rasher and eggs to match if I would polish off a few lines for him. I agreed, and at his dictation wrote as follows:—

"Dear 'Liza,—I send you P.O.O.[16] for seventeen shillings. Things are flat. Such a many of us on the road. Three of them at one lodge here last night, so that nobody got more than eighteen-pence. I did better at St. Albans. Hope to do something when I get South of London, which will be about Friday."

For obvious reasons I suppress names and addresses, and I feel it more incumbent on me to do so because he liberally kept his word as regards the honorarium.

We grew chatty over our comfortable repast, and he was kind enough to commiserate with me when I assured him of the stagnant state of the leather-dressing trade, and of my inability to get employment at it.

"You appear to be doing pretty well," I ventured. On which he laughed, and winked in a friendly manner.

"So might you if you liked," said he.

"How?"

"By working the ticket," was my friend's reply.

Now, I had heard before of "working the ticket," that is to say, of lazy and dishonest handicraftsmen who attached themselves to trades benefit societies, for the sole purpose of providing themselves

16. Post Office Money Order.

with the proper credentials for demanding relief and assistance at as many of the trade "houses of call" as existed on a tramp route.

If the appointed relieving official sent his distressed brother to a job in the vicinity, the latter was compelled to take it, or forfeit his "travelling ticket;" but it is easy enough for an unprincipled rascal to make himself objectionable in a score of ways as well to his fellow workmen as his master; and in a few days he is informed that his services are no longer required, and he is free to tramp again until his jolly progress is once more arrested for a short spell by a provoking offer of honest employment.

At the same time I had always understood that no more was to be made by the nefarious dodge than enabled the crafty one to live from hand to mouth—certainly not enough to afford such luxuries as getting drunk on gin over night, with rashers and eggs next morning.

But I found that there are tickets and tickets.

The one which my friend held, and which he took from a breast pocket, carefully wrapped in brown paper, showed that he was a duly elected member of the "Loyal United Brotherhood,"[17] the lodges of which society, like those of the Odd Fellows and a score of others that might be mentioned, may be reckoned by thousands in all parts of the country. My informant was a hatter by trade, but he never made hats, "only when he was out of luck and couldn't help himself."

"I pay three and fourpence a month contribution," said he, "and I've got a route book and know every lodge and every lodge night. All the rest is easy as kissing your hand. You are entitled by the rules to eighteenpence a day while on the road. But that isn't your pull. You get your pull out of the lodge members. You are free to go to any of 'em, and p'raps you find thirty or forty respectable members—tradesmen and that sort. Well, in the regular rules, the secretary says, 'is there any case for relief?' Then you have your say, and you get your eighteenpence, and it is your own fault if you can't work on their feelings with your story for twice as much more. Why, I've got as much as seventeen shillings at one lodge."

I should like to have had further conversation with him, but we were going contrary ways. "But we will have a drink together," said

---

17. No friendly society of this name existed. Greenwood probably used this fictitious name to spare the actual society from embarrassment.

he, with the air of a man who well knows his way about; and he took me to an old-fashioned brewery (Pryor was the name, if I am not mistaken),[18] and there declaring ourselves tramps and wayfarers we were supplied with as much small ale as we could drink from a measure, and with no more than "Thanky" to pay for it.

Thus cheaply refreshed, I pushed on towards Welwyn, and for several miles came on nothing noteworthy, unless worthy of being recorded was the spectacle of a queer kind of disagreement between an old Irishman—genuinely on tramp and in search of work—and his dog.

They were from London, and the dog, a bob-tailed, raw-boned, ragamuffin kind of common cur, had, it seemed, played his master a trick which, if not unpardonable, was certainly embarrassing. As the Irishman gave the facts, the animal must have overheard him express his intention of going on tramp, and secretly resolved to accompany him. Like the cunning villain he was, he had unsuspectedly skulked in the rear until his master was fair in the country, and then he ventured to reveal his undesired presence. He declined to retreat. When peremptorily ordered to go home, he raced on ahead for a mile, and when his irate master came up with him, again coolly trotted on a bit further. Two days had elapsed, and they were no nearer a treaty of peace than ever, and when I left them the man was sitting on a stile, taking his dinner of dry bread, and cutting off bits of crust to pelt him with (and which the dog, with an expression in his eyes that told of his consciousness of being master of the situation, snapped up ravenously and acknowledged with a meek wag of his tail), alternately throwing him a morsel, and shaking a warning forefinger at him, swearing by all that was good that he would "take the consate"[19] out of him by drowning him in the very next pond they came to.

---

18. Pryor Reid and Company were brewers in Hatfield at the time of Greenwood's visit. The Pryor family also owned large breweries in Shoreditch and Baldock in the nineteenth century. Whitaker, Allan. *Brewers in Hertfordshire: A Historical Gazetteer*. Hatfield: University of Hertfordshire Press, 2006, pp. 56, 105-6, 120-21.

19. Conceit.

A mile or so further, and I reached a bridge that spans the road, and beneath which there tumultuously tumbles a stream, broad and brisk; and while idly contemplating the eddying shallows and the enviable fish coolly disporting amongst the smooth brown stones, there arose from the tangled bushes that grew on the brink the startling apparition of a man naked to the waist, demanding to know if I had such a thing as a lucifer match to give him. A second glance seemed to explain the real position of affairs. He had been washing his linen, and was waiting while it dried, spread out on a hawthorn bush. I invited him to come up and get the match, and, after enjoining me to look up and down lest there might be a policeman coming, he complied. He was a strong-looking, well-conditioned young fellow, and talked like one whose education had not been entirely neglected. He sat on the stone coping of the low bridge, dangling his dilapidated legs, and with his nude upper part toasting beneath the noonday sun, and spoke freely of his affairs. He was a stableman, and had lived in some rare good families. Somehow, however—and he spoke of it as a curious and unaccountable freak of his nature—he got sick of it. A man had better be a horse, a precious sight. Work, work, work, and nothing but it in a stable. He left it to go on what he might call his own hook. He had made an ass of himself "touting" for a better swell on the moor at Doncaster, and had got the jacket whipped off his back, and the skin too a'most. He always, since he was a child, had a fancy for being along with horses, "and yet," continued my shirtless acquaintance, pensively wagging his head, "if a man's heart went along of his wrongs and injuries, Jews don't hate pigs more'n I should hate horseflesh: cuss the horses—they've been the ruin o'me, and brought me to what you see!"

"Betting on them?" I inquired.

"No; through waitin' on 'em;—leastways, when I say it was horses that brought me to what I am, that ain't quite right. Don't let me tell a lie if I can help it: it was a mare—a bay mare, belonging to Lord ---'s stable down at Melton Mowbray. If ever there was a hanimal with a devil in it, it was that mare."

"I wonder his Lordship kept it," I remarked.

"Oh no, it ain't a wonder," he rejoined. "The beast was all right to everybody else but me—as kind and gentle, the artful warmint,[20] as you please; but from the very first day I went into that stable, I looked at that mare and she looked at me, and I thought to myself, I don't like the look o'you, my lady, and I shall have to keep a stiff hand on you. Well, sir, she seemed to know my thoughts, and to take a regler spite agin me, and to hate me like a human creetur. She'd start in her stall when she heard me coming, and shiver and whinny as though I was the devil. Ha, ha! 'pon my soul I sometimes think that's what she took me for."

"Perhaps she had reason," I ventured.

"Well, don't you know," continued the grizzly-muzzled rascal, "it wasn't gallus[21] likely that a man was going to be beat by a horse. She would never let me alone. Biting me, kicking me, getting me into corners to give me orful squeezes whenever she got the chance; why, as a matter o'course, it come to be regler war between us. She got the worst of it, the brute. Of course, I couldn't leather her, she was such a fine-skinned 'un she'd show a flick with a silk handkesher; but there was a dozen ways of gettin' at her. There's ways, don't you know, of serving a horse: you can drive 'em wellnigh mad with pain and yet not show a mark. The most simple things will do it, bless you. You can poke a darning needle into 'em, or you can shove a few crooked pins in the nose-bag, and little things like that, and nobody be the wiser: I mean to say, if you go about it careful and don't act the fool. I did, worse luck. I ain't going to tell you what it was; but they watched me, and I was bowled out and chucked out of a hay-loft clean on to the cobble stones in the mews. That accounts for me being lame of one of my legs."

During the delectable narrative there came up other two tramps—the one a bulky, ragged image of laziness, who said he was a blacksmith by trade; and a decenter looking agricultural labourer. The blacksmith begged a match, and flung himself

---

20. Vermin (varmint).

21. A Scottish dialect word which implies mischievousness or impertinence, but is invariably used to characterize behavior of the lowest classes. Its meaning in this context is obscure.

down amongst the wayside nettles to listen as he smoked his stumpy black pipe, and the labourer leant over the bridge, saying nothing, but occasionally spitting emphatically into the water. "He might have broke my leg, don't you know—the great hulking coward," said the villainous stableman in conclusion. "If he had broke your neck, dang ye, it would have been nowt too bad," rejoined the rustic, facing about fiercely. "Ho! Indeed. Ha! Well, just you wait till a horse takes a spite against *you*, and then you talk;" and he went off down the bank, to try if his shirt was yet dry, and I left the rustic arguing with the still prostrate blacksmith on the unreasonableness of his expecting ever to fall in with a job if he wanted to lay down for a sleep every mile or so.

On again for a mile or so, and then all unexpectedly to have my further progress arrested in a somewhat startling and unlooked-for manner. Standing at his half-open garden gate, there was a tall and thin, sharp-visaged gentleman, who hailed me with a peremptory "Hi!" and irresistibly hooked me as it were towards him with a crook of his forefinger.

Eyeing me with severity and suspicion through his gold-rimmed glasses, said he, "Did I not see you a short time since on the bridge down yonder?"

I meekly admitted the possibility.

"In company with three ruffians, who, if they had their deservings, would be on the treadmill?"

Evading the question of deservings, I pleaded guilty to the three ruffians.

"A parcel of lazy, idle, prowling vagabonds, who would go a mile on another road if they was any danger of finding work on the one they chanced to be on; and you are as bad as the rest, I'll warrant!"

I humbly replied that he was mistaken, and besought him to believe that I was on the road with the most industrious intentions.

"D'ye mean to tell me," asked the gentleman, sharply, "that you would cheerfully set about a job if I found you one?"

This was embarrassing. Confound him and his "job!" as if my hands were not already full of work. But what could I reply? It was not without growing alarm that I informed him I should be thankful of the chance of earning a honest shilling.

"What kind of work have you been accustomed to, sir?"

was his next question, asked in a manner that was terribly magisterial.

I hope to be forgiven, but the temptation was strong. Had I professed to be a carpenter, a glazier, a house-painter, or any other kind of handicraftsmen, he might have insisted on testing the truth of my statement by setting me to work at once on his own premises, and it was evident that he was a person who might not be so trifled with with impunity. For all I knew to the contrary, he might be a justice of the peace, with power to consign to limbo any unfortunate without visible means of existence. The only way of escape was to lay claim to a trade it was not likely he would find me employment in. I at first thought of calling myself a dancing-master; but suddenly bethinking me that though he looked himself as little like a dancer as could well be imagined, he might have daughters inclined to the frivolous pastime. I changed my mind, and gravely informed him that I was in the undertaking line of business. But the fates ordained that I should not escape.

"Can you dig?" was his next query.

I should be happy to try, I told him, but that the handling of little nails and a tack-hammer was irreconcilable with blistered hands, and that, therefore, I must beg to be excused.

"I tell you what it is, my fine fellow!" exclaimed the gentleman, growing angrily red in the face, "I begin to think that you are one of the picking and choosing sort; but let me advise you not to try your tricks on with me, for I won't stand it. I offer you work and you refuse to do it! Come along with me."

I went with him into his garden, which was an extensive one, but considerably neglected. Grass was growing on the gravel paths, and the flower-beds were rich in weeds.

"You are willing to work for your bread, you say," said the gentleman; "prove it, and weed this very nicely—it won't take you more than two or three hours—and I'll give you three-pence!"

I felt that I would have given many threepences for liberty at that moment to drop the tramp, and in my proper person give him the benefit of my opinion of him and his shabby offer. Threepence for three or four hours of garden weeding under a hot June sun! He went his way, promising to come back by-and-by to see how I was getting on. As there was a contract between us, I suppose I am still liable under the Masters' and Servants'

Act[22] for leaving my work unfinished. Had it been small salad instead of grass, I might have eaten all that I picked of it from the time of commencing until my generous employer was out of sight, when I resumed my bundle, and by a short cut over his garden palings, took to the road again.

Through Welwyn and on to Stevenage, meeting with no further adventure and no more material for penwork, unless I were required to write an essay in praise of beer. Not on the habitual tippling of the beverage in question as it is known in populous places, but on the blissful satisfaction that attends the consumption of one cool pint of country ale, quaffed from a blue earthenware jug on a blazing afternoon, and on a highway where the alehouses are two or three miles apart, and the dust of the white road seems to enter into the system and to work out again at the pores, as brimstone is know to do; a pint to the exact quantity, as though a moderate brother of Bacchus himself had prescribed it. Half-a-pint would be a mockery; three-quarters would demand a repetition, which would be too much; but the full, mild pint, with the heady head, just admits of what Mr. Swiveller[23] called a "modest quencher," with a drop left to contemplate while one gratefully "flavours" the wholesome drink to the mouth, and takes breath for the remainder. It is stuff stout enough for a nightcap, too, this hot weather. My bed at Stevenage cost me twopence more than at Hatfield, but it was at a wayside cottage; and I never hope to sleep sounder, or wake more perfectly refreshed.

---

22. Many Acts with this name were passed during the 18th and early 19th centuries to regulate relations between employers and employees. The author's reference to these statutes is perhaps an ironic allusion to the fact that in his time, they were not dead letters, but were widely used to limit the efforts of trade-unions to organize in the work-place. For a contemporaneous example, see "A Barrister." *Servants and Masters: The Law of Disputes, Rights and Remedies in Plain Language.* London: Horace Cox, 1894.

23. Dick Swiveller is the good-natured, but slightly raffish, clerk in Dickens' *The Old Curiosity Shop* (1841).

CHAPTER IV.

A "REGLER" TRAMP'S INVITE TO A DAINTY BAN-
QUET—ONE OF THE HABITUAL TRAMP TRIBE—
HEALTH AND STRENGTH AT A DISCOUNT—THE
WAYSIDE ALE-HOUSE—LONDON MAID-SERVANTS—
ECCENTRICITIES OF TRAMP LIFE—TRAMP MAD-
NESS—CONVERSION OF TRAMPS—A WARNING TO
BACKSLIDERS.

"THIS is to Give Notice, That if a person residing somewhere
between Hitchin and Shefford was, on or about the 21st of June,
deprived of a speckled hen of the Dorking breed, he may, by communicating with J.G., care of the publisher, receive payment for
the same."

This is for conscience sake. For all I can positively assert to the
contrary the poultry in question may have been honestly acquired,
though at the same time I feel bound to confess that the attendant
circumstances were somewhat suspicious. I will, however, relate all
that I know concerning it, and the reader then can form for himself a judgment on the case.

In the afternoon following the night on which I passed
that never-to-be-forgotten night at the common lodging house
in Back Street, Hitchin, I was passing a plantation that
skirted the high road, when, suddenly thrusting aside the nut
bushes, a tramp of unmistakable sturdy-vagabond type revealed
himself.

"Old chap!" said he, addressing me in an affable tone of voice,
"do you happen to have any bread in your bundle?"

Now it chanced that I had some bread with me. Disliking the
harsh home-made article such as one usually gets in country villages, I had, before leaving Hitchin, purchased a twopenny loaf at
a baker's shop there.

"Yes," I replied; "I've got some. Why do you ask?"

"Because," said he, "I can make it worth your while to whack
it with my mate and me, if you'll keep it dark."

"How do you mean, worth my while?"

"Do you like roasted chicken?" asked the sturdy-vagabond,
with a grin.

I replied that I did.

"All right, then," said he, with a cautious glance up and down the road; "come along o'me, and I'll put you up to a feed you don't get every day."

Moved more by curiosity than by any desire to participate in the dainty banquet so mysteriously hinted at, I followed my conductor; and in the depths of the wood discovered the "mate" he had spoken of busily employed in digging, with his great clasp knife, a hole in the ground to bury a chicken's head and feet and some speckled feathers. In a second hole, a short distance off, were some glowing wood embers, atop of which the bird itself was fragrantly baking. It was a nice fowl, and though the preparations for cooking it were necessarily of the most rough-and-ready kind, there was a neatness about the order of things that bespoke the possibility of my two friends not being unacquainted with such al fresco culinary feats.

"Ain't he a beauty?" remarked the gentleman who had first accosted me. "Bust me if I could help buying him. A cove coming along in a cart offered him so wery cheap, that I was tempted to buy him, though I hadn't a penny left to buy tommy[24] to eat him with." On which his comrade winked at me and broke into a guffaw that tended to confirm my already growing suspicions that matters were not so straightforward as they might have been.

Anyhow I deemed it judicious to decline to share the savoury meal with them. While, however, I excused myself on the ground that I already had eaten my dinner, I yielded up the biggest half of my twopenny loaf, reclining on the grass to smoke my pipe, and have a little friendly conversation with them while they ate.

They were scarcely the kind of fellows I should have cared to have been alone with in such a solitary place, had it been dark night instead of noonday. The talk turned on looking for work, and I enquired what was the particular kind of job they were in search of. On which the "mate," whose shaggy moustache by this time was richly anointed with chicken grease, and who at the moment had a leg on the point of his knife, delivered himself of an ugly oath as he replied, "We ain't wery nice about what it is. We take things easy, we do. 'Tain't no good being partickler in these times."

---

24. Soldiers' slang for bread, also encountered by C. W. Craven: see below, pp. 183 and 186.

A sentiment which his comrade heartily endorsed, adding with a villainous grin,

"Anything wot turns up; that's the kind of job we're looking arter. All I know about it is, that I ain't going to starve in a land o'plenty. I'll work sharp enough if I can fall over a job wot I fancy, but I ain't going without wittles, whether or no."

It was evident that I was in the position of "a certain man who went down to Jericho,"[25] and was revolving in my mind the easiest way to escape from my bad company, when the most ruffianly of the two remarked:

"You ain't been on the road long, any fool can see."

"How's that?"

"How's that! why, you wouldn't be wearing a flannel shirt as good as what that other one o'your'n is if you was regler on the road. Not but that I dessay [it's][26] wery comfortable," he continued, with an ill-disguised wink at the other, "and I should like to have the feller to it. What do you say, Joe?"

"I'd sooner have the walue of it," Joe responded; "if it's as good as it looks, it would fetch a dollar."[27]

And, I suppose by way of satisfying himself on the point, he unceremoniously thrust his dirty, greasy fist in at my bosom. Clearly it was time to be off. It would, however, never do to let them imagine that I was afraid of them. I made some careless remark as to the folly of trusting to appearances, and then observed:

"Hark! Is that *your* dog?"

"Dog?" They were up on their feet in an instant.

---

25. "But he, willing to justify himself, said unto Jesus, And who is my neighbour? And Jesus answering said, A certain man went down from Jerusalem to Jericho, and fell among thieves, which stripped him of his raiment, and wounded him, and departed, leaving him half dead." Luke, 10:29-30. Thus begins the parable of the Good Samaritan. The author is clearly thinking here of the thieves who robbed the traveler, rather than the Samaritan who rescued him.

26. In the original: "its."

27. Slang for five shillings.

"There's one somewhere near, I'll answer for it. I've a rare quick ear for a dog," said I, puffing at my pipe, "but what's the matter? If it isn't your dog, it doesn't matter whose it is, does it?"

They appeared to think that it did, for one rascal bolted at once, and was soon lost amongst the trees; while his companion, only pausing to gather up the fragments of roast chicken and bestow them in his ragged cap, speedily followed his example, leaving me, much relieved, to find my way back to the high road.

On again, meeting with nothing to break the monotony of my afternoon's hot and dusty march but still one more of the common cadger kind, and who would have received no more notice in these pages than the rest, but that he was the most perfect specimen, both as regards "get up" and impudence it had been my lot to meet with.

"I shouldn't ask you, sir, only, as is well known, a pipe do take away the gnawing from want of wittles, which, lor o'mighty knows, is my case, genelman; and *have* you got such a thing as 'arf a pipe of terbacker?" Through a break in the hedge I had observed him some time before he was aware of my approach. A robust and sturdy rascal of middle age, and of the habitual tramp tribe beyond a doubt. When in the distance I first made him out, he was dangling his long legs on a gate, with his battered old billycock[28] cap tipped over his eyes to shield them from the sun. When I came up with him, he had between his lips a short black pipe with an empty bowl, and was wearily slouching along as though his feet had known no rest since he set out at early morning.

In reply to his application, I made answer that not only was I possessed of half a pipe of tobacco, but enough to fill several pipes, as I had purchased an ounce of tobacco in the village half-a-mile off.

"That's lucky," he remarked, rubbing his hands fawningly; "a bit of terbacker, genelman, when a poor feller can't get a crust, is a gordsend on a hempty stomach."

"I should feel ashamed, if I were you, to beg of a man as poor as yourself."

---

28. A low-crowned, round, felt hat: Greenwood wore one when visiting Lambeth as the "The Amateur Casual." See above, p. 54.

It was worth several pipes of tobacco to watch the varying expressions of the man's countenance as I administered to him this mild rebuke. Presently, with a short laugh, and with a bit of a scowl, he remarked—

"'Ow's your brother Job?"

I replied that it was unknown to me that I had a brother of that name.

"It's Job Blunt *I* mean," said the tramp; "if you ain't one of the Blunt family,[29] may I be butchered."

"Why *don't* you work?"

"'Cos I can't fall acrost a job; *that's* why, since you're so pertickler in asking."

"I am afraid," said I, "that if you did as you say, 'fall across' a job, you would be more likely to lie there and go to sleep than to get up and do it. I've met with your sort before. I tell you what, though, if you really want a pipe of tobacco, I'll give you one with pleasure, if you will tell me honestly when it was you last worked for a meal."

And thinking it probable that it might take him some time to call to mind the bygone event, I handed him my tobacco. He filled his pipe, with deliberation, and lit it, and after a few whiffs at it, replied—

"The last time as I worked for a meal, likewise a lodging, was this 'ere blessed morning'. Ser-'elp me, it's true," he continued, remarking my look of incredulity. "You're a open-spoken kind of cove, and I'll be open-spoken to you. It warn't no fault o'mine, mind you, but it is true that I did three hours' work this morning—hard work, fit only for a horse to do—which it was, stone-breaking for my last night's lodging and three-quarters of a pound of bread for breakfus'."

"At the workhouse?"

"At the work'us," he repeated with manly candour.

"And not for the first time?"

"Not by many a 'underd, in town *and* country."

"You are dependent on chance for the means of a living?"

---

29. "Blunt" was flash slang for money. The tramp had clearly seen through Greenwood's disguise to some extent, as he is suggesting that the latter has money.

For a few moments he regarded me with perplexity in his eyes, and finally scratched his head and laughed.

"Who you are and wot you are I don't know, and us two being alone, ser-'elp me I don't care, and so I tell you plain," said the tramp, "but I'm challenged to be plain spoke, and I'll stand to it. You're right; you've drawed me like a picter. My living *is* all chance. But you're wrong as to the idle part of it. Idle! well, I like that!"

"But you never do any work?"

"I was never brought up to no trade, if that's wot you mean," replied my six-foot friend in an injured tone, "which [is][30] no reason why it should be chucked in my teeth. Therefore," he continued, the brilliant idea evidently suddenly occurring to him, "why should I put myself for'ard for a job, and p'r'aps shove out a man wot was reg'lar brought up to it, and has more right? How would *you* like it? S'pose somebody should come along in *your* line, whatever it might be. S'pose *I* was to come along and got there first some morning, and put myself for'ard and got you the sack! No, fear. Why I should hate myself."

I had no remark to make on this noble outburst of generous sentiment, and presently, as we sauntered along the shady lane, he began again—

"Oh, no, it ain't work, mine ain't! It's like picking buttercups to tramp a dozen miles on a stony road with the luck dead against you, and not a penny or a pen'orth to be picked up anywheres. It never rains, I s'pose! or freezes, or blows, or snows! It's wery pleasant, when you gets used to it, to make your ways to a place, a village, say, or a town, making sure of a bit o'grub there, and finding as soon as you sets your foot in it the pleeceman or the beadle, who politely sees you through the jolly place and bids you good-day at far side of it, into p'r'aps a moor or a stretch of wild country afore you. That's only a lark, all that, I s'pose?"

"You appear to forget that you have your health and strength," I ventured to remark.

He laughed in pure bitterness of spirit.

---

30. In the original: "it's."

"Oh lor, oh lor!" he replied; "I set *myself* down as hignerant, but ser'elp me! What's the good to me of *my* health and strength? It's a dead loss to me. If I was a sickly-looking sort of chap, if I had a lame leg or on'y one arm, it would be more valuable to me than health and strength, as you call it. Let them have health and strength, as wants it, jiggered if I do. I ain't got no use for it. It's on'y an aggrawation. It would be all right if they would take a nat'ral view of it, and think what a awful lot of wittles it takes to fill up a man as big as wot I am; but no, they'd sooner give to a weazel of a feller with one leg in the grave p'r'aps, and no appetite at all to speak of. 'Pon my soul, mister—if you will excuse the obserwation, I've had that there 'health and strength' dinned at me till I'm fairly sick of it. When I gets a lodgin' at the casual ward, the task-master he ses, 'Oakum, no; give him half a dozen bushels of stones to break; he's got his health and strength.' If ever I gets— which has happened afore now—took before a magistrate under the Wagrant Act,[31] I know what's a coming before he opens his mouth, 'A great hulking rascal like you, in the prime of health and strength;—a month, with hard labour.'"

"I wonder that you do not grow disgusted."

"'Pon my word I often wonder so myself," he replied, laughing, as though I had uttered a good joke; "it's just enough to make a feller do anything, and that's a fact."

And so we parted; but happening to look back after I had walked about a hundred yards, I found that he had altered his mind, and was now lying on his back on a wayside bank, with his billycock adjusted over his face as though it were his present intention to go to sleep.

No more tramps of a noteworthy kind that day, but in the evening I think I heard again of my two friendly chicken-roasters. It was at a lonely wayside ale-house, with an elderly woman in charge; and she was telling a gamekeeper, who had looked in with his gun for a pint, of two impudent fellows, one of them carrying a knobbed stick, who had called and asked for water, but finding

---

31. The Vagrancy Act of 1824 (5 Geo. IV, c.83) allowed the authorities wide leeway in prosecuting those without visible means of support under summary jurisdiction. See above, pp. 14–15 and 115 note 19.

her alone demanded beer, and on her refusing had turned over the settle[32] outside and kicked it into the road. "I'd like to 'a fell in with 'em!" remarked the tall gamekeeper grimly; and although it was not for me, who had broken bread with the rascals, to say anything, I most heartily wished that he had.

By-the-by, I have said that no other tramp worth mentioning turned up that day, but I have forgotten one—the only one throughout my march who begged of me.

A dozen times at least I was solicited for "'bacca"—for "a mite as big as a pea for the tooth," for "just enough for a blow and a spit;" but the man in question was the only one who asked me if I had "a bit of grub to spare."

I think I never saw a man with narrower shoulders for his height, or with eyes deeper sunk in his head, or one the working action of whose jaws was more painfully evident when he spoke. I came on him using a stone as a hammer, and endeavouring to replace the heel of one of his old boots that had come bodily away from the upper leather.

If he told the truth he was a man to be pitied.

For many years he said he had held a hawker's license, and sold tin-ware; but a year ago had "got into a bit of a mess," for the first time in his life, he declared, and was sentenced to three months' imprisonment.

"They'd better give me a year—ten years," said he dolefully; "for they stopped my license 'cause of my conviction, and won't grant me another. If they had, I might have been getting a honest living now, instead of wandering about the country in this state."

"But do they always stop the license of a hawker who gets into trouble?" I asked.

"Always; it's the law. I have met with plenty who have been served so. They won't give a man a license, and if they catch him selling things they put him into quod[33] for not having one. It's bound to be quod first or last; there's no escape from it."

"There's the workhouse," I suggested.

---

32. A seat, most usually a wooden bench.

33. Prison.

"Yes!" replied the poor, lean scarecrow, causing the hinges of his jaws to stand out in bold relief as he ground his teeth against the institution in question. "The work'us gives a man like me shelter for the night and a lump of bread, and for that it keeps me working till eleven o'clock next morning, when all the jobs are picked up, and I can do nothing but get on the road again and get to another town and another work'us. That's my life, and it's the life of scores. They drop into the way, and they can't drop out of it."

I lay awake a long time in my humble bed at Shefford, where I slept that night, thinking of this poor hopeless wretch, and speculating to what extent—providing he spoke the truth—the existing system of poor laws are responsible for the plague of tramps with which the country is afflicted.

Eccentricities of tramp life crop up now and again. I had been afoot not more than an hour next morning when, entering a humble wayside ale-house to procure a breakfast, I found two young women sitting over an early meal of bread and milk. They were decently attired in clean cotton gowns, with modest untrimmed straw bonnets of rustic village fashion on their heads, and substantial nailed boots on their feet. Under the table was a bundle of considerable size, tied in a red plaid shawl, and evidently their joint property. They whispered together and eyed me askance, and presently one of them blushingly asked if I could tell them the nearest way to London. To the best of my ability I gave them the required information, and so we slid into conversation.

When I told them that I was from the great city, and was tolerably well acquainted with the manners and customs of the inhabitants, they became more confidential still. They told me that they were from a place near Kingsthorpe, where they had, until recently, been in service at adjoining farm houses, at a wage of six pounds a year; and that the object of their present migration was to better themselves.

"Have you friends in London?" I asked.

"Shan't want any friends when we get there," replied the elder one confidently.

"What makes you think so?"

"A girl can do without friends when she can earn fifteen or eighteen pounds a year," said she; "a girl must be a fool to bury herself in a dull, miserable country place with only six pounds a year, when she can get three times as much in London service and see all the life besides!"

And then with much eagerness they both began to question me if it was true, as they had heard, that in London maid servants got out at least one evening in a week, and were at liberty to go to the theatre or to a dance; and whether all the nursemaids took their young charges to the parks for an airing every day; and whether the military bands played there from morning until night. They had been on the road three days, and in that time had walked more than thirty miles; preferring to save their money to enable them to pay their lodging and look about them when they reached the metropolis, rather than spend it in railway travelling.

It was scarcely possible to exaggerate the gravity of the situation. They were well-looking, well-grown girls, both of them; the youngest, not more than eighteen, was almost handsome. Both of them were evidently as innocent of the world and its iniquitous ways as two calves in a meadow, and here they were guilelessly tripping to the stronghold of ever so many roaring lions, the business of whose lives it is to keep a ravenous eye on exactly the kind of prey these two damsels afforded. It would have been an act of Christian charity, had one been empowered to do so, to have called in the village constable there and then, and insisted on their being conveyed back to Kingsthorpe without an hour's delay. Being incompetent to take such a step, I did the next best thing I could: I assured them that they had been grossly imposed on; I threw the wettest of blankets on their glowing anticipations; and informed them that there were already thousands of young women in and about London, who, with the best of intentions, could earn scarcely enough to feed and clothe themselves; and that, all things considered, not one in a dozen were as well off as a country servant in a respectable situation. But I might as well have addressed myself to the old case-clock ticking in the corner. They knew it better: it wasn't what they had been told—it was what they had read.

"But you mustn't believe those silly romances you read in story books," I persisted; "you'll be sorry if you do, take my word for it."

But at this point I was ignominiously defeated, for the youngest girl triumphantly produced from the pocket of her gown a penny morning paper of the previous Monday, and drew my attention first to the long list of servants wanted at handsome wages, and then to the two or three columns or so of theatres and other places of amusement, open every evening. They whispered again; and I distinctly caught the words, "What does he know about it? What *can* he know, a poor fellow like him?" And for fear, I suppose, that I might further persuade them, they hurriedly finished their bread and milk, and taking up the big bundle, wished me an abrupt good morning.

On again, and after an hour or so met with another case of tramp madness, but of a different kind. This time it took the shape of a travelling photographer, with his apparatus mounted on a kind of Bath chair. He was a young man, with the kind of long hair and exposed throat that denote the inborn genius, and he was sprawling amongst the roadside ferns, with his chin on his elbows, scowlingly regarding creation. He had with him his wife and child. She, a poor wasted and wan young creature, weather-stained, and with her shoes worn to rags, sat by his side, suckling her lean baby. They were from Hammersmith, she told me, on a business tour, but had been doing badly as yet.

"You see," said the young woman, with a glance at her husband that revealed her fathomless belief in his immense talent, "he is not used to this kind of thing. My husband is an artist—a painter, and his idea was to make a tour with this instrument to take views of country mansions, and by that means get introduced to some of the leading families, who would give him employment at his proper profession."

"And you find the speculation does not pay?" I remarked, sympathetically.

"Well, the fact is, trade is dull everywhere."

But at this up starts the genius with the flowing locks and the Byronic collar.

"What the devil do you mean?" he demanded, glaring at me with such proud scorn in his expressive eyes as should have withered me in my shoes. "Trade! I leave trade, let me tell you, sir, to the vulgar herd; you understand, sir," he repeated, with cruel pointedness, "to the vulgar herd! Come, Peggy!"

And he shook his tangled locks and adjusted his slouch hat artistically, and stalked off with majestic strides; while his wife, depositing the baby in a niche in the photographic conveyance, laboriously pushed the latter on before her in a manner that showed she was used to it, but somewhat limpingly, for the road was stony in that part, and for all the defence her old boots were, she would have been better without them.

On again, and at a place called Cotton End I was hailed from a field by a stout fellow in a kind of velveteen shooting jacket and a black billycock, who was accompanied by a slender gentleman in sombre attire, and with a neat clerical tie.

"'Old 'ard for a minute, my friend," exclaimed the person in velveteen, laying an arresting hand on my bundle;" " 'Old 'ard, if you please. My companion here would like to have a few words with you!"

Instantly there flashed to my mind that little affair of the roast chicken in the wood.

The law's vengeance had pursued me by a short cut, and this was a magistrate!

But my fears were speedily allayed when the slender gentleman produced from a black bag he carried, a bundle of missionary tracts, and selecting those that seemed to him to apply especially to my case, handed them to me, politely remarking, in a manner which I suppose he meant to be complimentary:

"Read these, my erring brother. They can't possibly make you worse, and they *may* do you good!"

I sat down at once and commenced on one which was headed "A Warning to Backsliders!" and began "Friend! Judas was a man as thou art." This naturally paved the way to a pleasant conversation, during which I ascertained that the gentleman in black had a mission for the conversion of tramps and wayfarers, who are expected to gather pretty thick in the fields at this haymaking time; and that the individual in velveteen was his appointed bodyguard and protector. I would have given a shilling to see the pair of them tackling that proud young photographer!

On again, and still on: meeting with nothing further worth mention, until Bedford town was reached, which was the end of my tramping for that journey. And at Bedford I met the welcome friend who brought me a change of raiment; and at Bedford I shaved and dined and slept, and returned next day to the paths of respectability.

Chapter Six

"A Night in the Workhouse" by C. W. Craven

In: *A Night in the Workhouse, Cliffe Castle, The Secret of the Rock, The Story of Old 'Three Laps.'* Keighley: Author, 1887. Pages 2–7

H aving had a desire for a long time to obtain an insight into the vicissitudes of a vagrant's life, I determined to put a plan into execution which should secure to me at least one night's company amongst the guerrilla element of modern society. How I succeeded will be found in the following narrative, the accuracy of the incidents of which I am prepared to vouch for.

OBTAINING A TICKET.

This necessary preliminary to a night in the Workhouse is very easily accomplished. I found no difficulty in obtaining a suitable rig-out in the shape of an old pair of corduroy trousers, a pair of [worn-out][1] shoes, together with a dilapidated coat, specially slashed for the occasion, and a greasy nebbed[2] cap. Thus

---

1. In the original: "worn-ont."

2. Peaked.

suitably equipped, I perambulated to the police-station, hung about the door hesitatingly for a moment or two, and then screwed up sufficient courage to enter the office. My appearance was greeted, in cheerful tones, by the officer in charge, "Come forward, young man; do you want a ticket?" To this I answered modestly, "Yes, if you please, sir." In reply to his interrogations I gave him the following information concerning my august self:—Name, Charles Burrell, on the road from Bradford to Burnley; trade, mechanic; age, 28, height, 5ft. 5in. This was written upon a ticket, with which I was duly presented, a duplicate being kept in the officer's book. I thanked him kindly, and betook myself rapidly up Oakworth Road to the Workhouse.[3]

THE PORTER'S LODGE.

On attempting to enter I was debarred by the stern fixity of the iron gate. After waiting a few moments a window was opened to my right, and a pompous voice exclaimed, "What is it?" I presented my ticket. Again the questions were asked, "Where are you from? Where are you going to? What trade are you?" to all of which I answered as in the first instance. The assistant porter (for I found out afterwards that he wasn't the regular one) then exclaimed in a surly tone, "Pipe and matches!" "What?" replied I. "Pipe and matches!" "Yes, I'll have a pipe and matches." "I want your pipe and matches." "I haven't got any." "Then pass on." I passed on, and after missing my way several times, found myself in

THE OUTER ROOM,

The dimensions of which were about 4 1/2 yards square. Here a regular pauper was in charge, who at once told me to undress myself. Whilst doing this, a piece of dry bread, about 4oz. in weight, was thrown on a board, with the exclamation, "Thear's yer

---

3.　　The Oakworth Road Workhouse, erected in 1858, was the only such institution in Keighley, a Yorkshire town dominated by the textile industries. The 1881 Census showed the workhouse to have 223 residents, including seven staff. In this year the town had a recorded population of 33,540. See http://www.workhouses.org.uk [accessed 18 December 2007].

Tommy."[4] On getting my coat, waistcoat and trousers off, and dis-covering my underclothing, the attendant exclaimed several times, "*You* don't look as if you hed been on t'road long anyhow." "No!" says I, "this is the first time." He then told me to take my shirt off, and trip myself entirely. "Why take my shirt off?" I asked. "Because ther might be sum o' them *thear things abaght*," he replied. "Are there many of those things round about these quar-ters?" I further interrogated. "Nay, ah doan't think ther'll be so monny, we mostly stove 'em when we find onny." With this answer I was somewhat comforted. When I had undressed myself to a state as naked as when I was born, I was told to tie my clothes up, and place them alongside a series of similar bundles laid against the wall. I was then furnished with a couple of rugs and ordered into

THE INNER OR SLEEPING ROOM,

and the lock turned on me. All was dark as pitch. My bare feet slipped on what I afterwards found was the vagrants' spattle[5] on the stone floor, and the sensation was cold and slimy. It made me think of snails, and worms, and other loathsome creeping things. I felt glad when my hand clutched the boarding on which my limbs were to rest for the night. The men in the room were con-versing freely with one another, and after a time I ventured to inquire if there was any room for me. The one in the partition nearest the door answered that I could sleep alongside him, but must be careful not to upset the tin of water at his feet. I made my way as best I could to the place indicated by the sound of his voice, and got my foot accidentally into the tin of water, but soon extri-cated it. Then covering my naked body as well as I could with the rugs given to me, I laid myself on the hard slanting boards, with bare wood as my pillow, to experience

---

4.　Here the workhouse bread was referred to using the soldiers' slang "Tommy," a word James Greenwood also heard: see above, p. 170. Other vicarious vagrants encountered "toke" or "pannum": see above, pp. 59, 61, 96.

5.　Obsolete version of the word "spittle."

TWELVE HOURS' MISERY.

Do as I would I was unable to make the rugs entirely cover me. There was a cold draught, and I was alternately seized with cramp and neuralgic pains. Now and again I could observe the dim naked forms of the vagrants as they passed to the tub where circumstances of necessity were performed. Needless to say the stench arising from this was anything but pleasant. When the night had progressed somewhat, the noise arising from snoring and the men talking in their sleep was incessant. One fellow kept calling out "Sixpence." Another said, "You are there, and I am here, and we've another night and day to do," &c., &c. As the eight o'clock bell rang for the regular inmates to go to rest, there came a sound of sweet music from the outside, as if a batch of church revivalists was indulging just before separating for the night. The vagrants wondered where the singers came from, and one of them exclaimed, "'The Workhouse Door.'[6] Have you ever heard it sung? I heard a young woman sing it the other night, and liked it very well." The conversation turned on various topics. Two of the vagrants had been in Skipton Workhouse the night previous, and one of them related how his bread had been carried away by a ravenous rat as big as a cat. The leading features of the Skipton Workhouse were the severity of the labour in stone breaking, and what a "clever beggar" the porter of the establishment was. Other topics were the new waterworks at Barrowford and Colne, and the probabilities of getting a job there. Also what sort of task-work would be likely to be given to us the day following. The tramp next to me claimed that he was

SUFFERING FROM DIARRHŒA,

And that the agony he was undergoing was most excruciating. He had asked three times that day to see the doctor, but every time the attendant pretended not to be able to make out what he had said, and the only effort made to relieve the pain was by giving him a tin of warm water to drink. He stated he had travelled from Wakefield, where he did manage to obtain a bottle of medicine;

---

6.   A broadside ballad with this title was collected by C.H. Firth, the 19th century student of popular culture, and is included in the holdings of the Bodleian Library.

but at Keighley he had been treated "worse than a dog." From him I learnt that he had been where he was all Sunday, without putting his clothes on, and that he preferred being inside to outside on that day, because people stared so much, and shunned a tramp, particularly if he was badly dressed. He had passed many a Sunday without even breaking his fast. He intended making his way towards Burnley, where, he stated, there was no vagrants' ward, but that tickets were given for a lodging-house.

I DID NOT SLEEP A WINK ALL NIGHT,

And kept fancying "some o' them thear things" were creeping over me. By the time the welcome streaks of morning dawn appeared through the window, my bones felt terribly sore, and I was half starved to death. At about a quarter to seven the key turned in the door, and the order was given for us to "get dressed and bring your rugs in here." Seven naked forms then flitted about in search of their clothes, and commenced to dress. I found the piece of dry bread I had left untouched the night before still remaining. I was asked by one of the vagrants if I wasn't going to take it, and replied in the negative, saying he could have it if he cared to do so. He appeared exceedingly grateful, and at once commenced to devour it. The feet of my fellow-lodgers were of all sizes and shapes, and I had never seen such a collection of corns and bunions before. I found in my pocket a small paper of tobacco, which I shared out as best as I could. After getting dressed we carefully folded up the rugs we had slept in, and piled them up in a corner of the room. A few then produced small pieces of soap, which they had secreted about their persons, and endeavoured to wash themselves at the bath, into which at different times I had observed several spit and blow their noses. Whilst

WAITING FOR BREAKFAST

I had a good opportunity of noting the appearance of the room we had slept in. I judged it to be about 8 yards long by nearly 5 yards wide, and at one end was a passage, in which was placed a slipper-bath, a long towel on a roller, and the cess-tub. The boarding on which we had laid was divided into three partitions, each of which was supposed to provide accommodation for three vagrants. Two or three windows, strongly barred on the outside, gave a moderate light to the place. The walls were newly whitewashed, and I noticed several inscriptions written thereon in a legible hand, including the following:—

"Dirty days hath September,
April, June, and November;
From January up to May,
The rain it raineth every day;
From May again until July,
There's not a dry cloud in the sky;
All the rest have thirty-one,
Without a blessed ray of sun;
And if any of them had two-and-thirty,
They'd be just as wet and twice as dirty."[7]

Also,

"If I could stretch from pole to pole,
And grasp its icy span,
Although this is but a dirty hole,
'Tis better than dry scran."

"Dry scran," I was informed, meant dry bread. Amongst my [companions][8] were a tailor, aged 67, decently dressed, a compositor, also respectably attired, and a band-maker, while the remainder could scarcely be classified, except as labourers. Several of them had worked in the town on previous occasions, and on explaining myself as a native of Keighley, I was led into conversations which were remarkably interesting. Breakfast was brought in by a pauper attendant, and consisted of seven pieces of dry bread on a board, each piece weighing 8oz., one for each vagrant. These were placed upon the stone floor, while in a surly tone the man who brought them exclaimed,

"THEAR'S YER TOMMY."

Talk about the haughty pomposity of parish beadles![9] It was nothing in comparison with the attitude of the pauper as he

---

7.   Actually based on a poem attributed to Thomas Hood (1799-1845).

8.   In the original: "campanions."

9.   Craven refers, inappropriately, to the "parish." See above, p. 122 note 6. *The Oxford English Dictionary* defines a "beadle" as "An inferior parish officer appointed … to keep order in church, punish petty offenders, and act as the servitor or messenger of the parish generally; a parish constable."

deposited our breakfasts upon the ground. A rusty can was then brought in, containing about two quarts of cold water, which was to serve as a drink for all of us. A strong feeling of indignation rose within me as I observed the miserable fare, and the contemptuous manner in which it was served out. Although I was told I should need it before the day was finished, I gave my share away, whilst the others seized upon their portions eagerly and devoured them with apparent relish, more than one, though, complaining that in England vagrants were treated worse than criminals were in any other country. After a sufficient time had been allowed for breakfast, we were ordered out to

PERFORM OUR TASK WORK.

Two were relegated to some lighter labour, whilst five, amongst whom was myself, were set to corn-grinding. We were placed in a room, consisting of but two narrow passages at right angles. Here protruding from the wall were six wheels with handles attached, and nothing else but the dead wall was discernible. After being ordered to grind away at these, we were locked in. Some of the machines were dreadfully hard to turn, whilst others were not so bad. Fortunately, mine was one of the latter, and I was very much envied by the others, when they observed how easily my wheel went round. One of the vagrants, who had been at the game before, had made the calculation that to grind the requisite four bushels of corn, it was necessary to make 8,800 turns at the wheel. He adopted the process of counting the revolutions, and every time he reached 100 he made a note of it on the wall with a pencil, and then rested himself on the wheel handle before commencing the next century. The old tailor performed his work very methodically, if rather slowly; but all were agreed that they would not kill themselves with the job. The "comp,"[10] who performed next to me, was very weak, and could scarcely work his machine. The most aggravating part of the affair was that none of us could observe how much work had been accomplished.

---

10. The compositor, referred to above, p. 186.

THE ATMOSPHERE WAS VERY WARM,

And in midsummer must have been nearly stifling. Being in want of something to drink we thrust a tin through an aperture in the window, with a request to one of the paupers to fill it with water. The tin was taken away, but no water appeared, and nearly an hour passed before our wants were supplied in this respect, and then only because of repeated knocks and shoutings. Drearily the hours passed until twelve o'clock, when we were liberated for dinner, consisting of thick soup, which I could not bring myself to taste. From one to five o'clock corn-grinding was again our portion, after which the night was spent much similar to the last one. I was greatly pleased when my time expired and I was again a free man. I quickly travelled down Oakworth Road, and immediately on reaching home cast off my tramp's garb for ordinary attire.

MY IMPRESSION

Of the general treatment of vagrants is that the system is much too severe. Making every allowance for the shortcomings of the class constituting them, I am of of opinion that the lowest of mankind deserve better treatment than that accorded to pigs, dogs, and other animals of creation. The food furnished was scarcely fit for these last mentioned, whilst about the harsh treatment the less said the better. It is a disgrace to any civilised country. The only redeeming feature I deserved was the general cleanliness of the place. When I noticed anything dirty it arose from the habits of the vagrants themselves. I would not again for a substantial sum, be placed in a similar position, if I had any choice in the matter, nor shall I forget for a long time to come, my experience in the Vagrants' Ward of the Keighley Union as an "Amateur Casual."[11]

---

11. Craven ends his pamphlet by referring to James Greenwood, who wrote under the pseudonym "The Amateur Casual," see above, pp. 27–28.

Chapter Seven

The Casual Ward System:
Its Horrors and Atrocities.
Being an Account of a Night In the Burnley Casual Ward, Disguised as a Tramp
by J. R. Widdup

Manchester: The Labour Press Society, 1894

I t will now be some five or six years since a tramp appeared, one bright sunny morning, at a window of the house in which I was then living, and holding up a can in one hand, and a small packet containing some tea in the other called out and asked me if I would give him some hot water. I motioned to him to come inside, which he did, when I asked him how it was he came to be there so early (it was about five o'clock). He replied that he had been sleeping out, as he preferred to do this when the weather was warm rather than go to the casual ward, and that he was going to try to get a labouring job, where some houses were being erected in the neighbourhood. I gave the man some breakfast, and told him I hoped he would be successful in his search after employment.

This happened on a Saturday morning. On the afternoon of the same day I was attracted outside by the noise of a number of people running past the house. I asked what was the matter, and was told that the police had just pulled a drowned man out of the canal. I put on my hat and walked off in the same direction as the crowd was going. When I got to a stable in which the dead body had been deposited, I asked a policeman if I could see the man, adding that I thought I knew something about him, for I had a presentiment from the first that he was the fellow who had begged some water of me that morning. I was admitted into the stable, and on seeing the dead body found that such was the case. The poor fellow had probably been unable to get a job, and rather than set off tramping again he had decided to put an end to his existence by throwing himself into the canal. I gave the police all the information I could, and eventually they succeeded in tracing the dead man's relatives, who, it was found, were a moderately well-to-do working-class family.

Since that time, whenever I have gone near a casual ward, I have always thought of this incident, and wondered what sort of treatment the poor fellows were subjected to who went inside those places. I felt sure that the casual wards could be very little better, if any, than prisons, when a man would even sleep out of doors rather than lodge inside one: and I have often been seized with an almost uncontrollable longing to pay a visit to one of these places myself, disguised as a tramp, for the sake of getting to know what actually did take place inside.

I was walking home with the Secretary of *The Socialist* Board,[1] one evening after a meeting, when he said he had a proposal to make to me, which he thought might be the means of doing some good if I would only carry it into effect.

"What is the proposal?" I asked.

"That you should disguise yourself as a tramp," he said, with a laugh, "and present yourself for admission at the Casual Ward."

I immediately fell in with the idea; now I thought I have an opportunity of exposing what goes on in these places, as I can give a full and exact account of my experience in *The Socialist*. The matter was brought before the Board, and after they had agreed to the proposal, which they did very readily, I set about to prepare myself for the occasion.

The first step for me to take was to obtain the necessary clothing. I had decided on representing myself as a painter, but on second thoughts it struck me that painters in the spring of the year are fairly well employed, and that the ruse might not work and I might be found out. In my [dilemma][2] I thought it best to confer

---

1.   Widdup's account was originally published in *The Socialist and North-East Lancashire Labour News*; see above, p. 31.

2.   In the original: "delimma."

with the Board Secretary, who decided that it would be better for me to represent myself as a "comp,"[3] adding that if I did so he could find me a portion of the clothing necessary to my make-up. This I at once agreed to, and in a very short time I was dressed in a pair of trousers remarkable for their ventilating capacity, a waistcoat with one button on, which a rag gatherer would have looked at with [supercilious][4] contempt, and a frock coat which had certainly ceased to perform ordinary duty long before I was born. In this attire, with a ragged scarf thrown round my neck, and a pair of boots on my feet in which I might have ventured to embark but for the fear of serious leakage, I certainly looked a very rough specimen of humanity, and I only now needed a hat to correspond with my general attire to give me the appearance of a complete "professional." The hat was soon forthcoming, and after I had sumptuously regaled myself on the best viands in the house I set out for my destination, accompanied by the Board Secretary.

On arriving at the workhouse gates, I parted company with the secretary, after bidding him good night, and entered the yard. On reaching the building in which I was to lodge for the night I found the door half open. I rang the bell. No answer, however, was made to my first entreaty for admission, so I rang again. I was not long in getting an answer after ringing a second time, for immediately a ferocious-looking black dog came bounding towards me, and stood, at the door, barking and growling in a manner which clearly indicated that he meant business if I stepped forward without being invited. From the moment when I reached the door, I could hear an altercation going on in which it seemed to me that a female was taking part, whom I could hear saying "Well we cannot do anything with you here in that state. You know you should not come here like that." I was somewhat surprised at hearing the voice of a female for I was not aware, as I afterwards learned, that women too were admitted to the Casuals.

---

3. A compositor. C. W. Craven encountered a compositor in the casual ward at Keighley; see above, pp. 186 and 187.

4. In the original: "supercillious."

After waiting a while at the door, the dog was called back, and I was told to go in. I went in and sat down in the waiting room. A drunken, dirty looking woman was seated opposite me. It struck me at once that she was an "unfortunate," one who had been made what she was by the pernicious influence of a system which had compelled her to sell her body for bread. It was impossible to make much of what she said, but I heard her ask for the doctor, protesting that she was "all right." The female attendant stood before her, looking as if unable to make up her mind whether to admit the poor woman or not, and repeating what I had already heard her say. She spoke kindly and pleasantly, and I could not help thinking there was a touch of pity in her words.

I did not remain long, however, in this room, for soon a bullying looking young man came swaggering towards me, and told me to "get into the bath room," pointing the way in an imperious manner. I went into the bath room, and from there into the stoving room, where I found three men already waiting. I did not speak to them nor they to me. They stared at me very much, which I did not wonder at when I looked at my clothes, for I certainly appeared a disreputable and ruffianly-looking individual.

We waited in that room about half-an-hour, when a voice cried out, in a stentorian and imperative tone, "Come this way!" We went that way, and it was fortunate for me that I was the last, for I had not the remotest idea what we were wanted for. We passed out of the bath room and walked up to a small window at the other side of which was seated the porter. A number of questions were put to us in turn, and our answers were taken down in writing. When it came to my turn the porter looked at me very hard, and I was afraid he knew me.

"What is your name?" he asked

"Samuel Wilkinson," I replied.

"What is your age?"

"Twenty-eight."

"Where were you last night?"

"Preston."

"Where are you going to?"

"Bradford."

"Where do you belong to?"

"South Salford."

"What do you do?"

"Compositor."

"What!" he said, staring at me very closely.

"I'm a compositor," I again replied.

"Have you ever been here before?"

"No," I replied.

"Have you any property?"

I replied that I did not know what he meant.

"Have you any property?" he said again. "Have you anything about you."

I now understood what he meant, so I dived down into my trousers pockets and brought out twopence. Then I went into a pocket in my frock coat, and produced a clay pipe.

The money and the pipe were put aside; the porter called out number 28, and ordered me to go into the bath room.

When I got there one of the men was just stepping into the bath, and the others were undressing themselves. I could now understand why a rush was made when the order was given to appear before the porter. It seems that even these poor fellows who are at the bottom of the social scale, are not altogether unacquainted with the value of cleanliness. It was to get into the baths first, to have the advantage of cleaner water, and a cleaner towel than those who came after them that the rush was made.

I took off my clothes and left them lying about in the stoving room, thinking that they would be stoved[5] and disinfected. I noticed, however, that the other casuals made theirs into a bundle, so I tied my scarf around mine. I then waited until one of the baths was empty (there were two) and then I went into the bath room, and found to my surprise that I had to take my bath in the same water as had just been used by one of the other casuals. I did not like this and would have protested against it, but two of the attendants were watching me very closely, and I feared that if I complained they might find me out. I thought it best therefore, to say nothing, and stepped into the dirty water very reluctantly.

I was standing in the bath, wiping the upper part of my body (I will not say drying, for the towel was almost as wet as if it had

---

5.   The verb generally means to be dried in a stove. However, Widdup and Mary Higgs (see below, p. 212) seem to use it in its larger sense of storing in a heated room. See also above, p. 183.

been soaked in water), when I accidentally let one end of it fall into the water. I wrung it out, and was just thinking that I might as well wring the whole towel when one of the attendants, he who had ordered me into the bath room just after I entered the building, cried out, "Step out, there! G--- d---, step out, here; step out!" motioning at the same time with his head in the direction of the door. I thought he meant step out of the room, and a fear ran through me that at last I was found out. However, I was reassured again that I was as yet undiscovered when I heard him say, "Step out of the bath." I had not heard exactly what he had said, although I heard plenty of oaths, and what was more, a remark which no one dare print. Accordingly, I stepped out the bath as I was told, but it was with difficulty that I held my tongue. The beastly expression which he had used had stung me to the quick, and it was only the fear that if I said anything, they might discover whom I was that prevented me from telling him what I thought about him. I soon found out that it was impossible to take the water off my body with such a towel as I had, so I hung it over a rail fixed to the wall, and put on a coarse rough prison shirt, as I saw the others doing, which was large enough to hold two men my size. I then strode off into the stoving room (which all the while was without steam) brought my clothes and shoes out, and walked into the corridor.

An attendant then conducted me to one of the cells.

"Here you are," he said, as he opened the cell door, "Your bed is here."

"But," I said, "there is someone in."

"That is your bed." was his laconic reply.

I again repeated that there was someone lying there, when he replied that my bed was in the corner, adding, with especial emphasis, before he closed the door—

"There's your bread."

Of course, as might be expected, this conversation and the banging to of the cell door awoke the man who was lying on the bench, which was fastened to the wall.

"Halloa, mate," he began, "what o'clock is it[?]."[6]

---

6.   Widdup does not use a question mark here.

Then he made some remarks about being tired, and about his bones aching, finishing up by again asking what time it was.

"It is somewhere between nine and ten," I replied, "But where is my bed," I said.

"Bed," he replied, "They don't keep 'em here. There's your rug. Get down on the floor and make the best of it."

"Have I then to sleep on the floor?" I asked.

"Yes, if you can sleep there," he said, "It appears the cells are filled."

"Is this my bread?" I said, as I took up a piece that was almost as hard as wood, which I found at the bottom end of the plank bed on which he was lying.

"Yes," he replied, "that's it I suppose."

"But where is yours?" I asked.

"Oh, mine is on the shelf, in the corner there but I don't care anything about it."

This remark convinced me that I need not fear that he would take mine, as well as his own, which I did not wish him to do, for although I felt sure that I could not eat such unpalatable stuff the moment I first handled it, yet I wished to bring it away with me to show what it was like.

"If you want to drink," he said, "there's some water there."

I turned to where he pointed and found a pot which looked very much like a preserve or marmalade jar, but I was not tempted to drink.

"How shall I arrange these rugs[?],"[7] I asked.

He then showed me how to wrap them round me so as to get the greatest possible amount of warmth out of them, afterwards bursting out into a violent fit of coughing which almost shook the whole building.

I could now see much better than when I had just stepped into the cells out of the lighted corridor. I got down on to the floor, and after covering my feet up with a thin counterpane, I adjusted a dirty, thin bag stuffed with straw, which I had for a pillow, and settled down to make the best of my position.

As might easily be imagined, I did not sleep. The floor was as hard as brick, and was exceedingly damp and cold. The pillow was

---

7.   Again, there is no question mark.

very troublesome, as the sharp prickly straw hurt me very much. Besides, it smelled very bad, which did not surprise me when morning came, as I found it to be very dirty, one part of it in particular appearing as though someone had vomited on to it. This, however, was no doubt caused by the dirt from the heads of those who had lain on it previously, the casuals not washing their heads when they take their baths. I made some remarks to my mate on the bench above about feeling cold, adding that it was a shame that men should be compelled to go there because they could not get work. I then questioned him as to where he had come from, when he had worked last, and in what his employment consisted. He told me he had walked from Skipton that day, and that on the Monday and Tuesday previous he had been working in Bradford as a labourer. He said he did not know where to turn when morning came, and he only wished he had somewhere to go where he could get work.

"It is very hard to be out of work, when one really wants to work," I said.

"You're right, mate," he replied, "only those know who have tried it."

"But if all were of my mind there would soon be an end to this system," I said, "and those who will not work today, and have so much to say about others being lazy because they cannot obtain work, should have a try at doing something useful themselves."

This seemed to frighten my friend very much, and I could not get another word from him. Perhaps he had never heard such revolutionary talk in a casual ward before, and did not know how far it was safe for him to continue the conversation, for he had not seen me, nor I him it being dark all the time. He rolled about a great deal, and coughed a lot, but he would not utter a single syllable more.

Soon after this the workhouse clock struck ten, and in a short time the lights went out in the corridor outside the cells. The busy bustle of the attendants ceased, and nothing was to be heard save the coughing and the subdued talking of the casuals. One of the men in a cell next to mine, said to his [pal],[8] just as he seemed to be arranging his rugs on the floor—

---

8. In the original: "pall."

"We shall have a better bed in heaven, Johnson."

Johnson, however, made no reply to this remark, which showed that his friend had made up his mind that he was sure of getting to heaven, and that he would have a better position too when he got there: but in a short time I heard him say—

"Are ta warm, Bill?"

To which Bill replied rather sharply, "How can I be warm sleeping on the floor[?]"[9]

After this, I did not hear any further conversation, but the place was by no means silent, the violent coughing of the casuals being kept up all the night through. It would be impossible to describe what my feelings were as I lay on the cold, hard, damp floor, with my head only a few inches from an [outer][10] wall. Thoughts of all kinds flashed through my mind, but ever uppermost and foremost were pictures of tyranny and oppression which I had read about, or heard of, at some period in my life. I realised, for the first time, what imprisonment really meant, and what an outrage it was to imprison a man for life. No doubt it was the surroundings which induced these thoughts in my mind, which only served to intensify the miserableness of my position. The hours seemed to go very slowly: and as I counted each quarter chimed by the workhouse clock, I wondered if the morning would ever come.

About 12 o'clock it began to freeze rather hard, and the cold affected me so much that at last I began coughing and sneezing, and I feared I should have an attack of influenza. One poor fellow I heard coughing and expectorating above all the others, and I knew he would not have to sleep many more nights in the casuals to get the bed that Bill had remarked about to Johnson, assuming, of course, that he passed the recording angel all right. After a fit of coughing he would cry out, "Oh dear! Dear me! Oh, deary me!" and make other such remarks which indicated that he was in great pain, and which made me [feel][11] all the more miserable. He was

---

9.   For a third time, Widdup does not use a question mark.

10.   In the original: "out."

11.   In the original: "fell."

not the only man, however who coughed a great deal, for there were others whose cough indicated severe bronchial and asthmatical affections and which told pretty plainly that the poor fellows were being slowly murdered. I did not wonder at their coughing, for I felt that if I were to have a week in the casual wards that I should be almost as bad as they. My shirt was very damp, for I had not wiped the water off my body after the bath, the towel being so wet that it was impossible to do so. In addition to this my shirt and rugs, which were made of a greasy, dirty-looking material, smelled very strongly of sweat. I could understand this well enough, for the shirts would in the great majority of instances do double duty, acting as towels as well. They were by no means clean in another sense, for during the night I had an experience which made the flesh creep on my bones, and which told me pretty plainly there were live stock about. I have an impression that these would come from the bag of straw, for when morning came, on putting my hand to my cheek, feeling something moving there, I felt and afterwards saw sufficient to convince me that if I had only known the night before what I then knew, I would have kicked that bag of straw into another corner of the cell, and I should have benefited from the point of view of cleanliness by so doing.

At last morning came. All night long I had lain awake, [it][12] being impossible to sleep under such horrible conditions. I had never been warm and about five o'clock I broke out into shivers. This frightened me very much, and I got up and paced the narrow cell with the stinking blankets wrapped as closely round me as I could hold them. I was fairly pleased when I heard the bell going somewhere about six o'clock, and when I [heard][13] a voice call out "Take your clothes in," as an attendant opened each cell door. I lifted my clothes into the cell from out of the corridor, where I had to leave them the night previous, and it did not take me long to get rid of the stinking, greasy-looking garment which I had had for a shirt, and get my own shirt on to my back. As I was dressing myself, I wondered if my clothes had been stoved

12. In the original: "It."

13. In the original: "hear."

and disinfected, as I had been told the clothes of the casuals were. I certainly believe that they had never been removed from the cell door, for, to all appearances, they were exactly as I had left them the night before. I cannot, however, say for certain that my clothes were not carried away; but I was awake all the night through, and I certainly never heard anyone walking outside in the corridor which I should have done had anyone been for them. I am strengthened in the belief that they had never been removed, by the fact that from the moment of entering the cell, in which I was lodged, to the time of leaving it, the steam pipes were quite cold, despite the fact that it had been freezing hard during the night. I believe also that the steam pipes in the cells are a continuation of the rows of pipes in the stoving room; and if this is so, as there was no steam through the pipes in the cells, it is hardly probable that there would be any steam in the pipes in the stoving room. It would be impossible to say, for certain, that my clothes were not carried away and disinfected, but judging from all the circumstances taken together, I strongly believe they were not. However I leave the reader to from his own judgement on the matter.

By the time that I had finished dressing myself I had been able to take a good look at the man who had slept on the bench above me. I saw at once that he was an out-door labourer, and his hands indicated that he had been working not long before. He asked me if I had had a good night. I replied that I had not slept at all.

"But I was so tired," he said, rubbing his eyes, as he sat up on the plank bed. "From Skipton to Burnley is a good walk."

"What shall we be put to now?" I asked.

"Oh, grinding corn," he replied.

I chatted with him while he made his bed up, which he did in a very neat and tidy fashion. By the time that he had finished, the bullying young man threw the cell door open and said, "Williamson, step out!" The man stepped out, but where he went to I do not know.

I was left alone for about ten minutes, when the same attendant came back, and ordered me to step out also. I did so and was admitted into the next cell, in which there were already two others waiting. One of the men was very talkative, and I was glad of the change. He seemed to have been fairly-well educated at one time, by the way in which he talked. He swore horribly about the bread which had just been given to us, and said he had never been in such a b--- "spike."[14] At Rochdale, where he had stayed the night previous, he said he had had hot tea for breakfast, with bread and butter. He was a curious customer, and everything he said ended with a reference to this b--- "spike." He seemed to be very anxious to know if he would be put to task work "in this b--- 'spike.'" Of course I could not tell him, and the other man who was in the cell did not know either.

For a while we were all silent. At last our talkative friend began by shrugging his shoulders and remarking that it was very cold, finishing up with the usual complementary[15] expression. "Last week," he said, "I was a Roman nobleman dressed in armour." Then he made an imaginary parry, feint, and thrust, as though he was fencing with someone, after which he related that he had been a "super" at the "Manchester Ryal" for eighteenpence a night, and that on the Saturday previous he had been engaged in the performance of "Rienzi" as a Roman nobleman. He then told how they fought with Barton M'Guckin's men, finishing up with a history of the movement lead by Rienzi against the Roman nobles in the 14th century, and a review of all the first-class lyric artists of the day.[16]

After remaining in this cell for a time the door was flung open, and the porter told us to "come out." We were then marched down the corridor until we came to a number of other casuals. The porter then led the way, and we were told to follow him. We went outside into the yard, and walked along the building side until we came to the Workhouse. We there halted, and the porter told several to step out and follow him. He soon came back and told us to follow him again. I was afraid we were going to have to

---

14. "Spike" was a widely used term for the casual ward, although this is the first time that it appears in the texts in this volume.

15. The author perhaps means "complimentary."

16. *Rienzi* is an early opera by Richard Wagner, based on the novel by Edward Bulwer-Lytton. Barton McGuckin (1852-1913) was a distinguished operatic tenor of the period. A "super," short for "supernumerary," is, in modern parlance, an "extra" on the stage or in film.

labour for the builders at the new Workhouse Hospital, for I knew if we were that there was sure to be someone there who would know me. However, we were turned into the timber yard, where a number of us were put to sawing large blocks of timber which are cut up and sold for firewood.

The man who was put to work with me was a very disreputable-looking individual, and I soon felt convinced, from what I saw of him, that he would not have hesitated at doing something dreadful if it had suited his purpose. He was certainly one of the worst types of [ruffian],[17] which capitalism produces, that I have ever seen. Two other men, working behind me, appeared to be fairly decent fellows. One of them was very well dressed, and he had on a print collar and front. I noticed this man greasing his shoes with the fat used for the saws.

"Are you softening the leather?" I asked.

"Well, no, not exactly that," he relied, "you see it makes them look better, and I am going into the town."

"What is your occupation?" I asked.

"I'm a cabinet-maker," he replied, "I have a friend in the town who will give me a few shillings to start me on my way, and I am going to see him at noon."

"Do you find work bad to get?"

"Yes, it's bad to get," he said.

I felt sorry for this fellow. He was not a lazy man, by any means, for he worked with a will at his task. I told him I hoped he would soon be able to get work, and he replied that he hoped he would.

After working about an hour the old men from the Workhouse began to appear. They stood round us and chatted freely all the time. I cannot refer to all that occurred while we were sawing timber, but more than once I had evidence of the truth of the remark that "a fellow feeling makes us wondrous kind."[18] If I explained what I mean by this, I should certainly make the lot of the casuals much harder than

17. In the original: "ruffianism."

18. From David Garrick's "Prologue on Quitting the Stage in 1776": "Their cause I plead—plead it in heart and mind/ A fellow-feeling makes one wond'rous kind." In his *Poetical Works*…. London: George Kearsley, 1785. 2 vols., 2:325, lines 3 & 4.

it is at present, and this I have no particular desire to do. One of the old men approached me, and with childlike simplicity told me all about himself. He said he was 84 years old, and that he had worked all his life up to about ten years ago. He then showed me some money had in a purse, afterwards remarking quite suddenly

"I say, young felly, yo' look like a broken dahn gentleman."

He winked, laughed and shook his head at this, as though he would say I know [sic], and then went off.

We worked until about eleven o'clock when we were told to "knock off and go up with the others." Accordingly we ceased working, and went towards the entrance of the building in which we had lodged for the night. As the men went in together I took the opportunity to slip out of the yard and walked off as fast as I could. I noticed a good many standing about at the gates as I came out. There did not seem to be the faintest ray of hope in their countenances, and probably not one of them knew where to turn to for work. There was nothing for them but to start off again, tramp, tramp, tramp, day in and day out: and I felt as I was coming away from them that such a life would soon make me as ruffianly and as devoid of energy as they seemed to be. I got home tired and hungry, for I had not eaten any of the bread (?)[19] given to me, and after having a hot bath and a good breakfast, sat down and wrote the following:—

Burnley, Saturday, April 21st, 1894.

Dear Sir,—I will give you the twopence and the clay pipe left by Samuel Wilkinson, of South Salford, last night. With the former you may purchase a cigar or half-an ounce of tobacco, and have a smoke at the expense of the editor of *The Socialist*.

Don't forget to purchase a *Socialist* on Friday next, price one penny, or 1/8 post free, for one quarter.[20]—Yours truly,

THE EDITOR.

---

19. Widdup adds a parenthesized question mark to express his doubts as to whether the "bread" that he was given was really worthy of the name.

20. A longer-term subscription was not to be recommended. The *Socialist and North-East Lancashire Labour News* folded at the beginning of 1896, after an existence of twenty-eight months.

To the Porter, Burnley Casual Ward.

---:0:---

In the foregoing account of my experience in the Burnley Casual Ward, I have simply described the treatment to which I was subjected as it actually occurred, and there has been no attempt at exaggeration whatever. I now wish to make a brief examination of the casual ward system, and the method adopted of treating an unfortunate class of men and women, who are mainly made what they are by the evil effects of a system of society over which they alone have no control, and which they are powerless to alter.

I do not wish it to be supposed that I have discovered any means of dealing with the casuals, which would effectually eliminate them as a whole, other than, of course, an entire economic and social change such as the establishment of a Social Democratic State would bring about.[21] If these men and women were put to productive work under municipal auspices it would probably mean that the employees of private firms would be displaced by the competition, and that while one class was set to work, another would be thrown out of work, and would, in all probability, become tramps themselves. Of course, if the authorities could be compelled to find work for all those who were displaced by their setting the unemployed to work, it would eventually lead to the whole community working for themselves. But as a direct, and immediate improvement, the community can see to it that these unfortunate men and women are not punished as they are at present, because the industrial arrangements of to-day are such that work cannot be found for them. If they are compelled to tramp about in search of employment, as undoubtedly they are, it is the duty of the community to assist them, and not to make their lot in

---

21. Widdup, and his newspaper, were supporters of the Social-Democratic Federation, a Marxist political organization founded by H. M. Hyndman. The Federation gained prominent support from leading socialists in the 1880s, but was beset by infighting. In 1900 it was one of the founding organisations of the Labour Representation Committee, which became the Labour Party in 1906. See Crick, Martin. *The History of the Social-Democratic Federation*. Keele: Keele University Press, 1994.

life more unbearable by subjecting them to a course of treatment
as bad as the treatment of prisoners in jail. With this end in view
I suggest the following alterations:-

> 1st. –That no casual be compelled to bathe in the same
> water as has been used by another. (This change has
> been effected in the Burnley Casual Wards since this
> unclean practice was brought to light.)
>
> 2nd. – That each bather be provided with a clean towel.
>
> 3rd. – That the baths in their present form be entirely
> abolished, and a hot and cold shower bath substituted in
> their place. This would be a safeguard against the trans-
> mission of disease from one person to another.
>
> 4th. – That a wire mattress be provided for the casuals
> to sleep on, in all cases.[22]
>
> 5th. – That each casual's clothes be stoved, so as to
> destroy any vermin they might contain.
>
> 6th. – That the cells in winter time be kept warm the
> night through.
>
> 7th. – That a proper breakfast be provided for the casu-
> als, instead of a piece of unpalatable bread and a drink
> of water.
>
> 8th. – That a certain amount of useful work be set to
> each casual so as to cover the cost of his maintenance,
> by the ratepayers, and that on completing the work, he
> be allowed his liberty.

---

22. Contrast Mary Higgs (below, p. 217), who found that wire mattresses were
"disliked for cold" by the female tramps among whom she mixed.

9th. – That the system of setting a man to grind corn, which he cannot see, for an indefinite period, be entirely abolished, as a task of this kind is simply severe punishment of a prison like character.

It might be said that if these improvements were made the casuals would increase. But even assuming that this would be the case, if they paid for their cost of maintenance, as is here proposed, their increase would not be a greater burden to the ratepayers than it is at present, nor even as great. It is often asserted, by those who uphold the present system, that the casuals are a lazy, vagabond class, who do not want work. Well, admitting that they have become so bad at this, it is pretty certain that the present method of dealing with them is not, by any means, calculated to make them better: its effect is rather to make them worse, and any improvement of the casual ward system is justified on those grounds. One thing is quite certain that capitalism has made the casuals what they are, and that if they were not in their present position, another body of workers would be. Seeing this, and recognising that it is only possible to abolish the cruel position in which they are placed by abolishing the system which produces them, it becomes the duty of the more fortunate workers to assist them, at present, as far as possible by improving the casual ward system, and also by working unceasingly for an economic change which will mean the establishment of a juster [sic] social system, in which casuals and casual wards will be no more.

Chapter Eight

"The Tramp Ward"
by Mary Higgs, writing as 'Viatrix'

Contemporary Review, 85, (January/June 1904).
Pages 640-67

H AVING, with a friend, spent five days and nights of the
summer of 1903 as a Tramp among Tramps,[1] I was led to
pursue my social investigation a little further. The reasons
were many. It was suggested in several quarters that our
experiences might be exceptional, that they were the result of
testing isolated workhouses, that mismanagement in detail was
possible. Abnormal conditions might prevail by accident. It might
also be that in the larger centres of population cleanliness and food
were both better managed. Also the time of year at which we went
was one when the tramp ward was empty; we did not come in contact with other tramps and learn their character. It was possible
that conditions which pressed hardly on us were easy to them. It
seemed very desirable to ascertain exactly the winter circumstances in some large centre of population. There were reasons
which made the one we chose exceptionally interesting as an

---

1.   Higgs, Mary. *Five Days and Five Nights as a Tramp among Tramps: Social
Investigation by a Lady.* Manchester: John Heywood, 1904.

experiment. The story of our Tramp was a matter of public knowledge; the personal assurance of Guardians had been given that the
evils mentioned did not exist. They had examined and convinced
themselves that, as regards the destitute poor, their workhouses
were free from blame. Not only so, but the workhouse tramp ward
chosen had been frequently mentioned in the public Press. A large
"sleeping-out" problem existed in the town. It was suggested that
it might be desirable to relax regulations so as to make it easier for
destitute persons staying there to go out in the morning to look
for work. "It was thought that in this way men who shunned the
casual ward might be induced to enter it in preference to sleeping
out." So said the public Press. The experiment of slightly relaxing
the rules was tried. Very few availed themselves of it. The
Guardians also opened the wards early, but very few men came,
"the applicants were mostly men tramping in search of work," but
all who applied had slept in the neighbourhood the night previously.

The Clerk added that "the experiment made it clear to the
public that there was no necessity for the men to sleep in the
brickfields."

Here evidently was an exceptional Board of Guardians, bent
on meeting a public need. With such a desire on their part, probably ideal conditions would prevail. An ungrateful vagrant class,
"men in search of work, but who don't want to find it," nevertheless refused to flock to the provision made for them. They obsti-
nately preferred brickfields after six weeks of relaxed conditions!
Was it ignorance or prejudice on their part? Or was it possible that
the Guardians were mistaken in thinking provision had been
made? One thing only could test the matter, another descent from
respectability, and identification with the claimants for relief. One
night as a tramp might give insight into real conditions. It is so
surprisingly easy to become a tramp that it is strange it has not
occurred to Guardians personally to test conditions by sampling
each other's workhouses, or at any rate by sending into them some
trustworthy witness.

So my friend and I started on a well-planned tour of investigation; we dropped out of civilisation in a town far enough away to
tramp from, and set our faces towards a place where friends were
ready to receive us. We told no lies. We were at 5.30p.m. so penniless that through a partial miscalculation we had only 3½d.
between us (besides two pennies husbanded for after needs)

wherewith to procure the substantial tea with which we wished to fortify ourselves! Consequently we could not afford 2d. for a cup of tea, and our first surprise was to find that a 1d. cup of tea was hard to procure. It was only searching in a poor neighbourhood that our evident poverty procured us, as a favour, a cup of tea each and four slices of bread and butter for our 3¹/₂d. The usual price was 2d. for a "pot of tea" in a small, poor, but clean, shop, and bread and butter was ¹/₂ d. a slice. When I asked the woman to give us ¹/₂ d. worth instead of a two penny plateful, she gave us two extra slices "free gratis for nothing." Evidently we were objects of charity, poor and respectable, and we appreciated her kindness. But considering the real price of food, we paid for what we had. Cheap cups of tea are a preventive of evils. Thirsty men and women must drink. Surely a penny cup of tea easy to be obtained might keep many out of the public-house. Of course we were ignorant of where to go to obtain cheap food, but so, maybe, are other wanderers who are not *habitués*.

Refreshed, but not satisfied, we began to search to S--- Street. No one knew where it was, so we had to resort to the usual refuge and "asked a bobby." He knew, and knew why we asked! After a moderate walk through a very poor neighbourhood we easily identified the place by a row of six men propped up against a wall waiting, and one woman hovering near. We found, somewhat to our surprise, that the hour of admission was one hour later than that which prevailed in other towns we knew. Seven o'clock is late on a winter's night, and it may be you will suffer from cold, snow, or sleet, if you arrive as a stranger at six o'clock. Besides, what about early admission? However, no one was being let in, so we took a short walk and returned. All the loiterers had disappeared inside, so we followed. We were, however, only admitted to further waiting under cover in a curious ruinous shed. It was a very cold place; the roof would let in water through holes in the skylight; it was, however, a fine night and only moderately cold. So we joined two women, and saw the men, about 15 by that time, arranged in a row against the opposite wall. Two women were sitting on a step, and one on the handle of a wheelbarrow. We sat on the edge of a plank with our backs against a hole that gave a view of a place which we afterwards found was under the tramp ward, apparently used for bricks. A married woman, somewhat respectably dressed, came in with her husband. One by one men dropped in. The women spoke little, but a buzz of conversation went on among the men, whose numbers grew to over 30. Two facts struck me. Hardly any one was old; most were in the prime of life, and with a few exceptions, if you had met them in the street, you would say they were ordinary working men. Some few, however, were evidently of the "moucher" type. We waited, growing cold, for a full half hour in this draughty place, and then, as the hands of the office clock pointed to seven, we women were told to crowd into a corner near the office window, "married people first," and an official in uniform proceeded to take particulars. Husband and wife, in the case of three couples, had to give name, age, where they came from, and destination and occupation. Then began, as each candidate came forward, a process which I can only describe as "bully ragging." If the unfortunate applicant stated the facts in a meek and ordinary voice, this official asked, "Have you been here before?" If the answer was "No," "See that you don't come here again," "Sponging upon the rates!" and various other expressions not to be repeated were used in a hectoring tone of voice. If the reply was "Yes," he became threatening and violent in language. One married woman ventured the reply, "Not since before Christmas." He flew upon her and used insulting language. This preyed on her mind so much that in the course of the next two days she frequently said to us, "I only said 'not since before Christmas,' and he said I sauced him." One poor woman with a bandaged head was summarily dismissed. "Get out with you, you ---" "Off with you --- sharp!" Threats of five days' detainment or of "gaol" for "impudence" were used, and he announced as a clincher, "all you women will have to stay in two nights and pick 3lbs. of oakum."

My heart sank low. These must be desperate, well-known characters with whom I was to associate, the very scum of the earth, to be treated so. Even this habitual imposture could hardly justify the official language. The officer was evidently a "lion in the path" and not muzzled! But I was a decent, married woman rejoining my husband who was working in a neighbouring town, too far from him to reach him that night, without means to procure a bed, and seeking shelter simply in order not to be on the streets at night, and to proceed as soon as permitted. I gave particulars which were true, and in answer to the question, "Have you been here before?" could truthfully say "No." But this was not enough. "And what are you doing here?" "I am going on to my husband." "You've no business to be here imposing on the rates, do you know I could give you three months for it? I've a good mind to send you off and make you tramp to him to-night." I was so dumbfounded [*sic*], my friend says, that I replied, "I wish you would!" Then he proceeded to insinuate I was a woman of bad character; my eyes fell and my face flushed, and I suppose gave colour to his statement. Reply or justification was worse than useless. I grew so confused I could not state correctly the number of my children, but said I had "one or two." Evidently a bad character, leaving children up and down the country. "See you don't come here again. I shall know your face, and it will be worse for you if you do." I earnestly replied, "I won't," and was allowed to pass on. I waited at the top of a flight of steps while he "bully ragged" my friend for going about the country with such a bad character. He made her cheeks flush by insinuating she was no better. She said when she joined me, piteously, "Do I look like a prostitute?"

We entered together the tramp ward, a barn-like room, furnished with a wooden table and three forms. We found afterwards that it was the top storey of a converted mill. It was sky lighted, and divided into several rooms—a very large dormitory, a bath room with W.C.s,[2] an attendant's private sitting-room and store-room, and the day room we entered, which was approached by a flight of stairs from outside. The room was very slightly heated, apparently by a steam-pipe overhead, there was no fire, and a very cold draught from outside, when, as frequently, the door was left ajar. The table was so placed that the draught came to those who sat there. We were told to hang up our shawls and sit down. A very stately officer in spotless uniform received us, and marshalled us like soldiers, peremptorily, but not unkindly. We sat at [the][3] table and were given brilliantly polished tin mugs and spoons. Then each of us was helped to gruel, very good in quality, almost thick enough to be called porridge, and sufficiently salted not to be tasteless. A salt-box was on the table. We each received also a thick slice of good

---

2.   In the original: "W.C.'s."

3.   Word omitted in original.

bread.[4] We fell to with appetite after our slender tea and long waiting. Gruel was not so bad—for the first time! The table and floor were spotlessly clean. So far good. I did not at the time reflect that it is usually supposed to be bad to have a bath immediately after a meal. As soon as we had finished eating it was, "Now, women, come to the bath, two of you." My friend and I eagerly embraced the first turn, and were soon marshalled each to a corner of the bath room, searched (for pipe and tobacco!), and told to get into the six inches of warm water, which a notice told us we were entitled to, and carefully asked if it was too hot or cold. We had, however, only soft soap to wash ourselves with, and were told to wash our hair. This we had previously escaped; my friend had very long hair needing careful drying, and the prospect of wet heads was not cheering. If you wish to frequent tramp wards it is desirable to have short hair. However, there was no help for it, so with the officer standing by to hand a clean towel and enforce haste: "Come hurry up, women," I hastily bathed, dried my hair as well I could, and got into the garment provided—a modern substitute for a hair shirt, a coarse garment of dark blue bathing flannel of most peculiar shape; it just covered the elbows and barely came to the knees! The neck, of white calico, was dirty. I had to perform an act of self-sacrifice in leaving my friend the cleanest. Blankets and nightgowns are stoved[5] every night, rendering insect pests impossible, but unless I am greatly mistaken they are not washed often. My friend, who afterwards folded the blankets, found they made her hands filthy. It is not very nice to think of sleeping thus, but it would of course be impossible to wash the blankets every time. It might be possible to give a person a clean nightgown and the same one for two consecutive nights. As it was, we knew the

---

4.   Many of the vicarious vagrants encountered the word "skilly" or "skilley" to describe workhouse gruel, but Higgs does not refer to it. It is also unusual, perhaps unique, to find the bread described as "good." Below, p. 216, she finds it dry and, on eating it for the second time, "not appetising."

5.   Like J. R. Widdup (see above, p. 193), Higgs uses the word "stoved" in its larger sense of storing in a heated room.

second night we must be wearing someone else's. They were lumped and sent to be stoved. With regard to the blankets, every night the regulations have to be relaxed for one or two women unfit to be bathed. These sleep in their own clothes. They cannot be clean. But in the morning all these blankets were also lumped and stoved. Consequently, the next night you might be sleeping in your neighbour's blankets. Two women on one night slept without changing or bath. It would seem to be a simple precaution to wash the blankets from these beds, and thus in rotation wash all. However, these delights were yet to come. We folded our clothes and were marched through the sitting-room in our scanty costume to fetch from the store room pillows and blankets. An American leather very low pillow and a straw pillow with a white cover were allowed us, but the second night only the American leather one was allowed. This was much too low for comfort. One woman begged a white one, but we were stopped from asking,—it was only for women who had just washed their heads! It was a special favour to her.

We were then marched into the large dormitory and told to let down a wide board propped against the wall, one for each. A row of sleeping women occupied similar "plank beds." There were a few straw beds on bedsteads, but only for sick folk, and also some children's cribs. A gas jet or two burned all night and revealed the gaunt rafters and skylights. Now to test the delights of a plank bed! We were told to make it, "one blanket below and two above." So we meekly did so, and the officer retired.

Then began, about 7.30, a night which I can only describe as one of long drawn-out misery.

The human body is not made to accommodate itself easily to a plank bed, even with "three good blankets." If you lie on your back your hips are in an unnatural position unless the knees are raised, and then the air comes under the narrow double blankets. Try first one side and then another. Your weight rests on hip and shoulder squeezed into flatness and speedily sore. Add wet hair, a long pillow very hard, a garment that leaves arms and legs uncovered and pricks you all over, and conditions are not easy for sleep. Double a blanket under you four-fold, get another round you, and place the third on top double. This is more tolerable, but still cold. My back is still sore after three nights in a soft bed. Do not imagine either that we slept more uneasily than others. Everyone complained of the hard couches, though some said even they were preferable to wire mattresses, on which you "couldn't get warm." A simple expedient would provide an efficient remedy. If a strong hammock were fastened in a frame bedstead by eyelets on pegs, this could be removed and stoved, and washed, if necessary, and it would give to the body and allow of easy sleep. But even on this uneasy couch sleep might have been obtained but for a number of disturbances which made the night a prolonged torture. The end of the room was occupied by a large cistern. At intervals, day and night, a flush of water was sent along a pipe for sanitary reasons. A very good arrangement; but we happened to be at the cistern end of the room. Anyone who knows how a cistern behaves can imagine the peculiar noises that issued. It seemed possessed by a demon bent on preventing sleep. It would s-s-siss for a few moments, then gurgle, then hiss, then a rush would come, followed by a steady tap, tap, tap, that speedily became maddening. Water on the brain with a vengeance! Wet hair and running water in combination! This proximity to the cistern was, however, an accident, carefully avoided the second night, but several poor unfortunates would always have to suffer it. It was, however, a minor evil compared with others. The beds were so close that they almost touched, quite unnecessarily, as the room was large, but so we were ordered. Your neighbour breathed right in your face, and you had all the twisting and turning of a sufferer on each side to add to your own. Most of the women had bad colds, and you succumbed yourself under the double influence of contagion and chilliness. Then your coughing and sneezing added to the common misery. Only the women there for the second night lay still—apparently, but not really, asleep. Later, I knew why: sheer fatigue and exhaustion prevented restlessness. But all of us newcomers turned and squirmed; some sighed and groaned; others gave vent to exclamations of misery. "My God, what a hell-hole of a place," said a woman, roused from uneasy slumber for about the sixth time. Far the worst thing of all, which made it a punishment fit for Tantalus,[6] was the interruption to slumber. Nominally, women could be admitted till 10, but really, for one reason or another, they were admitted till past midnight, under protest. An officer was in charge,

---

6.   Tantalus, son of Zeus and king of Sipylos, was condemned by the gods to be continually taunted by visions of food and drink which always evaded his grasp.

and in each case her manner of procedure was as follows: She turned the handle of the door with a loud noise, marched in the newcomer (after previous cistern gurglings connected with bathing operations), and ordered her in a loud tone of voice to let down the plank bed. Down it came with a bang, startling all sleepers. Then she administered some rebuke mixed with orders, left the new unfortunate and shut the door sharply. One newcomer was a poor old Granny, very bad with rheumatism, whom she loudly accused of drink, probably with truth. This old woman sighed, groaned and moaned, "Oh! deary me," "Lord help us," most of the night, and was in real pain. She got out of bed twice with numerous sighs and groans, taking a quarter of an hour at least each time. Bed after bed was let down and dragged across the floor. A woman came in very late, could not settle, was moved to a straw bed, was too frightened to sleep (perhaps d.t.),[7] and finally was allowed to go out in the middle of the night. No doubt the post of this night-watching officer was tiresome and onerous, but a little thought might have brought about considerable improvement. If a number of spare beds were placed ready over night, and scoldings administered in the day room, if doors were opened quietly, and orders given softly with some considerations for a room full of weary sisters, one would have been thankful. As it was, people grew more and more restless; someone was constantly wandering about, or sitting up and coughing or moving uneasily. It was nearly impossible to snatch more than a few brief moments of restless slumber before, with early morning, sheer weariness reduced us to quietude. Then at 5.30 we were roused by the mandate, "Now then, women, all of you get up, be sharp now." A hasty obedience, swift and unwavering, is enforced by several stern sanctions. In the first place before you lies a day of service, the conditions of which can be made hard at will. Behind that is the possibility of being detained four or, if Sunday intervenes, five days, for "cheek" or "impudence."[8] No one could face such a prospect with

---

7.   Suffering from *delirium tremens*.

8.   Compulsory detention for two nights, or four if it was the applicant's second visit to the same workhouse in a month, was required by the Casual Poor Act of 1882 (45 & 46 Vict., c.36). The period of detention extended to three or five days if it included a Sunday. See above, p. 18.

equanimity, yet for every slight cause it was possible. We had an object lesson before us of the tender mercies of officials. A poor woman, a silk weaver by trade, who had been reduced to live by casual labour at charing, or by selling bootlaces, had entered the previous night. She was ignorant of the two nights' detention, and had a cleaning place to go to. When she found she was to be detained she begged and prayed to go, and the officer was moved by her tears to take her to the matron and give her liberty. But this took time, and she reached her charing place too late. Work was denied her, and she wandered about all day, and came back rather late to claim her second night, having difficulty in re-finding the place, and having nowhere to go. I have every reason to believe her story was true, for she repeated it to us again and again, it fitted in with her character and history, and she had no motive for deceiving us. But for this offence of returning, after having asked off, she was condemned to remain five days: her story was not believed, though she begged with tears to go out and seek work. One officer, indeed, spoke to almost all in a most peremptory, and one might even add, insulting manner, casting doubt on the truthfulness of what was told her. Reply was useless, as it would only provoke penalty. She hurried people up and ordered them about. One woman, an old hand, on the second morning said, "Come, come, you needn't be so knotty[9] with us," but no one else ventured anything that could be interpreted as disobedience or "impudence." She turned a deaf ear to one poor, tired woman whose feet were swollen, and who wished to remain another night, and tried her best to order poor old Granny out. "You won't stay here," "You can walk right enough," "you won't come over me with your tales." Fortunately for us her *régime* was limited. We had altogether dealings with three officers; one was careful and stately, strict but kind, only not considerate in the matter of protecting our sleep. This one was "knotty," and the third far more kind; fortunately her share of us fell at dinner time, but of that more anon.

I should remark that I felt considerable sympathy for these our taskmistresses. Even with a cosy sitting-room, and stove, and sofa, it must be an irksome and disagreeable task, and our "knotty"

---

9.   Meaning hard and rough in manner.

friend looked weary. By the end of the time she had sufficiently differentiated us to tell us before leaving "not to believe" the others. But I think she was to a great extent harsh and wrong in her judgments; at any rate, the assumption that all were lies was wrong. My friend and I are accustomed to judge characters of this class, being engaged in Rescue work,[10] and having destitute women constantly in hand. You cannot live a while two nights and a day in fellowship with women, under pressure of hard circumstances, without eliciting confidence. The women who went out after one night with us we did not know; they ate, or did not eat, a hasty breakfast and departed very early—about 6.30 probably—some of them to join husbands. But the following may be taken as a truthful description of our sisters who remained. The main impression on my mind is a double wonder at their patience in affliction, and at the qualities revealed in them, and a wonder whether, if I had selected a similar number of better class friends, and placed them in like circumstances, they would have borne the test as well.

Our morning ablution had to be performed with cold water and soft soap, and our clothes were restored to us mostly stoved (in which process some are said to be ruined, becoming limp and creased). Breakfast, the same as supper, was meted out to us. Gruel a second time with dry bread is not appetising. Oh, for a drink! The room was cold, and only cold water from the bath tap available; it tasted of metal polish or soft soap.

We sopped our bread in our porridge, and knowing we had the day to face, ate all we could. No one ate all the porridge and bread. We were not exceptional, hardly anyone ate much. Some kept their bread and munched it at intervals through the day. The porridge, including some nearly full mugs, and what remained in the can, was simply thrown away. Naturally enough when the officer left us, and we waited for the taskmistress, the conversation turned on food and treatment. Those who knew other workhouses

10. Higgs devoted her time to a range of voluntary agencies, and is best known as a 'prime mover' behind the National Association for Women's Lodging Houses: Chadwick, Rosemary. "Higgs [née Kingsland], Mary Ann (1854-1937)." *Oxford Dictionary of National Biography*, 27, (2004), pp. 78-79.

declared that this was "the worst they knew." In the course of the day we heard the merits of most of the workhouses near, and of some far away. It may be well to summarise as follows: The comparative merits of a tramp ward depend first on drink;—the women feel dreadfully the need of drink, especially after hard work. Coffee or tea makes all the difference to dry bread. Gruel is not drink. Some can bring in a bit of tea and sugar, and as a favour beg hot water; but it is often denied them. We procured it once, and it was once denied in our hearing. We had but a screw[11] of tea and sugar, and some had none.

The second requisite would seem to be food, but it seems that only a few can eat the gruel more than once a day. It is played with and left by most. Hence dry bread and a morsel of cheese at dinner is the real fare. As the quantity of food allowed is that which will sustain life in an adult, semi-starvation is the result. The tramp men who brought back the stoved blankets eagerly and hungrily hid under their jackets the pieces of bread the women had left.

Now to commence, after a night of misery, with a freshly-caught cold, to sit in a cold and draughty room with no fire, and feast on gruel and dry bread with a possible drink of water is punishment, not charity or alleviation of misery.

The third merit or demerit of a tramp ward is the bed. Straw beds are a luxury, wire mattresses are disliked for cold, plank beds for hardness; the floor is preferable, as there is more room.[12]

The fourth and perhaps the most important item is the character of the officers. Any who have even a drop of the milk of human kindness are remembered with appreciation. But they seem rare. Not, I believe, that there are many intentionally unkind. "They know not what they do." The constant habit of dealing for so brief a period with individuals prevents the formation of the customary links of human kindliness; the worst characters return, the best stay a very short time and are lost to sight; any act of kindness meets

---

11. A small amount, wrapped in paper.

12. Contrast J. R. Widdup (above, p. 204), who recommended that all casuals be provided with wire mattresses. See also above, pp. 212–213.

apparently with no reward. Kindness for kindness' sake is difficult; a peremptory official habit is easily acquired. There may be texts in an officer's sitting room, and yet the Christian qualities of fortitude, patience and self-sacrifice may be better exhibited to one another by the tramps outside her door than by the inmate in authority. Some workhouses are to be avoided like poison. There positive cruelty and insult reign, but the slightest resentment might be interpreted as "insubordination," and earn prison. A cast-iron system administered in a cast-iron way may, without intentional unkindness, be responsible for a vast sum of human misery.

The taskmistress came and asked us if we could wash or clean. Three of us were set to pick oakum. I could not volunteer to stand over the wash-tub, and besides, I wished to unravel the mysteries of oakum-picking and learn the histories of my comrades in misfortune. So we three sat on a wooden bench in a cold room, and three pounds of oakum each were solemnly weighed out to us. Do you know what oakum is? A number of old ropes, some of them tarred, some knotted, are cut into lengths; you have to untwist and unravel them inch by inch. We were all "'prentice hands." One woman had once done a little; we had never done any. After two hours I perhaps had done a quarter of a pound, and my fingers were getting sore, while the pile before me seemed to diminish little. Then I was asked if I could clean, and gladly escaped to a more congenial task. One woman only picked oakum all day, she was the one who was penalised. She had never done it before, and did not nearly finish her quota, though I helped her a little later on. Fortunately it was not demanded, but it might be at the will of an officer.

It will easily be perceived that long before this any dream I had of ideal tramp ward conditions had vanished. I was instead filled with amazement that any enlightened and Christian men and women could consider this a refuge for destitution, and wonder at a preference for brickfields and liberty. Prison treatment would be preferable; but my wonder was still to grow.

For the prevailing idea in my class of society, which I to some extent shared, was that tramps as a class were so incorrigible, and so determined to lead a nomad existence, that the life had somehow a mysterious charm for them, and the only thing was to severely penalise vagrancy in order to deter men and women from it. Viewed in this light it might be desirable that the treatment in a tramp ward should be made equal to that of a prison as a deterrent. A suspicion had been gradually growing in my mind that there was a destitution that was not voluntary vagrancy, and an actual forcing of lives into nomad existence. But I had not realised the pressure our system exerts in the direction of a wandering life.

Let me introduce you to my companions and assure you I shall ever regard them with affection and respect.

There is first of all "Granny," a poor old body of 70 sorrowful years. Once she had a little home of her own, and brought up a family of five sons and daughters. But her "old man" died. Still her son supported her, and she led a precarious existence, much plagued by "rheumatics," until one day, not long ago, the place where her son worked was burned down, and she lost her stay[13] and was turned adrift. She had mother-wit enough to beg her way, people gave her tea and pence. She "paid her way" in tramp wards, taking in a little tea and sugar, and "tipping" officials with a penny for hot water. She offered me a halfpenny for a screw of sugar. She had begged unsuccessfully of a child at a door before coming in, the mother stood behind and refused. "As if a spoonful of sugar would have hurt her," Granny scornfully said. One thing remained to her—liberty—but to keep this she was forced to walk from town to town, sampling tramp wards. She had not done it long, but it was too much for her. One arm was too painful to be touched, it was hard to put on her tattered garments, she provoked the wrath of officials by dilatoriness. Her legs were a study. Each leg was swathed in bandages, her feet wrapped in old stocking legs and bandaged, and men's boots put over all, a long—long process. Poor old soul, she wanted to end her wanderings, and told us, I believe truthfully, that she had tried to get into two workhouses but had not succeeded. Knowing the reluctance of officials to admit paupers out of their own parish,[14] I can

13. Place of residence.

14. The settlement laws (see above, pp. 11–15) remained in place when Higgs was writing. Higgs refers to the "parish," but the poor law union had replaced the parish as the unit of settlement as long ago as 1865. From this date, parishes were no longer responsible for the costs of the upkeep of their own paupers; this removed some of the iniquities of the system. See Caplan, Maurice. "The New Poor Law and the Struggle for Union Chargeability." *International Review of Social History*, 23, (August 1978), pp. 267-300.

well believe it. She was really ill when she came, besides the possible complications of having been "treated" to a drink of whisky.
She could hardly stand, had a cough and looked feverish, and only
fit to lie down; we had to help her on to her feet several times.
Perhaps her ailments bulked large,—most old people's do,—but
she did not after all groan so very much, considering. She was
ordered out, but she said with truth that she might "fall down in
the street." It did seem likely she might just go wandering on "till
she dropped," so we all advised her to stay and see the doctor who
might order her into the House. She seemed to have only a mazy
idea of how to go to work to get in, but she took our advice, saw
the doctor and was allowed to stay another night, but not ordered
in, as she could stand. However, she might the next day, after
being turned out, herself apply for admission, and this we all united to advise her to do. The one effect her wanderings had produced in her was a deadly hatred of workhouse officials. In the
afternoon, after singing a hymn, I comforted her by telling her her
wanderings might soon end in a better place. She was not sure of
going to "heaven," but she felt sure she should meet many of these
her tormentors in hell, and "then," she said, "I'll heave bricks at
'em!" I couldn't help suggesting "hot bricks" as appropriate, and
then talked to her about "loving her enemies." "I can't help it," she
said, "if it keeps me out of heaven; I hate 'em—I hate 'em all!"
Poor old soul, she lay on a form most of the day, obviously ill, wor-
ried out of the bed on which, in the absence of an officer, she laid
her poor old bones. The officer next morning truly said that the
workhouse, and not the tramp ward, was the place for her; but she
scoffed unbelievingly at her story of having tried to get admission.
Yet Granny continually told us she longed to get in and have "a
good bed," and one can imagine a poor old body like that, with no
one to speak for her, might have difficulties with a relieving officer. But we had to leave her behind us, though one longed to take
her by the hand, and see her safely in. I was not in a physical condition to stand the long hours of waiting from 6.30 a.m. till the
office at which she would be admitted was opened. We advised her
to stay as long as she could and then go there.

   Next in order was a married woman, whom I would gladly
own for my own relation. Her husband was on the men's side.
"That's my old man," she said, on going out, "I know him by his
cough." She had been well brought up and had sisters in good
circumstances comparatively. She and her "old man" were com-

fortably ensconced in a workhouse where, as a good steady worker, she was probably not unwelcome. But she heard her sister in a
distant town was dying, and they took their discharge and walked
there and back, close on 70 miles, arriving in time and staying for
the funeral. She was very, very weary with the long tramp, accomplished within a week. I believe they were re-entering the workhouse. This woman had a pleasant face and manner, and took several opportunities of doing small kindnesses; she did not grumble,
she only mildly complained of the task set her. I think she had
cause—she was set to scrub a very long and wide corridor. She
steadily scrubbed away for hours; she had no kneeling pad, and it
was "hard lines" on poor food and in a tired state. How many of
us walk 70 miles to see a dying sister, and, weary and sorrowful,
work without complaining, and with a cheerful face, and an eye for
others' sorrows?

A woman who interested me much was also a married woman.
Once she had been waitress in a hotel frequented by the gentry, a
place I knew well, and travelled with her wages in her pocket to
buy clothes. She was still better dressed, a shapely woman, with a
face almost handsome, graceful in her movements and a capital
worker. Her husband did not look a bad specimen of a working
man. Her story was that they had had a comfortable home; he was
once a singer in a Church choir. But his particular branch of trade
failed, and he had to seek a growingly obsolete kind of work where
it was to be found. They had tramped north in vain to find it, and
were now tramping back to their old neighbourhood in the hope
that things would be better. This woman also did not complain,
and behaved in a self-respecting manner, not a foul word or
reproach; she worked steadily, but was very weary and restless at
night. She had a heavy cold on her and grew worse instead of better. I seem to see her sitting wearily up in bed, unable to get the
needed repose. They had walked long distances recently.

A more doubtful character was "Pollie," who apparently was
well known to the officials. She was left stranded, as her husband,
one fine day, being let out of a tramp ward before her, left her
behind. She complained bitterly that the men were let out so long
before the women, they had time to get "miles out of the road." If
she caught him he would "get three months." Meanwhile she
intended to visit a sister who would give her a few shillings, and
then make tracks for another sister. Her face was not unhandsome,
but her nose betrayed the real reason of her misfortunes, and her

tongue was ready, and not too clean. She knew the workhouses far and wide, and had had her tussles with the authorities. She had thrown her bread and cheese at a matron who gave her it after hard work, giving another woman a workhouse diet. She had been in prison for "lip." She was, in fact, a tramp proper, and with a little drink and boon companions, probably foul mouthed and violent. But she and Granny were the only ones who used expressions not polite to give point to their opinions, and that only occasionally. We were no restraint, unless our interior character insensibly sweetened the atmosphere, for no one, not the most travelled, suspected us. We had been "on the road," could refer to workhouse reminiscences, and "knew the country" far and wide. We freely rewarded confidences by real bits of history. As we sang in concert, probably that was thought to be our "line of business." We were complimented on our voices, I, like the husband above mentioned, had once "been in a choir." I feel sure we should have got a good living "on the road." A tramp man who passed us told us he thought we should have been "miles further by now." He watched us, and made in the same direction. I twitted my companion on the loss of a chance for life. It might be thought our speech would betray us, but I do not know that it was more educated than that of one at least of our companions. We were with "all sorts and conditions of women," but not the worst.

There remains to be described a little Scotch woman, also married. She had been a servant, and was a "neat-handed Phyllis."[15] Born near Glasgow, she married south. Work failing, she and her husband had tramped the weary miles to her friends in the hope of work. They had returned, *via* Barrow, and were bound further south, so far seeking work and finding none. They had become habituated to tramp wards on the long march, and could tell the character of most, and the stages of the journey.

These were the only ones we got to know intimately. If they were tramps, with one exception they were made so by circumstances.

Shall I picture my brave little friend and companion, who worked on hour after hour with a splitting headache caused by a

---

15. An image from John Milton's "L'Allegro" (1645), line 86.

sleepless night? She had to clean the officer's room thoroughly, and to scrub tables, forms, floor, everything in short, in the large day room and down the stairs, a big piece of work. Meanwhile the two married women scrubbed the big dormitory and the bath room. The Scotch woman was told off to wash, by her own request, and related gleefully how she managed to wash and dry some of her own clothing before the officer came and told her to "mind out and wash nothing of her own." We were meanwhile growing dirtier, and more in need of a bath than on the first night. One woman washed a pocket handkerchief and dried it on the steam-pipe. Nothing else was possible.

I was taken away after two hours oakum picking and set to clean. While waiting for a bucket I saw a fire. Welcome sight. I dried my boots and warmed my feet, wet from the previous day's tramp. I was provided with materials, shown where to get water and set to clean, "scrub, mind you," two lavatories, two W.C.s[16] and a staircase with three landings and three flights of stairs. I was also to clean the paint in the lavatories, etc., and do the taps and the stair-rods. Of the latter task, however, I was relieved by a pauper woman, who said her work, of which she was thoroughly sick, was constantly to clean brasses. I like cleaning, and set to work with a will, only one soon comes to the end of one's strength after a restless night and an insufficient breakfast. I found I must moderate my speed or I should not last the day out. Men were doing a cistern in the downstairs lavatory, and kept passing and re-passing with dirty boots as fast as I cleaned. My taskmistress, after one inspection, left me alone to it. I fetched bucket after bucketful and completed my task to my own satisfaction, and hers apparently, by 12 o'clock. She was not unreasonable, but a little sharp. She sent me back to dinner in the tramp ward, and "hunger sauce" enabled me to finish the bread and cheese allotted, washed down by tea. We all brought out our husbanded treasures, and the kinder official let us have boiling water. The man in the office sneered at her and remonstrated, "You are soft!" "I can't help it," she replied. May God bless her, for it can hardly be imagined what a warm drink was to a thirsty soul, even without milk and with little sugar. We gave Granny some, and all ate our frugal

---

16. In the original: "w.c.'s."

meal without repining and with thankful hearts. We were allowed an hour, and resting my head on the table I snatched a few moments of most badly-needed rest. Then it was time to work. I was taken to the House and given a new task, to wash out an office. The little Scotch woman dusted the board room and my room. All had to be ready before three. I finished to satisfaction in good time, being once rebuked for sitting to do the last piece of floor (I had been on my knees without a pad for hours), and once for not saying there was no coal in the coal-box. But these were gentle rebukes. I was now very tired and could hardly carry my bucket. I slopped the water a little, and perhaps my taskmistress saw I was tired; at any rate she laid on me nothing further, but sent me back to the ward.

There my friend's task was by no means ended; she was on her knees scrubbing painfully, a quarter of the floor yet to do. I tried my hand, but was not quite "in the know," so I sang to her to cheer her and the others. Even old Granny cheered up to the sound of "When ye gang awa', Jemmie,"[17] an old favourite of her youth. It was easy without offence or suspicion to pass to hymns that might leave some ray of comfort in sorrowful hearts, and to get in a few words about the bourne "where the wicked cease from troubling and the weary are at rest."[18] I could not help considering that probably nowhere in the wide world were there souls more dear to our suffering Saviour than such as these, who were sharing the life He chose on earth. Granny used to sing, "Oh, let us be joyful, when we meet to part no more," and all were ready for the "Kindly Light" to lead them home. I have discovered that this and "Abide with Me," with "Jesu, Lover of My Soul" are tramps' favourites. Could the deep-seated religious sentiments of the human soul choose better expression?

The little Scotch woman loved some of the "songs of bonnie Scotland." In spite of scrubbing, my friend chimed in, and the hours passed. I grew rested in thought and body. Then our taskmistress appeared just as the floor was finished: she had for-

---

17. A Scottish ballad first transcribed in 1827. Also known as *Huntingtower* and *The Duke of Atholl's Courtship*.

18. From "Burial Hymn" by Henry Hart Milman (1830), line 7. The other hymns cited in this paragraph are well-known.

gotten the store room; it was locked up and not cleaned. She chose my poor weary friend; but I could not stand it, and volunteered instead. I had watched till I knew how, so I set to work with a will and acquired a new accomplishment, how to scrub a floor with sand and soft soap! My performance "gave satisfaction." At last all was finished, and we awaited the next meal, not with eagerness, for the third time of gruel and dry bread "pays for all," but at any rate with hunger. It was a long, long wait from 12 dinner to somewhere about 6. A slender breakfast at 6, dinner at 12, and hard work left something lacking; the morning gruel was slightly sour also, and I began to have uncomfortable feelings. Nevertheless, after a seemingly long wait, during which we all grew quite "chummy," and I extracted much information and confirmation of personal histories and social condition, at last supper arrived, and I finished the gruel with appetite, but could not, without a drink, eat dry bread.

Then another wait. We all grew tired to utter weariness. I longed even for a plank bed. We sat in various listless attitudes, half starved, cold, too weary to talk. There was nothing to see, sky-lighted as the room was, nothing to do but pick oakum, which still lay in measured heaps on the floor, no literature save the "regulations for tramps" on the walls.

This, then, was the kind of thing which left no "necessity for men to sleep in the brickfields!" I questioned the married women; none of them knew anything of any relaxation of rules. Evidently in their world it was not a matter of public knowledge that a man might enter earlier and go out after one night.[19]

At last it was bed-time one more, and we were "officered" to our uneasy couches. We were allowed to remove our shawls to the room where we slept,—a great boon, as I smuggled mine into bed, covering my bare arms, and securing a little more comfort. But I was sore from the night before, and no position gave ease. It being near the week-end, few came in, as it meant an extra day's detention; but the same ordering and bumping went on. I shall never

---

19. This refers to the relaxation in 1892 of the provisions of the Casual Poor Act, which allowed men to leave the casual ward after one night if they were looking for work. They could not return, on pain of four nights' detention. See above, p. 214 note 8. See also above, p. 18.

forget my next door neighbour who came in rather late and was near enough to touch. She was a respectable woman of the barmaid class, slightly grey, and therefore rather old for employment. She was well dressed. She was out of a place, and had applied at a Shelter too late to be admitted, and was sent here. She had never been in such a place before, and her astonishment at the conditions amounted almost to horror. We told her how to make the best of her bed—none of us near her were asleep. She twisted and turned her wet, grey head on the hard pillow, sneezing with a commencing cold. She sat up and lay down. "My God," I heard her say, "one can't sleep in this place." And with reason, for though the interruptions were not so numerous, they were sufficient to effectually break sleep. Granny did not groan so much, but she got out of bed, was scolded and had to be helped in. "Don't be so soft," I heard the hard official say, as she gave an involuntary small scream when one of her aching limbs was touched. It was true she had given trouble, but she was old, feeble, and ailing. It would not have been hard to be kind. I was myself by this time ill. The last meal of gruel, coming as a distasteful meal on a tired body, had not been digested. Sickness came upon me, and I had to be a disturber of the peace by three times getting up, and parting with my hardly-earned supper. Each time, paddling over great bare spaces in scanty attire, I grew colder, but I was in terror of attracting the attention of the officer, being considered ill and detained. Anything rather than another day in such a place of torture. As on the night before, some slept the sleep of utter weariness, most groaned and twisted, some lay awake. I never understood so well the joy of the first dim daylight, the longing of those who "wait for the morning." A woman sat up, "I'm dying of hunger," she said. It was the poor woman condemned to stay five days. What would she be at the end? I felt a mere wreck. Only two days ago I was in full health and vigour. It was no absolute cruelty, only the cruel system, and meagre and uneatable diet, the lack of sufficient moisture to make up for loss by perspiration, two almost sleepless nights, "hard labour" under the circumstances. Before me lay home and friends, a loving welcome, good food, sympathy and rest. What about my poor sisters? "I have nobody, nobody in the wide world, I wish I had," said the poor soul next to me, new to such treatment. A good-looking woman beyond had never been in before. I shuddered for those I should leave behind, new to such conditions.

Is this the treatment England gives in Christ's name to His destitute poor? What if some are "sinners[?]"[20] He chose such, and "Inasmuch as ye did it not to one of the least of these my brethren, ye did it not to me."[21] My heart burned within me, Thank God for every bit of suffering, that I may bring home the truth. A public newspaper states, "The Guardians only hear *ex-parte* statements, those of the men themselves." Supposing they speak true?

During the afternoon one poor woman had said, "If only the rich Guardians, and the heavy ratepayers, knew how their money was spent, and how us poor things had to live, they wouldn't allow it." They felt bitterly the irony of so many officials being paid to order them about and get the maximum work out of them, while they were practically starved. The conclusion of the whole matter is: the more rigidly the system is enforced in its entirety, the more hardly it presses on the destitute poor, while it makes no provision for their need. It is not even preventive, and it is costly. Morning dawned slowly as I pondered, and the welcome call came. My neighbour slept, her face drawn in sleep as if with suffering, her profile and grey tossed hair as she lay on her back, as the easiest position, and appeal of sorrow to the eye of the Watcher of men. She woke with a start and moan.

No help for it. "You women all get up, be quick now; be quick and hurry up, Granny." Short, sharp, decisive marching orders. Sick and shivering, with aching head and body sore from head to foot, I did my best to hide any sign of illness that might come between me and liberty. My companion suffered also from violent headache, neuralgic pains, and an aggravated cold. "Pollie's" face was drawn and tired. No one complained much. I heard only one grumble at having to wash an already smarting face with soft soap. One produced a precious bit of white soaps and lent it—a kindly deed. Granny got under weigh with many a groan, very slowly. "Hurry up, women; three of you have not put your boards up. Now then, Granny, don't be all day." We will pardon her, for she has been on duty all night, and is also tired; but surely the woman

20. Higgs did not use a question mark here.

21. A re-wording of Matthew, 25:10.

who said, "Come, now, you needn't be so knotty with us," spoke
true. We had little chance or time to speak much. It was only the
early cold grey dawn of a winter morning, but already the message
had come up that husbands were waiting. Gruel and bread for the
fourth time! No one going out did more than pretend to eat it,
some pocketed the bread. Neither my friend nor I could have
touched it if you had offered us a sovereign, my soul loathed it so
I could hardly bear to look at it.

The poor woman condemned vainly hoped for release; she
wept, but this only hardened the officer. She was not to be "come
over" this way. "Don't you believe her." Granny must swathe her
poor old legs and do, she had better get into the workhouse. We
had to leave them to their fate. I shall never forget the last few
moments of waiting. A raging passion for freedom took possession
of me. I dared not ask to go a moment before I was ordered to for
fear lest it should be construed as "impudence." May be I wrong
the officer, but she interpreted so easily any appeal as interference.
Oh to be free! Oh, to lie down anywhere under God's free sky, to
suffer cold and hunger at His hand. "It is better to fall into the
hand of God than the hand of man." We both agreed we would
face a common lodging-house and its pests, or even the danger of
prison for "sleeping out," rather than pass again through such an
experience. Do I exaggerate? It must be felt to be realised.

At length we escaped with "Pollie," leaving Granny and the
victim with the newcomers. It was very early, and about two hours
lay between us and succour; my friend was almost too tired to walk.
But the free air was round us. Thank God for a fine morning! We
are "on the road," and nothing in front can be so bad as what lies
behind. We are tramps and "mouchers," we can beg, for we need
pity, sing for our living, sell bootlaces and turn over the money; even
if we steal, prison only awaits us, and it cannot be worse; our companions who have tried it prefer it. One thing we could not do—we
could not at that moment work for an honest living. It is physically
impossible. By hook or by crook one or two restful nights must be
put between us and the past. Strength to work has gone. One might
perhaps tramp, for the air is reviving, and people are kind to a wayfarer. Do you wonder at our national tramp manufactories?

For this is what it amounts to. An obsolete system, adapted to
the times when population was stationary, is supposed to meet the
needs of a population necessarily increasingly fluid. Labour shifts
from place to place where it is needed. Individuals drop out or are

thrust out. There is never, on any one night, in our great centres of populations, sufficient provision for this ebb and flow. The houseless and the homeless are a great multitude, as sheep without a shepherd. Day by day they make a moving procession. The decent man or woman who is stranded joins them, at first with the honest intention of gaining a livelihood. If it cannot be obtained what is he to do? The common lodging-house can never be a sufficient provision for this need. It would never pay the private owner to provide the maximum number of beds required. Our friend "Pollie" grumbled that in many lodging-houses the price of a decent bed was 6d., and "then you could not be sure it was clean."

What is needed may take away the breath of a conservative public. It is nothing less than the entire sweeping away of the tramp ward, and the substitution of Municipal Lodging-houses, coupled with strict supervision of all private ones. The maximum need with regard to sleeping accommodation on any one night in a great city must be met. Shelters, sanitary and humane, not charitable institutions, but simply well managed "working people's hotels" must be run privately and supplemented publicly, providing accommodation for everyone. To meet destitution, these should be supplemented by "Relief Stations" on the German plan, where supper, bed and breakfast can be earned.[22] Freedom need not be interfered with beyond demanding work sufficient to pay. Payment should be on the graduated ticket system. The tramp proper hates work. If once a national system sufficient for destitution were inaugurated, the man who would not work could be penalised. A Labour Colony is his natural destination. The classification of workhouses and their adaptation to various necessarily destitute classes, such as epileptics, feeble-minded and the aged, might remove much destitution, placing it under

22. In Germany, public relief was supported at the local level from the late 19th century onward. Such public support for the indigent was particularly important during the economic downturns of 1894-95, 1901-03, and 1907-09. It was not punitive its in application but had the objective of moving the recipient toward gainful employment and independence; Hennock, E.P. *The Origin of the Welfare State in England and Germany, 1850-1914: Social Policies Compared.* Cambridge: Cambridge University Press, 2007, especially pp. 308-10.

humane conditions. But the immediate and crying need is for the abolition of an old, inhumane and insufficient provision for the suppression of vagrancy, in favour of adequate provision for the modern fluidity of labour, coupled with honourable relief of destitution, neither degrading nor charitable.

Chapter Nine

The Spike
by Everard Wyrall
London: Constable, 1909

"The Spike" is the tramp's name for the Casual Ward.[1]

CHAPTER I
I SET OUT

I HAVE been told that the experiences related in the following pages read more like romance than actual truths. I have been contradicted point-blank by those who had ends to serve by contradiction; that was inevitable. Also, many who have no idea of the manner in which a man enters a casual ward and what he frequently has to go through before he gets out again, have frankly said that such things are impossible. I thought so too until I experienced them; indeed, I scarcely could believe at times that I was really in civilised England.

---

1.   This was Wyrall's own annotation.

It is an undisputable fact that our methods of dealing with all questions relating to the care of "Weary Willie"[2] and the thousands of paupers thrown upon the rates, are woefully behind the times; this also was very apparent to me. Much of what I have written appeared in one of our most influential London daily papers,[3] and I am able through the courtesy of the editor to re-publish them almost as they appeared in print.

If any further doubts as to the veracity of my statements exist in the mind of the reader, attention is drawn to the following paragraph which headed the articles as published:

"The following article is based on the *actual experiences of* the writer, who has for the time being become a tramp, his object being to examine the conditions of work-houses, and the people who frequent them."

*　　*　　*　　*　　*

One damp grey January morning, before London was properly awake and the milkman had delivered the last of his tin cans, I crept out of a warm and comfortable bed, with a none too inviting task before me. For it was the morning on which I had decided to set out on my first tramp *as a casual*.

On the floor in the centre of the room—they were hardly clean enough to occupy a chair—lay a pile of ragged and dingy clothes. A pair of battered boots and a greasy tweed cap completed the outfit, the strangest it had ever been my lot to own.

First I drew on a pair of socks—they also had been respectable at one period of their existence—then in turn a ragged vest, a flannel shirt, a pair of worn trousers and a threadbare coat; the dilapidated boots, a yellow scarf twisted coster-fashion round my throat, and the tweed cap completed my attire. I have forgotten to mention that I had not shaved for four days.

---

2. "Weary Willy" and "Tired Tim" were tramp characters created by Tom Browne and featured in a comic strip published in *Chips* between 1896 and 1910. The name and persona of "Weary Willy" were later adopted by the famous circus clown Emmett Kelly.

3. The *Daily Express*.

Opening the door gently for fear of rousing the house, I took one last look round my cosy room, then stole quietly down the stairs into the street. For the time being I was homeless and friendless, with just enough money in my pocket to take me to the outskirts of London and to provide myself with a good meal, should I find myself in difficulties. A thin rain had begun to fall, and it was one of those dismal mornings frequently experienced in London which seem to affect everything and everybody; and although I had no apprehension of anything serious, yet I felt that the weather was an unpleasant prelude to my voluntary tramp.

As I stepped into the street, it would be difficult to exactly describe my feelings. I immediately wanted to hide myself, and yet I was all enthusiasm for the task I had undertaken. Nevertheless as I strode through the streets with the tweed cap drawn over my eyes, I felt for all the world like—well, just as I wanted to look—a poor wretched being, one of the submerged. It was my rôle for the nonce, and the more I looked the part the better it would please me. I had yet to learn how deeply one can be made to feel poverty.

The streets were as yet but thinly populated, mostly by night-walkers—men who had walked about all night, homeless—and tired policemen who hung about the corners. So I too thought I would hang about. I wanted to feel the first pang. I had not long to wait. Soon the thoroughfares became busy with bright-eyed clerks hurrying to their City offices, keen-eyed shopmen stepped over the wet roadway, smart typists hurried along to 'bus or "tube." And from these came the *first pang*. For I noticed they drew away from me as, with bent head, I slouched along the pavement. Immediately they seemed to shun me, I had a wild desire to run after them and tell them I was not what they thought I was— then I remembered. But then it was that my eyes were opened to the exceeding bitterness of poverty.

When I recovered from that first shock, I began to make my way towards London Bridge Station. But still the continued gaze of the public took effect on me. I could not get rid of the desire to hide myself. Then I reflected that by so doing I should miss much of what I had come out to seek. So I ground my teeth and strode on, trying hard not to notice the way they edged me to the kerb-stone and thrust me into the gutter. Once I thought I would take a 'bus, but I fought against such a weakness, and trudged on. What a boon the night must be to those poor homeless souls who find themselves shunned as I was on that dreary morning. Darkness! It hides many sins—but is also kind and covers up tatters and rags.

At last I reached the station, but even then I found I was the object of much suspicion. Policemen, porters, passengers—everybody in fact—seemed to look me through and through as if I had no right to be there. Pity lingered mostly in the eyes of little children. No one in this life has a better knowledge of your true Pharisee[4] than the beggar in rags.

I have forgotten to state that I carried a brown paper parcel containing a writing tablet, a pencil, a map, and a sweater: the latter to don should I elect to sleep beneath a hedge or in the corner of a friendly barn, for the time of year was mid-winter.

At the end of what seemed an age, my train steamed into the station, and making a dive for an empty carriage, I took a corner seat farthest from the platform, thankful indeed to get away from the suspicious scrutiny to which I had been subjected.

When I left my little room I had had many qualms as to whether I looked the part sufficiently. My journey to the station had dispelled any such doubts. If it had not then, the following incident, which happened soon after I had taken my seat in the carriage, would have sufficiently convinced me as to the disreputable figure I cut.

The train was on the point of starting, the guard had already blown his whistle, when the door of the carriage was thrown violently open, and a man in a silk hat and frock coat made ready to jump in. Suddenly his eyes rested upon me—the door swung to with a slam, and I was alone.

Twenty minutes later the train ran into the suburban station which I had selected as the real starting point of my tramp.

CHAPTER II
"THE NIGHT COMETH—"[5]

AS I stepped away from the station my spirits began to rise. I have always been fond of walking, both for pleasure and

---

4.   The Pharisees were a Hebrew sect criticized by Jesus (Luke, 11: 37-54 and Matthew, 23:1-36). The term has since carried implications of hypocrisy and dishonesty.

5.   "I must work the works of him that sent me, while it is day: the night cometh, when no man can work." John, 9:4.

exercise. And now that I was through the first dreaded part of my task I began to revel in the open countryside: houses became less frequent as I left the station behind me. But the rain still fell heavily and my clothes and the parcel I carried suffered accordingly.

At various intervals along the road, I passed, both coming and going, men of the stamp I was imitating. Sometimes they looked at me with a questioning expression on their none too clean faces, but I did not stop—it was too early as yet to slacken my pace. I had previously marked on the map I carried, a little country town where I imagined there must be a workhouse, and I had still ten miles to cover.

I wondered what time it was, and after enquiring from a passing van-man, found to my astonishment that it was but ten o'clock; I had imagined it to be at least noon. Therefore, I took shelter in a small plantation, hoping that the rain would soon cease.

Presently the clouds lifted slightly and the rain became less heavy, so that I once more stepped on to the road and continued my journey.

On the way I munched a few biscuits and a thick piece of bread and cheese. I thought I should get a decent feed in the workhouse, though I knew I should have to work for it.

After two more hours I began to near the little village of C---: this was apparent from the number of houses by the wayside.

But no sooner did I come into close touch with my fellow-beings than feelings of shame and a sense of being "out of it" came back to me, and I hurried through the one little street without a pause, though I was almost gasping for a drop of water. As soon as I was clear of the village and beyond the sight of the nearest house, I looked about for a sheltering tree, and standing as close to it as I could, for the rain had once more begun to fall heavily, drew out my map and took stock of my surroundings. I found I had still five miles to go, and I calculated the hour as two o'clock. As I leant against the friendly tree, I heard a slow, uneven tread upon the wet roadway. Then a bent and limping figure came into view—that of a man walking evidently with pain. I might have struck up a conversation with him, for he passed quite close to the tree behind which I stood, but as yet I was shy of strangers, and knowing that at night I should have to make the acquaintance of many I did not know, preferred to do my little tramping alone.

When he had disappeared in the distance I again ventured out, and without undue hurrying made my way towards D--- where I imagined I should find a workhouse.

By now I began to feel tired. The country air and the fact that I had been on my feet since early morning told on my strength. I longed for a drink of water. I knew I should have to go through one more village before I reached D--- and I determined to ask at a house or shop for a drink. Perhaps the reader might wonder why I felt thus shy knowing that my disguise was of my own choosing. But the truth was I knew I was in such a disreputable state that I unconsciously exaggerated it to myself: also it is not easy to permit oneself to be taken for a member of that great family—the submerged. As yet I had spoken to one man only—the van-man in the early morning. And I was pleased to find that the village I was just entering was almost deserted; the rain I suppose kept them all indoors. Looking about, I saw one tiny general shop, and summoning up courage opened the door and asked the woman who apparently kept it if she could give me a glass of water. After eyeing me suspiciously, she called out to someone to bring a glass of water. I suppose she thought she dared not leave me alone in the shop. Thanking her, with I suppose more genuineness than she generally experienced from such a class as she imagined me to be (for her stony features somewhat relaxed themselves), I hurriedly left the little shop and continued my journey. My next stop would be a long one.

Night had begun to fall and already the street lamps were turned up when I entered D---. A lad was coming towards me, and from him I enquired the way to the place I wanted.

"Tommy, where's the workhouse?"

The lad looked up with a dubious expression on his face—first at my unshaven chin, then down at my torn and muddy trousers, and a wave of pity swept over his face. The silent sympathy of little children is very sweet.

He still seemed puzzled, and I repeated the question.

"Keep straight on, s-sir." He had to blurt the last word out. He could not come to a compromise between clothes and voice.

"Keep straight on." What a travestied phrase that is to the poor outcast. They tell you anything when you are in rags.

By now the water had begun to ooze from my boots. The rain had long ago penetrated my thin overcoat, and had commenced a frontal attack on my undercoat. The water trickled down my face.

I trudged on, almost worn out, and cold and hungry. Heavens! I fancy such a life all the year round!

It is comfortable to contemplate the workhouse from before a roaring fire with tea and toast at one's elbow. In front of it, without a farthing in your pocket, your scanty clothing in rags and these drenched with rain, homeless and friendless, its proportions are considerably magnified. And this was how I felt, for all at once a grim, weird mass of stone loomed up out of the darkness. There was no mistaking it: it was the workhouse. I was on the very threshold of what I came out to seek. What would happen to me? I had no fears, but a certain feeling, born within us all, of hatred of the unclean and dirty, rose up within me, and I shuddered as I passed in at the iron gate. At that moment the place appeared horrible to contemplate; but it offered relief, held out prospects of food and warmth, and somewhere to lay my tired limbs.

I entered the gates alone!

*   *   *   *   *

In a whitewashed outhouse, on to a seat which ran round three sides of it, the fourth forming the doorway to which there was no door, I sank down exhausted. Under such conditions one might be forgiven for wanting to die. Then on the gravel path, which swam in water, the fall of heavy feet reached my ears.

"Is this where yer waits, matey?" Two tramps poked their noses into the shed. I said I thought it was, and they came and sat down by me. It was my first contact with the genuine article.

When one of them began to shrug his shoulders I edged away: when he rubbed his nearly-bald head I shrank still further away: when the other wheezed out a consumptive cough I got up and walked up and down the shed.

For an hour we waited there, soaked to the skin, shivering and hungry. Once a weird-looking individual came to look at us; I was told he was the "tramp-major"—an inmate whose duty it was to look after Casuals. Then he went away, and again we contemplated each other in gloomy silence. Again the sound of footsteps. A short, stout man with a bullet-shaped head stood in the doorway.

"I suppose you men understand you'll be kept for work all day to-morrow?" He had a way of firing off his words like penny crackers.

"Yes." In our condition we should have given a similar answer a thousand times over. Hunger sometimes makes men foolish. I wondered what the poor wretch who could not work, who had no strength, would have done. Surely the authorities would not have turned him out into the rain! But I was to find that out!

The man disappeared, reappearing a few moments later on the further side of a tiny box-shaped window built in to one of the walls. Through that window the inmates had to hand over their only belongings in this world.

"Name?"

"Age?"

"Trade?"

"Where from?"

"Where to?"

"Hand over your belongings."

One of the men handed in a little rain-sodden bundle, the outer cover of which had at one time been a respectable handkerchief.

The second man, from the pocket of one of the three coats he wore, produced a small canvas bag.

We were then searched.

"Follow me!" And the man turned to the door of the outhouse.

The air bit keenly as we stepped outside and followed him. How we shivered!

He stopped in front of the door of a low heavy-looking building. The tiny slits of windows were iron-barred. They looked like prison cells.

As if we were loathsome, he stepped aside for us to enter, came in after us and locked the door.

As the key turned in the door I longed to tear it out—too late. The first moments of the loss of one's liberty can scarcely be written down; the soul falls back upon itself, that is all.

The dim gas threw weird fantastic shadows on the four walls of the casual ward, for such I deemed it to be. The flooring was half of red brick, half of wood, the latter in the form of a daïs. Three stone steps led up from the ward to a brick passage, on each side of which were a number of small doors fitted with bolts.

In a corner of the ward stood the baths. The exquisite tyranny of "baths" is widely known,[6] also the effects which those who are forced to undergo them frequently feel. I felt sick at heart at the prospect of having to enter the one which was evidently to be mine.

"Strip—you men! Tie your clothes up in bundles, and make haste in."

I suppose we were keeping the good man from his own cosy fireside.

Thank heavens the water was tepid; but I shuddered as I used the small piece of soap and a grey towel, which had evidently done good service. But in a few minutes it was all over. There are, by the way, no doors to the bath-rooms; the officials watch the bathers in order to see that they really do wash.

(A case was reported in the papers not so long ago in which a sailor had been brought up before a magistrate, and charged, because he had refused to perform his task; he refused because he had been made to wash in a bath the water in which *had been used by three men*.)

As I crept out of the bath a woefully thin cotton shirt was thrown to me and to each of my companions. We were then ordered to pick up our bundles, and follow the dour man down the cold stone passage; that we were barefooted, and had just come from a warm bath, did not matter. *What* matters where the poor casual is concerned!

Outside some of the doors little bundles of clothes were already laid; loud snores and muttered oaths told the remainder of the story.

A door was unlocked and thrown open in front of me. I was told to place my clothes on the floor outside, and enter. I did do; but almost started back at the forbidding prospect in front of me. A low wooden bench, four evil-looking blankets, a hunch of bread, all dimly outlined in the fitful glare from the one small gas jet in the centre of the passage outside, and a window a few inches square, iron-barred—good heavens! it was a prison cell!

---

6.   There are several accounts of casual ward baths in this book, with which Wyrall may well have been familiar.

"Make down your bed there!" The voice of the prison warder over the most hardened criminal could not have been more cutting; the difference has yet to be learned by this official. I sank on to the edge of the "bed." He took it as a sign that I was going to lie down; the door slammed, the locks clicked loudly, the bolt shot—and I was alone. The cold brick floor sent an icy chill through my body. As I tried to arrange the well-worn blankets to the best advantage I envied the sentenced thief his straw pallet.

Thousands feel as I did that night, and in their broken-hearted wretchedness seek in prison that relief which should be given them in the place meant for that purpose—the casual ward.

I lay down, but not before I noticed that something hard and white beat every now and then against the tiny barred window. The rain had turned to snow.

For two hours I writhed in agony. The hard boards chafed my body, no matter which way I turned. The closer I drew the thin blankets the more intense the agony became. I fell into a dull stupor. Gradually my senses were slipping from me and I began to dream.

Bang! Bang!! Bang!!! The bottom of my wooden bench shook violently as I sprang up in terror. It still creaked and groaned. What to do I did not know. Then I sat on the bottom of the bed and listened intently; presently I understood. The bench was joined to that in the next cell. When my neighbour moved in "bed" mine moved also. I lay down again, but only to stare into the darkness—for sleep had gone from me—waiting for dawn, each minute seeming like an age. It came at last to the tune of a clanging bell, a bustle of feet, a jingle of keys, and an unlocking of doors. Mine was thrown open.

In the grey morning light I saw the outline of the "tramp-major," his arms full of thick hunches of bread. A piece of the latter was thrust into my hands with an order to "Catch 'old," the door slammed, and I was once more alone to contemplate the meal—and, the coming payment.

CHAPTER III
I PAY THE BILL, AND JOURNEY HOMEWARDS

FOR the space of half an hour I was left alone. Then once more the jingle of keys and the shooting of bolts announced the fact that the time had come to "pay our bills." A sharp voice in the ward called to us to "Come on," and after folding up the four thin blankets and laying them on the wooden bench, I opened the door and went down the stone passage to where the other men had already begun to collect.

In the grey of that winter's morning we formed a group of a dozen men down the centre of the ward. Some of my companions defied description; they can only be written down as "awful." In front of us stood a sour-looking man with the face of a bully and a coward, one who knew he had the whip hand and meant to use it. The thin lips denoted meanness and an uncontrollable temper. The eyes were sleek, cunning and watchful. He was the taskmaster. In his hand he held a long sheet of paper, and at intervals he rapped out the names of the men in front of him.

"John Butler?"

"Here."

"Thomas B---?"—then he looked up. "Hullo! here again, are you—you vagabond? All right!" and a cruel light flashed in his steely eyes.

"Donald McAlister? What's this?" and he bent his eyes closer to the sheet; "Veterinary surgeon? Oh! are you? Where's your certificate? Are you a M.R.C.V.S.?[7] Bit of a come down, ain't it, my beauty? What are you doing here?"

Donald McAlister hung his head and muttered he "didn't know."

Workhouse officials have no respect for "feelings."

Having called the roll, the taskmaster folded the paper and placed it in his pocket.

"Thomas Brown, you are to scrub out the ward and the cells, and move your lazy bones a bit. If I catch you skulking, I'll stop your dinner."

"Dinner" I subsequently found consisted of a tin of hot water, a few ounces of bread and an ounce and a half of cheese.

"You six men will saw timber—a pleasant little job, much too good for the likes of you. You four—follow me."

---

7. Member of the Royal College of Veterinary Surgeons, the standard qualification for this profession.

I was one of the four. I wondered what exquisite piece of devilry he had reserved for us. We walked, or rather slunk behind him
in no pleasant frame of mind, and soon found ourselves in front of
a strongly-built corrugated iron shed. The small windows were
heavily barred, and massive bolts were on the door. But some of
the panes in the window were broken, and through these apertures
the snow blew in in clouds.

Flinging open the door of the shed the taskmaster pointed first
to a number of piles of stones which lay on the ground inside, then
to a close-meshed sieve.

"Each man will break a pile of stones—two hundred-weight—
and pass them through that sieve."

We literally gasped as the enormity and almost impossibility of
the task dawned upon us. The mesh of the sieve was less than a
quarter of an inch; some of the stones were at least twelve inches
in diameter.

When I made this statement in the newspapers indignant letters from workhouse officials were received by the editor, saying
that two-inch sieves were always used. But in this instance it was
not so. I very carefully noted the mesh, knowing that a grave scandal was being committed in forcing the men to break the stones
small enough to pass through the meshes. It was but one of the
many abuses which exist all over the country.

"When you've finished," added the tyrant, "you can go." He
knew the task was well-nigh impossible. "If you don't break them,
I'll 'run you.'" In tramp language, to be "run" is to be handed over
to the police.

With loud protests one of the men started forward:

"I'm an ex-soldier; I've four medals. I've served my country,
and curse me if I'll do it."

With a snarl the taskmaster turned upon him.

"Get on with it, or it'll be the worse for you."

I have forgotten to mention that one of the men was the poor
old man who limped along the road and passed me on the previous day while I was sheltering beneath the tree. He was also one
of those who had been selected to break stones. And now he began
to plead:

"I'm lame in one foot, and can scarcely stand. I'm aching in
every limb. I want to see the doctor. I—," but all to no purpose.
One might just as well have spoken to the stones piled up on the
floor as to that brutal taskmaster.

"Can't see the doctor, he's gone."

"I've a sore arm," said one of the other men, pulling up his tattered coat sleeve showing a long raw scar; "and," pointing to a heavy bar of iron having a square end, "I—."

But the door slammed in his face, and the bolts shot on the outside.

Of the ghastly tasks imposed on the poor casual stone-pounding is the most horrible. For, let it be understood that stone-pounding is entirely different from stone-breaking. Pounding is carried out with long heavy bars of iron having square ends, the length of the bars being about four feet. They are of such a weight that only men in good health can use them properly. By the side of each pounder was a wooden box with an iron bottom. The stones were placed inside of the latter. Then, grasping the pounder with both hands, it was lifted about a foot above the stones and brought down with all the force at one's disposal. Nothing was given to us to protect our eyes, and one sieve had to do service for four.

For half an hour I tried my best to pound those stones, but I seemed to make little or no impression upon them. Then I began to feel a peculiar tingling in the palms of my hands, and my fingers became so sore that it was most painful to grasp the pounder. Finally, blisters put in an appearance, and these breaking, the chafings gave way to blood, which soon began to trickle down my fingers. I do not think my hands were particularly tender, because the hands of the other men were affected in much the same way.

The lame man worked like one demented—smashing, sifting, and piling up the fragments. It was a ghastly task. In his eyes I noticed something suspiciously like a tear, and he often cried out that his back ached. He now and then rubbed his wrinkled face as a sharp chip of stone struck him.

The ex-soldier stood with his hands thrust deep into his trousers pockets surveying his scarcely-begun task. He stood in that attitude for more than half the day, alternately cursing the taskmaster and commiserating with himself. It's a way men have.

The workhouse clock struck four. We had been allowed to cease work between the hours of twelve and one, and "dinner" had been served to us. At the end of that painful hour we were taken back to the shed and again locked in, with many admonitions and warnings.

And now the time had come when we should be judged for what we had done.

The ex-soldier was still grumbling. "I'd like ter break 'is bloomin' neck. It's a disgrace, that's wot it is—jist because I'm poor." And he sat down, but before doing so, slung the sieve to the other end of the shed.

The lame man bent over the few remaining fragments lying at the bottom of the pounding box.

"Thank 'eaven I've nearly done, and that devil can't run me."

He had refused dinner, and had worked all the time. The fear of being "run," and for ever branded as a jail-bird, had taken hold of him.

The man with the sore arm looked at the ex-soldier. "'E can't run yer, mate—why, 'e—" the door opened, and the taskmaster appeared.

The lame man was nearest the door; he was judged first. "Humph! You've nearly done, you can go in."

The poor fellow nearly took to his heels.

"You two men who haven't finished can stay out here 'till it's dark."

He referred to the man with the sore arm and myself.

"You"—to the ex-soldier—"you've refused to do your task, you're one of the lazy ones."

He stepped to the door and beckoned to someone who had hitherto remained out of sight. A blue-uniformed figure stood in the doorway.

"Arrest that man. He is charged with refusing to do the work laid down by the Local Government Board in exchange for 'relief.'"

"Relief! You ---" almost screamed the poor fellow.

"Come quietly, mate," whispered the man in blue. "You'll be better in chokey[8] than in this 'ere 'ole. Chokey's all right compared with this. They deals with yer too summary 'ere."

The ex-soldier was "run."

As he was led away the eyes of the taskmaster gleamed with satisfaction. What a triumph!

My companion and I worked at the stones until it was almost too dark to see the pounding boxes, and then they fetched us back to the casual ward. It was "tea-time."

---

8.   Prison.

The eyes of my half-starved companions, seated in stony silence on the wooden bench which ran round three sides of the ward, glistened at the prospects of warm water and bread. Of such was to be our tea. In one corner of the ward was the drying room, where the clothes of tramps should have been dried, though no one had offered to dry mine. This drying-room was used also as a store-room. Outside the baths were a row of tin wash-hand basins and a pile of enamelled iron mugs, dirty and well-worn; the enamel was to be imagined, not seen.

As we sat gloomily regarding one another a key grated in the lock and the door of the ward was thrown violently open, admitting a queer-looking individual carrying a galvanised iron water-can filled to the brim with hot water. Dressed in yellow corduroys, a black crush hat on his nearly bald head, having but one eye and talking with a peculiar half-idiotic lisp, the "tramp-major" set the can down in the middle of the ward. He was followed by the taskmaster.

Outside the rain had begun to fall again, and the wind hurled itself at the half-opened door. The drops of water beat with a loud noise on the iron roof of the building. It beat also on the dark figure of a man whom I noticed had crept close to the door. I suppose the warm glare of the gas had caught his eye. And perhaps the shuffling sound of feet as the tramps crowded round the man with the can of hot water had also its attractions, for in the half-light I saw how eager was his gaze. His thin lips, blue with cold, were pressed more firmly as he shook the rain from his battered hard hat. A sudden rush of wind pushed the door wide open, and as the tramps gathered round the door of the store-room the man, scarcely knowing what he did, slipped in and took up his stand behind the last of the line. It was not my place to say him "nay," though I knew he would be discovered before long.

The taskmaster stood in the doorway with his arms full of portions of bread. To some of the hungry men he threw pieces of bread as one might a bone to a dog.

"Here—you—and you—and you—and—" The rain-sodden man stood before him. He had almost tossed a piece into the eager outstretched hands of the shivering man. Then he noticed who it was.

"Hullo! What do you want?"

"I want a night's doss, mister."

"You'll have to pound stones—two hundred-weight—and put 'em through the sieve."

"Carn't do that, mister. Truth I can't."

"Oh, why not?"

"Mister, I'm sixty-four." And the poor old man almost broke down.

"Can't help it. Break stones up to seventy years of age. I keep to the law, and that's the law. If you don't like to do it, out you go, or—seven days. Anyhow, get outside until six o'clock. Can't take you in before."

And out into the icy wind and drenching rain the poor wretch crept.

*   *   *   *   *

Silence, broken only by an occasional grunt, reigned in the ward. I was aching and sore in every limb, and my hands were almost raw. Some of the tramps drew their threadbare coats up round their ears, and wrapped themselves in their own gloominess. Others sipped the doles of warm water and munched their few remaining crumbs of bread, or blew down their cold fists and swore loudly, and often.

"They puts us in 'ammicks ter night, mate," ventured my neighbour. I thought anything different from the horrors of the previous night attractive, and hammocks held out a fair prospect of a night's rest. I answered in a monosyllable.

"Come on, you men."

I looked up. The sour-looking taskmaster stood in the door-way. "Go across the path and into that door."

One by one we slunk in and tottered up a few wooden stairs. The door below us slammed, and the locks clicked.

Locks are a great feature in workhouse life. By the light of a match we found we were standing in a small room, down the centre of which was fixed an iron rail.

"You fixes the 'ammick on that rail," they said.

"Yes, but how?"

The match went out. It was the only one we possessed amongst the lot of us. But by the light of that one match I had seen enough of those hammocks—their appearance was quite enough. I made up my mind to sleep on the floor. We groped about for the blankets, and found them laid on the floor in piles of threes. Thin and evil-smelling they were, too. And when we came to count the hammocks we found there were only seven for eleven men. It was a problem we could not solve. Only workhouse officials are able to overcome such difficulties—they ignore them. I sought out a corner of the floor, and taking off my boots and coat, made them into a pillow. Next, I wrapped the blankets round the lower part of my body and laid down to rest. It was something at least to have one's own clothes, for on this night they did not take them from us.

I have said that I laid down to rest. But what a misnomer, for it was one of the most awful nights I have ever experienced, compared with which the agonies of the previous night were as Paradise. I have slept in the open, through rain and in frost, I have laid down in an enemy's country within rifle shot of our foes,[9] but nothing will ever compare with that horrible night. Shut up like dogs in a kennel, all the horrors of degradation forced themselves upon me. Some talked and babbled in their sleep. Others snored so loudly as to draw oaths and execrations from those who tried to lose their senses but could not. The atmosphere was awful! Filthy is a fitter word. The long hours passed but slowly. Not once did I lose my senses; it was all too horrible, too abominable; and even now I find myself shivering at the thought of that dreadful experience. In all that night I heard one real human cry. It came agonised and but softly from a huddled heap that, like me, had preferred the floor—"Oh Heaven!"

I turned my face to the wall. For a few minutes under thirteen hours (I was able to tell the time by a clock which chimed out the hours from a neighbouring church) we were shut up in that room.

But at last the dawn came, and a man entered bearing an armful of thick pieces of bread. He threw the pieces one by one to the huddled heap, and went away again, but not before he had told us that in half an hour we should be free to go our ways.

As we filed out of the door and through the iron gate I had entered so hopefully a little incident happened which shows the tramp's idea of the treatment he received.

---

9.   Wyrall was a second lieutenant in the Army Service Corps during the second Boer War (1899-1902) and was on active service in South Africa. He also served in the First World War and later became a military historian of some note.

The lame old man, as he passed the taskmaster, who stood by the gate watching us out, turned on him like a tiger:

"Look 'ere, mister, if ever I get you outside this 'ere place I'll do fer you."

From that workhouse I got back to Town as quickly as I could; but how I managed it, seeing that the money I hid away behind a post outside the workhouse gates on the night of my "going in" had been found by someone else, and how, wandering in desperation about the streets of that little town, I at last found the editor of a local paper who supplied me with the necessary funds, I shall relate perhaps later. But those details have really not much to do with workhouse life, and therefore I have left them out of the story.

CHAPTER IV
I SET OUT AGAIN

CONTRARY to my expectations, the disagreeable experiences related in the foregoing chapters did not for ever sicken me of the work on which I had entered, for at the end of a week I determined to set out again and test the treatment meted out to the poor casual in other workhouses. Therefore I searched the map for a small country town in an exactly opposite direction to the first place I had visited.

Again, before the day had properly begun in London, I crept out of my comfortable room in Chancery Lane and down the stairs into the street. Again I went through the process of being shunned and pushed into the gutter, but I did not take it so much to heart as in the first instance—suffering hardens as well as quickens. Still I got out of Town as rapidly as I could, and felt more at ease on the highroad to the little country town I intended visiting.

All day I trudged along in the best of spirits, with but a solitary interesting and amusing incident to relieve the monotony of my own company.

Towards the afternoon, when just outside the village of D--- a young lady, on what to me appeared to be a new bicycle, rode by me at a rapid rate. I thought no more (unless it was that she rang her bell a little too vigorously) of her until I rounded a corner, and there before me, with her bicycle propped up against a fence, was the young lady, pumping with all her might (judging from the colour of her cheeks) at the back tyre. As I came abreast of her she turned to me with a perplexed expression on her face and asked if I would pump it for her. Taking the pump from her I soon saw that she was trying to inflate the tyre without having first of all loosened the valve. I pointed this out and she appeared grateful. Soon the tyre was quite hard again, and as I fixed the pump to the machine I heard the jingle of coppers in her hand. To my intense amusement and astonishment (for I had for a moment forgotten my disguise) she asked if I would "accept this," and tried to slide some money into my hand. However, I raised my cap, and without taking the money went on my way as rapidly as possible. A few moments later she passed me, not so much as looking back—but I wondered what she thought?

When within three miles of the town I reconnoitred a small inn by the wayside, and finding that the bar was empty, slipped in and asked the proprietor if I could get a cup of tea. This I was fortunate enough to obtain, and I sat down in a corner waiting for night to come. I had not long to wait, for the time was winter and darkness fell quickly. Then I started out on what was to be my second sojourn in a casual ward.

After a walk of three-quarters of an hour I found myself in front of the "spike." It was a forbidding place to look at, but perhaps the conditions inside would not be as bad as those existing in the last casual ward I had visited. Indeed I devoutly trusted I should have something better than bare boards to lie upon, also I wondered if hot water and bread was to be my diet. These things flashed across my mind as I pressed the electric bell, which connected the locked gate and the porter's lodge of the grim building before me.

A lock creaked, and in the huge door of the now night-clad "spike" a square blotch of light suddenly appeared. A figure stepped across the aperture and hobbled down the pathway towards me, bearing a twinkling lantern. The latter flashed in my face, a key was fitted into the lock, and I walked in.

A strange crippled figure wearing a black hat stared at me out of eyes that gleamed with suspicion, then looking round about him as if fearful of being overheard, he bent towards me.

"Jist you look after the porter, mate, he's a --- 'e'll run yer if 'e can." In a louder voice, obviously for the purpose of being heard, he said: "You'll find the policeman inside."

The policeman! Here was a new phase of pauper life—the policeman.

*   *   *   *   *

He stood inside the square, light-pierced gateway—a spectacle in blue, and silver buttons. His hands were thrust deep into his trouser pockets, while clouds of smoke, drawn from a clay pipe, issued from his mouth. "The arm of the law" appeared to be out for a holiday. For some seconds he regarded me in silence. There was something infinitely amusing in the sight of this big burly "hodge"[10] policeman, and had the circumstances permitted I should have laughed aloud. I think he must have guessed my thoughts, for suddenly he seemed to remember his official might-iness. Out went the clay, and from an inside pocket he drew out a black note-book. His rosy and apparently honest face above that hated black book was an incongruity I could not forgive—and he sank in my estimation.

"Wot's yer name?" I told him, and he wrote my answer down with the air of a State Secretary. I wondered if he could spell.

"'Ow old? Wot's yer trade? Where're yer goin'?"

I said that I was a clerk out of work, came from London, and was journeying to Portsmouth.

"'Ow long out of work? Carn't yer git work? Why carn't yer git work?" and his bright eyes twinkled suspiciously. "Ever been ter chokey?"

To these enquiries I replied as shortly as possible. My answer to the last question seemed to surprise him—I had *not* "been ter chokey!" However, he still persevered, asking questions which seemed to me quite unnecessary, and I had a hard task at times not to give my identity away. I could only imagine he wanted me to make some sort of admission which would entitle him there and then to march me off to the aforesaid "chokey." But I suppose I disappointed him, for presently he tried a different method. He

---

10. An abbreviation of the name "Roger" and a patronizing term for a rustic or agricultural laborer. See Freeman, Mark. "The Agricultural Labourer and the 'Hodge' Stereotype, c.1850-1914." *Agricultural History Review*, 49, (Part 2, 2001), pp. 172-86.

(metaphorically) got up on to the judicial bench, and assuming the bearing of a circuit judge, asked if I had "ever been prosecuted?" My answer to this was apparently not to his satisfaction, for his ludship had to descend upon himself and re-light his clay—the drop was tremendous.

All the while the porter of whom I had been warned stood looking on. He was a sharp-featured man, dressed in a dark uniform and a black peak-cap. His eyes gleamed with suspicion and mistrust.

"Suppose you know you'll have to break three bushels of stones in the morning?" he said, in a voice obviously meant to terrify me.

I knew it only too well. My hands still carried traces of the stone-pounding in that other place; the blisters were scarcely healed.

The "hodge" policeman whispered to the porter. I was told to go out of the gate and take the first turning on the right and wait at the second white gate. With many misgivings I went down the pathway, out of the gate, and turning the corner as directed, soon found myself in front of a large white gate, spiked at the top. I have since wondered why they let me out once I had entered, and the only reason I can think of is that that method was adopted in order to give me a chance of running away if I did not like the prospects of the task. Then of course the officials could not be blamed for turning me away—a very subtle scheme.

No sooner had I arrived at the door than I found the policeman awaiting me. He was now fully dressed in a belt and helmet. I began to have visions of a prison cell after all. He held the lantern in his hand. A quick step on the gravel path and the porter appeared, carrying a huge bunch of keys.

"Come this way." A door was unlocked, and I was led into a small stone-paved and stone-walled building. I have been careful in my tramps to notice every detail.

"Hand over your belongings." I replied I had nothing. On a small table were already half-a-dozen bundles.

I was then searched. It was a grim picture, and one which would have astonished many who believe in the efficiency and humanity of the present Poor Laws. Both the policeman and the porter "went through" my pockets. Their hands were passed down the sleeves of my coat, and even my cap was taken off and examined minutely. The corners of my waistcoat and the tops of my socks received similar attention.

Need poor men be treated in this way? Is it not enough degradation to have to seek relief, without being treated as a criminal? What right had these men to feel in my pockets? I was not a dangerous criminal. I had entered the workhouse of my own free will, and had done nothing that could entitle the law to lay its hands upon me. It is sheer brutality to kick a man when he is down, and the treatment I have described meted out to really decent men, who have been compelled to seek a night's shelter in the casual ward, is a disgrace to the country. One cannot be surprised that these officials are sometimes struck by the men whom they would treat as if they were the scum of the earth.

The searching operations over I was told to follow the porter. We went out of the door and crossed the courtyard, where I was handed over to the care of another individual—a semi-lunatic he seemed to me. I gathered that he was the "tramp-major." I particularly wish to lay stress on the fact that in almost every case I found the "tramp-major" to be either a semi-lunatic, a cripple or with some physical ailment; usually he was deformed. My suppositions are that they are selected from the inmates for this work because they *are* deformed and maimed in speech—they cannot then tell tales.

And so I followed this individual to my incarceration.

CHAPTER V
TWO MEN AND A BOY

I HAD just crept out of the dingy stone bath and had begun to rub myself down with a towel, which had already been used many times, when I heard a voice outside the ward.

"There's a man, a woman and a kid at the gate!"

My heart leapt. I had long wanted to know how children were treated in the casual ward. During my ablutions I was watched by the porter, who, when I had crept out of the dirty water, told me to tie up my clothes in a bundle, and then retired. I did as directed, and stood shivering in the cold, waiting for someone to bring me a shirt to take the place of my own. None came, and when I called out, a voice answered, "Put yer own on, mate." I needed no second invitation. Then the tramp-major appeared at the door. I have described his appearance already. In his hands he carried a lantern, a hunch of bread, and a mug of hot water. The bread and water formed my "supper." He said something I could not understand, but I supposed he wanted me to follow him. And bare-footed, over the brick floor, across a stone passage, into the brick ward, I did so. What a sight met my eyes! A row of tarred boxes—horse-boxes they resembled—with a tiny platform in each, which was to do duty as bed. They were built next to one another, five on one side of the ward, five on the other, *vis-à-vis*. There could be no such thing as privacy—an occupant of one of the boxes could see the man opposite. The platform in each box was about eighteen inches from the floor. All had been tarred, and I saw (and later felt) that the corners had not been swept out for a considerable time. Three greasy blankets were then given to me, and I was left alone. Luckily, I found that I was the only inhabitant of that ward, though in a room next door I could hear others. Harsh treatment, I suppose, accounted for the empty boxes. It was a great boon to me to be able to use my own clothes. Therefore, untying the bundle, I pulled on my socks and trousers, and making my coat into a pillow with my boots beneath it, covered my body with my overcoat and my legs with the three clammy blankets, and so lay down. But I wanted to see the man and the child, if the latter should be a boy. If a girl, I suppose she would be locked up with her mother, and Heaven alone knows what they would do with the latter.

Soon, by the distant slamming of doors, the sound of rushing water and a noise of bustle, I imagined the man to be going through the process of bathing. I was not wrong, for presently the door of the ward opened and a man entered, followed by a small boy. I raised myself stealthily on my elbow. I wanted to see the lad.

"'E flashed the bloomin' lantern in our faces, just as if we wos convicts, didn't 'e?"

"That 'e did."

The thin, delicate-looking lad, whose face told its own tale of hunger and exposure, was altogether a queer little bundle of humanity. Fair hair hung in tangles about his ears. A pair of bell-bottom pants, one leg slit up almost to the knee, both ragged at the bottom, hung about his thin legs, which peeped out at various places. Above the pants he wore a threadbare coat, and on his head a grimy cap.

"Feelin' sort o' bloke, that porter," said the man, sarcastically. From which I gathered that the porter, who had probably searched him as he had me, lacked sentiment of any kind. The man was a big burly fellow, black-chinned and attired in the dress of a travel-ling tinker. He, too, carried a hunch of bread and a tin mug of hot water, but I noticed the lad had nothing. Presently, however, the tramp-major entered the ward bearing in his hand a mug of some-thing hot, and handed it to the lad with a grunt which might have meant anything.

From my horse-box I could hear "Ah's" and "Oh's" as the poor little fellow gulped the warm stuff. I heard the father say it was broth. Then the voice of the lad was raised in entreaty for father to "'ave some," but this the man resolutely refused to do.

"Father" then prepared to "make down" the bed, They had decided to sleep together, as the night was cold. They would thus have six blankets between them.

What a terrible place for this poor child! What a beginning! During the time they were undressing and arranging the blankets, in fact, from the time he entered the ward, not a curse nor a muttered oath passed the lips of the man. In his own rough way he did not want to hurt the ears of his child. Poverty and hardship had not robbed him of fatherly love. I respected that man.

They lay down together. Through the long night—they always seem longer when the punishment is great—I heard little expressions of pain and discomfort from the boy. How his poor lit-tle limbs must have ached in that horrible box! Frequently I heard him twisting and turning about, as I lay awake staring up at the whitewashed ceiling—longing for morning.

It came at last, and with it the sound of a key in the door. They had brought us "breakfast." For the lad there was a mug of gruel, for us the usual water and bread. They have better food in prison. The boy found the gruel too salt, and would not eat it, so that his father finished it for him, while the lad took some of my bread and a drink from my tin mug.

Clang! Clang!! Clang!!! The bell struck on our ears, which told that the time of reckoning had come. The lad looked up anx-iously at his father, who turned away and muttered something I could not catch.

The door was opened, and the porter entered. In his hand was the dreaded list. I wondered what was to be my lot.

"John ---?"

"That's me," said the tinker.

"Come along!"

He went like a lamb. It is wonderful how hunger and poverty tame some men. In the arena the tinker could have broken every bone in that porter's body.

As the father went out the lad stepped forward to follow him, but he was ordered to stay where he was. I waited for the porter to call my name, but for some reason or other he did not do so, and went away.

"Is father gone to break stones?" I had no words for the lad, I could only pity him in silence. We sat down together on the edge of one of the tarred boxes, and he told me something of his story— a sad one it was too.

Crash! Crash!! Crash!!! the sharp ring of metal on stone struck our ears. The lad jumped up.

"Is that father?" The pinched white face looked up into mine as the ring of the iron floated through the ward window. The man was paying for two nights' rest in a tarred box, a few ounces of dry bread, a pint or so of hot water and the loan of three greasy blankets.

As I looked at the frail little form before me I wondered if they would impose a task upon him, also what had become of his mother. The prescribed tasks for women are many. Oakum-picking is one of them. This punishment tears the skin from the fingers, and makes the hands almost unfit for any other kind of work.

The door opened, and the porter beckoned to me with a "Come on." I patted the lad on the shoulder and went out.

The workhouse authorities had decided not to make me perform the task—they were "going to give me a chance," so the porter said. But I have my own ideas as to why I was not allowed to enter that stone-breaking shed.

As I accompanied the porter to the gates I asked him what would be done with the boy. He replied that he would remain shut up all day in the ward, but I could get no other information.

With a parting warning I was almost thrust through the open gates, and I was free to journey back to London. As I sat in the train I thought of those three—the man, the woman and the child. What a terrible existence! How hopeless!

CHAPTER VI
I SET OUT A THIRD TIME—IN LONDON

THERE is one workhouse, at least, in London notorious for its harsh treatment of the casual. And I selected this particular "spike" for the purpose of testing the task.

The appearance of my former experiences in print had raised a storm of controversy. Scarcely anything I wrote remained unquestioned, and the letters displayed an extraordinary ignorance, on the part of the public, as to the actual methods of dealing with casuals. Were it possible to have full particulars of the method adopted by each local authority in England, it would undoubtedly be found that some at least were more fit for barbaric ages than modern life. But the subtle cruelty of the taskmasters is a scandal, which should be done away with at once.

Therefore, when I set out to visit this London ward, I determined to have a witness, and selected for that purpose one of the staff of the ---, a morning paper.

In accordance with my fixed plans, I spent a few days at home after my last country tramp, then I once more allowed my beard to grow, and arranged a meeting with my companion at a little office in Fleet Street.

It was arranged that we should journey together until within a short distance of the workhouse, and then separate and enter one after the other in order not to arouse suspicion.

About eight o'clock we set out, selecting the Embankment as the route to the --- "Spike." Rags were new to my companion, and although he did not say much, I gathered that he was going through much the kind of thing I experienced when I set out on my first tramp, though the kindly night sheltered him, and I had to face the glare of day. For some time we tried to find the dreaded place, until at last we were bound to ask a policeman to direct us. He eyed us suspiciously and suggested that we should go to the police station for full particulars—a thing we certainly had not the slightest intention of doing. However, we managed to find the place, and then leaving my companion waiting round the corner (for we had tossed up as to who should enter first), I went forward and pulled the bell. A light shone over the gate, on which in very large letters the words "Casual Ward" were painted. The clanging bell echoed again and again. The door swung open almost without sound. "Am I too late?" I had to say something, and indeed, as I saw at a glance that the waiting-place was unoccupied, I began to fear I should be turned away.

"Sit over there," was all the reply I received. On one side of the stone-paved hall were rows of wooden forms, opposite the porter's office and window. The porter, a sour-looking man, went back to his writing. I wonder why it is that porters of casual wards are always more or less disagreeable in aspect! It would do no harm surely to treat the poor men, who place themselves in their power, with a little kindly attention and perhaps a cheerful word! Such things would go a very long way, but now, the casual looks upon all porters of "spikes" as his sworn enemies. With one exception I found their manner domineering and unnecessarily rough. They should have been placed in charge of cattle, not men. In memory of that one exception I wear on my watch-chain two pennies, given to me when I left the ward, to help me on my way. It is the *one* bright remembrance I have of a dark and miserable period.

As I sat trying to imagine what would happen next a violent clang at the bell startled me out of my reverie. It was my companion.

We had, of course, settled that we were not to recognise one another nor communicate in any way.

The porter went to the door and swung it open. "Sit over there." I wondered if he had learned that phrase with his alphabet. For fully twenty minutes he went on with his writing, and the only disturbers of that grim silence were the voices and merry laughter of passers-by.

"Come 'ere, one of you." At last the inquisition was to begin.

"What's yer name?"

"Who are you?"

"Where d'yer sleep last night?"

"Where 'ave you been living?" My companion feigned a low and dismal voice: he had elected to be questioned first.

"Well, you'll be detained two nights and a day, will have to take a bath and be searched, and break half a ton of granite." Half a ton of granite!!!

I saw him wince, and well he might. But he accepted, though his voice as he answered quavered slightly.

Half a ton of granite—not stone!!! I wondered if I should ever be able to do it. It was navvies' work, and difficult at that. But the porter's little joke was reserved for me—at my expense. I answered his questions in the voice I habitually assumed, then he wanted to know where I was going and what I wanted.

I said I was "looking for a job—I wanted work."

His eyes shone with a twinkle, by no means kind, as he replied, "Work? You'll get it—in the morning." With that parting shot he came out of his tiny office and went down the passage, leaving me to resume my seat on the form by my companion. The latter, in an undertone, attracted my attention. "I can't do it," he said. "I shall have to tell them who I am." But I reminded him that the honour of his paper was at stake, and he recovered immediately. The sound of rushing water proclaimed that the baths were being filled for our benefit.

As I stood shivering and rubbing myself down I noticed the porter outside "going through" my clothes. I inwardly wished him joy of his task. I then made a move towards my own shirt, but that luxury was not to be mine. A blue cotton shirt was handed to me with directions to "Put that on." I particularly noticed the condition of the garment, and from the fact that the sleeves were even then turned up, proclaiming the fact that they had been too long for the last wearer, came to the conclusion that it had not been washed since it had been worn on a previous occasion. A fine method of spreading disease! As I stood trying vainly to find the buttons I chanced to look at the wall, and noticed a printed sheet, hung in such a position as to attract immediate attention. I stepped closer, and then saw it was a list of convictions of men who had refused to do their tasks, or had in some way displeased the work-house authorities. One read as follows:—"For refusing to perform his task—ten months."[11] I wondered what kind of man he had been to deserve ten months, also who the magistrate was who had convicted him. Surely one who had no idea of the brutal task which

---

11. Under the terms of the Pauper Inmates Discharge and Regulation Act of 1871 (34&35 Vict., c.108) and the Casual Poor Act of 1882 (45&46 Vict., c.36), a workhouse inmate who refused to perform the prescribed work task, or who absconded, was to be deemed "an idle and disorderly person" and dealt with under the terms of the Vagrancy Act of 1824, which could include a term of imprisonment. See above, pp. 14–18.

had been set the poor fellow. Perhaps he had refused to be treated as a criminal! The history of his conviction would be interesting!

"Tie your clothes up in a bundle!"

We did as we were told.

"Now *you* go to number twenty-six, and *you* to number twenty-eight." As the cells on one side of the passage leading out of the bath-room were even and those on the other side odd, my cell and that of my companion were next to one another. As we tramped barefooted down the brick floor we passed, outside the other cells little bundles of clothing, some tied up with an old scarf, others with string.

*   *   *   *   *

I sat on the side of the bed trying my best to consume a thick slice of brown bread and a mug of gruel. I gave the latter up, but managed to dispose of some of the bread. I hid the remainder beneath the wooden bench. My meals in casual wards had been invariably of hot water and white bread. Now the change was not unwelcome. The gruel was certainly more nourishing than water.

Also on the wooden bench I found a straw mattress and pillow. In tramp language, it was at least a decent "lay down"—*i.e.*, bed. But the price—half a ton of granite!

A vision of huge blocks, which, willy-nilly, had to be broken, took all the enjoyment out of the better food and bed. The contrast between better conditions of accommodation and worse conditions of labour seemed to denote purpose. It is, of course, an indisputable fact that workhouse officials do all they can to discourage the use of the casual ward. It is a point ratepayers would do well to remember when they are called upon to elect guardians. The matter would well stand investigation.

As I sat munching my bread I noticed for the first time that opposite the door by which I had entered there was another at the end of the cell, fitted also with strong bolts. I imagined the door led into the yard, and on that account would be locked. High up in the wall above this door was a tiny window. In the daytime only a small ray of light would enter the cell.

Heavy footsteps sounded in the passage, a bunch of keys rattled ominously, the door of my cell slammed to, the bolts were shot, and I was safely caged for the night. I had no means of telling the time. One loses count in such circumstances.

Pulling the two blankets round me I lay down, only to stare at the little window above the door at the farther end of the cell. Sleep to me was always impossible. Weird thoughts come to one under such conditions. It is easy to understand how those who so often look want and hunger in the face are caught by Socialistic theories. If the poor outcasts who, night after night, seek their rest in such places, ever think of life and its riddles, strange indeed must be their day's reckoning up. I do not doubt that many of them, in the dark hours of the night, remember the time when, as little children, they prayed at their mother's knee. What a fit time to pull them to their feet once more and give them another chance! But no inducements are ever offered in Government institutions. The man is "down," and everything to keep him there and even drive him down still further exists in the casual wards of to-day. The silence of the night was now and then broken by dry, hacking coughs issuing from the cells around mine. I wondered how many of the inmates should have been in a hospital. Certainly a good many, from the consumptive coughs which echoed through and through that silent "prison." Once the moon shed a ray of light through the little window, and by the dim light I could see that closed door at the foot of my bed. And then a fascination to see what was beyond came over me. I began to wonder if, after all, it was fastened on the outside. As I could not hear that the porter was within easy reach of my cell I crept out of bed. Only those awful hacking coughs went sounding through the ward. Very gingerly I slid back the bolts and the door opened! Ugh!! a gust of icy cold wind swept by me. In the distance I could see something white which seemed to lie at the other end of a cavern—that was all. It was a ghostly sight, and I was glad to close the door again and creep back to "bed."

"Ten hundredweight of granite!" Would they make those poor wretches, whose coughs proclaimed the fact that they were living a life with one foot in the grave, perform such a terrible task? Had these poor mortals been refused the blessing of medical assistance? I have been present when they have implored the taskmaster to let them see the doctor—but all in vain.

The night went slowly, for I was anxious for the dawn to come in order that I might take another look through that door. But at last the little black patch of sky through the window grew greyer, announcing the coming of morning. Therefore, I crept out of bed, and once more carefully opened the door. Again the cold wind made me shiver, but I scarcely felt the chill wind, for my gaze was centred on what to me, at all events, was an awful sight. A square white cell with a stone floor, a foot or more below the level of the cell in which I stood, an iron grating let in to the opposite side of the "cavern" and measuring about three feet by two feet six inches (I carefully gauged these dimensions), the bars of the grating placed two inches apart, the bottom of the cavern almost covered with huge blocks of granite. This, then, was where men broke granite, and were themselves "broken"!

Creeping over the blocks I saw that outside the cell was a stone trough into which the granite, when broken small enough to go through the iron bars, would fall, for all that quantity of granite had to be broken small enough to go through the grill.

Sickened by the sight I crept back to bed. What devilish thing was this men were put to? Was it for this, for refusing to be "broken" in such a manner that men were given "ten months"? I wondered how any magistrate, *knowing* the conditions under which casuals work, dare convict men for failing to perform such a task. But there! I have put my finger on *the* one point—*they do not know*. They are told by the taskmaster that the men are lazy and will not work, ignoring the fact that such heavy work sorely taxes well-fed navvies, and perhaps the man they accuse of laziness has not had a square meal for weeks. It is, as Dr. Macnamara once stigmatised it, "stupid toil."[12]

*   *   *   *   *

A bustling sound all through the ward, and the coming and going of heavy feet, announced the fact that morning had come. The door of my cell was unlocked, and I was handed another tin of gruel and a piece of bread. This was breakfast. As soon as I had dressed and had eaten something of what had been given to me (for I did not know how soon I should eat again), I went into that

---

12. Thomas James Macnamara, M.P. (1861-1931) was at this time Parliamentary Secretary to the Local Government Board. He later became Minister of Labour. A prolific writer on education for young people in care, he was a strong supporter of vocational education and meaningful work for those in this group. We have been unable to locate this quotation in his work.

"cavern" again. Picking up one of the heavy hammers (there were two in a corner of the cell), I smote with all my strength at one of the blocks of granite. I made no impression whatever. I felt then quite sure that, if ten months depended on the breaking of those blocks, I should certainly be in prison before many hours passed.

During breakfast-time the doors of the cells remained unlocked, and I found it possible to communicate with my companion. He regarded the outlook as distinctly serious, for he was of my mind—that it would be impossible to break ten hundred-weight of that granite in the given time—by nightfall.

As I sat on the side of my bed wondering what would happen next I heard the porter coming down the passage. He stopped at the door of my companion's cell. Shortly after the two went back along the passage.

Soon, however, I heard someone returning. The doorway of my cell was shadowed and the porter entered.

"Go down the passage and into the room on the left!"

On entering the room indicated I was met by a comfortable, well-fed individual, who looked me up and down with careful scrutiny. What had happened? Had my mission been discovered? To my surprise I had to repeat all the particulars I had given on the previous evening.

"Ump! 'come down' pretty quickly, haven't you?"

I replied that I had.

"Well, get out of this as quickly as you can, and don't come back again. I'll give you this one chance!"

Was this a genuine case of pity, or had they "discovered" me? I should like to think the former, but in face of the questions I was asked I think it was more likely that in some way they suspected us. Nevertheless, I lost very little time in "getting out." It was the most awful place I had ever been in. Had I been made to "work" I should most certainly have been what the tramp calls "run," i.e., imprisoned, for I could not have broken that granite, and I am by no means a weakling.

Outside I met my companion, who had been treated in a similar manner.

*   *   *   *   *

A few weeks after the above adventure I decided that I would abandon my investigations into the methods adopted by the

Government in dealing with casuals, and see how private institutions dealt with such cases. The State did nothing, offered nothing; what would private charity do?

CHAPTER VII
THE EMBANKMENT CROWD

WHEN I turned my back upon the State Casual Wards and set out nightly in search of private charity a phase of London life revealed itself to me such as I had never given a great deal of thought to until I began my investigations. It was easy and not so hurtful to steal out of my chambers in rags and down on to the one place which on dark nights seems to hold all London's most wretched of the wretched.

* * * * *

There is one spot in the vast metropolis frequented by almost every Londoner. It is spanned by many bridges, edged by crowded thoroughfares, and carries at its side the waterway of the world—the Thames. That spot is the Thames Embankment. There you can see the millionaire motoring to his City office, where he makes vast sums. There the beggar holds his *levée*, proud sometimes in the possession of a greasy sixpence. Puzzled politicians throng its broad paths. Journalists and lawyers wander up and down the wide pavements, free for a few minutes from the rush of an editorial office or a stuffy court, while many a poor wretch, leaning over the stone parapet, gazes in despair about him and then longingly at the muddy water.

You can reach the Embankment from Herne Hill or Hampstead, but be careful to go in the daytime, unless you would meet that vast hunger-crowd I want to tell you about, for it was there I found myself one night after I had turned my back on the Casual Wards.

* * * * *

It was half-past-ten at night. The wind, biting and icy cold, cut its way though my thin and tattered garments.

Half-past-ten and a cruel night, with the prospects of a night in the shadow of some friendly porch, bridge or statue.

Half-past-ten—and a night on which tired and weary men crept into the Thames.

From all parts of London the hunger-crowd was wending its way to the Embankment. It is very dark and holds many nooks and crannies, and the police are kind.

Beneath one bridge alterations were bring carried on—alterations which necessitated the use of stacks of timber and blocks of stone. I was told by one man that if you are careful during the day to collect all the old newspapers you might wrap them round you at night and sleep fairly comfortable with a plank for your bed and stone for your pillow, but it is necessary to creep in between the wood and stone when the watchman's face is turned. It is also advisable to get out of reach of the "copper's" lantern.

I had come to Waterloo Bridge, and the depths of the dark shadows which cling to the stone walls and steps leading down to the Embankment hid many a dingy figure. I sank down on one of the seats which fringe the roadway, turned up my coat collar, and prepared to wile away the hours somehow until morning. I knew I should not be allowed to sleep—indeed, I was more mentally tired than bodily fatigued.

Many a time the almost irresistible desire to interrogate those around me tempted me to rise and wander up and down, but I put the desire from me. It is easier to fathom the mystery of the Sphinx than learn the true history of the lives of some of these men and women. They will tell you the superfluities of their lives—but the real story—never! There is also in many of them a dogged spirit of indifference to their sufferings—that feeling which grows when all hopes of better things have passed out of their lives for ever. Once, indeed, I heard a heart-broken confession. The man's hands were blistered through stone-pounding in a casual ward. He was beaten, but had not quite sunk to that depth of degradation when sloth and mental and physical stupor claim the man for ever. With his head between his hands he cried aloud in his agony.

"It's me own d--- fault. It's the cussed drink. Why don't they 'elp me ter keep straight?"

The seat on which I sat soon began to lose its occupants. Presently it held only one other besides myself—an old man curled up at the further end. Then he, too, raised his head, and turning half round looked across the road in the direction of King's College. I followed the direction of his eyes and saw a number of men stamping up and down outside that severe looking building. Soon they stopped and began to form a *queue*. There were a hundred at least.

The old man on my seat got up, and shuffling across the road took up his stand behind the last man. But I sat and waited, though curiously interested. Surely something extraordinary was going to happen, since a large number of men of the outcast type could not be drawn together but for some purpose—and policemen, too, had arrived to keep them in order.

"Ain't you goin' ter git a ticket then?"

I turned round. There in front of me stood a little man, of the type that Charles Dickens loved to write about. He was attired in clothes that had now become shabby-genteel, but his close-shaven chin and upper lip betokened a recent shave. Something of pride remained. His hard hat was dented, but evidently had been brushed. His coat collar was turned up to keep out the cold, but beneath it could be see the white of a collar. So I answered that I didn't know what he meant—which was indeed the case.

"Why, yer gits a ticket for soup and a night's doss. You do a little work—two hours in exchange fer it—and it ain't unfair either! An' though I don't like doin' it meself I ain't a-come down ter beggin' yet, an' I'll do a bit o' work in exchange fer a meal and a rest. Cold, ain't it, matey?"

I said it was.

"Yus, cold it gits—fer them as 'as no 'omes." And then he looked at me intently. "You ain't used ter this? No—no more am I. I'm a master butcher, that's wot I am. I 'ad a little bizness in the country, but it went all wrong. Some'ow I couldn't make it pay. Things got to wuss and wuss, an' they sold me up—an' then—well, I've done this a week now. They've give me a ticket each night since I first found out that they gives 'em away. It's all I've 'ad an' I'm glad I can pay 'em in work. But I've 'eard of a job ter day—an' things looks better. They're a queer lot over there," and he jerked his thumb in the direction of the waiting crowd, which seemed to increase minute by minute. "Yus, a queer lot! Never thought I'd know 'em as I do now. A queer lot, I can tell you. Well, come along, mate, an' if you're 'ungry you'll git a basin o'soup and a bite o' bread—an' you won't 'ave ter break no stones nor pick no oakum—only chop a little wood, an' you're able ter do that in comfort an' not shut up in a stone cell as if you wos a pris'ner!"

From which I gathered that the little man unable to keep from the Casual Ward had been in and had tasted the bitterness of State relief.

"Come over with me an' we'll do it together!" So with my new-found guide I crossed the road and took up my stand at the *queue*. By now the crowd numbered at least five hundred.

Five hundred of London's poorest of the poor. Even those who dwelt in top attics, whose bed was a pallet of straw and who could scarcely afford one meal a day, and counted the crumbs, were better off than these—for the attic was home, and these had none.

Five hundred wrecks of manhood, and still they were coming and the crowd was growing in numbers. (I have since learned that on some nights twelve hundred men have stood at that *queue*.) Also that the Society which distributes the tickets organises "drives"—sending all that are encountered to this one spot, the *queue* on the Embankment.

Truly the darkness of night hides many charitable as well as criminal acts.

A buzz of excitement went through the crowd as two men in dark clothes appeared, and stood talking to the policemen who kept the crowd in order. They waited for Big Ben to strike eleven—then each dipped into his pockets and drew out a large bundle of tickets. Beginning at the top end of the *queue* they gave one to each man. My readers may be interested as to the wording on the tickets. Mine read as follows: "Any destitute man present-ing this ticket as mentioned below (time) will be provided (space permitting) with temporary employment, in return for which he will be provided with food and lodging."

When I held out my hand for a ticket the man gave me a searching glance. I was told subsequently that every new face is carefully noted. I do not know whether he suspected my disguise but his eyes softened, and I experienced then a glance so rarely met with—one of real pity.

I was not there to "give in," but I stored that look of pity away in the "best drawer" of my mind. And I took the ticket for obvious reasons.

I was gazing with interest at the little piece of paste-board when I heard a now familiar voice—that of the little master butcher.

"No, sir, thank you, I'd rather not 'ave a ticket for the doss 'ouse—I—well, sir, it ain't quite clean, or rather the inmates ain't quite clean—and well—" (and here the poor chap's voice became unsteady) "I've got a bit o' pride left, an' I 'ope ter git work in the mornin'. Yus, sir, I got the letter all right—and, please the Lord, I'll git the job!"

As soon as some of the men had received their tickets they set off at a run along the Embankment, up Arundel Street, across the Strand into Kingsway. They were the men whose work would begin at twelve o'clock—midnight! They would first receive a meal of bread and soup. Then they would chop wood for two hours. At the end of their tasks they would again be fed and a ticket given them for a doss house. Some of the men whose meals and work were due at once, but who had been fortunate during the daytime in getting a meal, exchanged tickets with those who had not tasted food for many hours. Was there ever such a strange mart? Some sold their tickets for a half-penny and upwards to twopence.

What a sight it was!

"You comin', matey?"

The little man stood once more at my elbow.

Yes, I would go. I was much interested in this vast hunger-crowd. I wanted to see what private charity would do for them. And so we went along to Kingsway together.

CHAPTER VIII
WHILE LONDON SLEEPS

CHIP-Chip-Chip! The sharp sound of steel—forcing its way through wood. Sh—Sh—Sh—; the sighing of a hand-saw. These indications of work came to me—wafted through the open curtain of the Church Army Labour Tents.

Midnight would soon ring out from the clocks and church towers about the Strand, and already half London was asleep. But here was a little community which knew no rest. It was a battle of life, for this tent gave many a man a fresh start, a warm meal, and put new life and vigour into him, and sent him away with the knowledge that he could come again if he failed to get work.

The poor outcasts who were beyond manual labour, whose sloth and absolute indifference to all moral obligations compel them to slink into the nooks and crannies of the Embankment and other hiding-places of the poor, to die rather than do a little honest work, have no place in these tents.

I took particular notice of the men as I waited in the midst of them for admittance (for the work was divided up into two-hour shifts). They seemed to number amongst them members from every grade of society. The officials in the tents can tell of "the high" and "the lowly," sitting side by side chopping little pieces of wood—a pathetic demonstration of someone's wrong-doing—in many cases their own.

Most of them were gaunt and hungry-looking. Many had undoubtedly been men of fine physique—Public School men perhaps. Yes, indeed, even 'Varsity men, for some there were whose very profession (I should have said one-time profession) necessitated a University education.

Here was a man who from his clothes was obviously a navvy. He could not have been long on the road, for his clothes still bore the characteristics of his class—and the apparel of the "sub-merged" has no characteristics, or at least paradoxically its lack of characteristics is its chief feature. Not a few raw lads were among them. It was pitiful to see them at that time of life seeking relief.

My guide, the little master butcher, stood in front of me. I have been in many crowds—never in one with less to say than that little knot of men waiting to work and to be fed.

I wondered if any of these men had wives and children—wondered most of all what had brought them down. One's thoughts always fly to the one cause invariably put forward by the ready-to-blame non-helping person—drink. Personally I am sure there are many reasons other than that one. First of all, the trouble almost always comes before the drink. Only when a man can struggle no longer against adversity does he sling up his burden upon Sin's pack-horse, and take his way to the devil by means of the drink-fiend with all celerity.

Suddenly the gate which stood between us and the curtain of the tent opened, and a long string of men with a feeling-much-better expression on their faces filed out through our midst. Some of them bore in their hands another ticket—a white one this time. The other was red. They were tickets for the doss-house.

These cheap lodging-houses are dotted all over London. They are licensed by the London County Council and periodically inspected, yet to think of them almost makes one shudder. I once had a peep into a room with *four hundred* outcasts lying asleep, or trying to sleep on "beds" placed next to one another. It was an awful sight, no less terrible than the stifling atmosphere of the room.

As the last of the file of men passed by the first of our "shift" walked in followed by others in line. And now the tickets were collected, the name and occupation of each man taken, after which he was directed with others to the further end of the tent, where tables and forms were set.

I could not help contrasting this reception with my experiences of the Casual Ward, with all its hateful, degrading system. No one was asked to turn out his pockets, nor were the hands of the officials thrust into them as if they had been pickpockets. Their belongings were not taken from them nor were they spoken to as if they were something less than human beings. I saw nothing but kindly glances from the officials and helpers; there were no mean jests like one I have recorded in the first part of this book, no task-masters with hearts of stone and a conscience even less impressionable, no policemen and no indignities. All they seemed to know was that you were "down" and wanted a friendly hand; that you were hungry and tired; above all, that you were born into this world as they were, to live, come what may.

What a hotch-potch of humanity, that little crowd! The "gaunt fiend"[13] seemed to have laid its hand on all and sundry.

We sat round long deal tables. Each man was served with a bowl of soup and a thick piece of bread. How good that soup was; how it seemed to thaw the frozen parts of one's body and put new life into aching limbs! It was good to look at those faces bent in keen enjoyment over what was perhaps the first meal for twenty-four hours, in many instances three or four days.

The time allowed for meals having elapsed, the foreman called for sawyers and choppers. The strong men took to the saws and the weaker to the choppers. Very little of the hard labour and terrible strain put upon one in the Casual Ward was demanded of you here. No threats of a term of imprisonment were hurled at you if you could not do the allotted task. Consequently hardly one man shirked his work, but did his best with what poor skill he possessed.

---

13. A common metaphor for starvation. For example, "But my shoulders ache, and that gaunt fiend hunger throbs wild within." Whitelaw, Alexander (Ed.). *The Republic of Letters...* Glasgow: Blackie & Son, 1835. 4 vols., 1:239.

For the sawing a man stood on either side of a wooden trestle, on which blocks of wood chained together had been laid. A broad two-handled saw was then laid across the bundle, and all that was necessary for the men to do was to take hold of the handles and pull first one way and then the other, backwards and forwards, until the pile was sawn through. The pieces were then passed on to the choppers who sat upon little wooden blocks, chopping the newly sawn wood into little sticks of the length of the firewood usually bought in shops. The sticks were then piled up on a tray and properly bundled by men specially engaged for the purpose. Thus while London was asleep a little community watched—and worked.

For two hours and a half the work went steadily forward, then the saws and choppers were laid aside, and we took our seats once more round the table. Another bowl of soup and a piece of bread was given to each man, and then as we left the tent we were handed a bed ticket, which would admit us to one of the many licensed "doss-houses." My guide, the butcher, refused the ticket. He said he expected to get a job during the day (it was very early morning already), so I took my way to the address given on the little piece of paste-board.

CHAPTER IX
IN THE SHADOW OF THE SPHINX

I MET him one night as I sat on the stone steps which flank Cleopatra's Needle on either side. Something in the bent figure, prematurely aged, and a distinct carefulness in his attire, which at the best seemed many years old, induced me to enter into conversation with him. Immediately he replied to my first question I knew him for one of the real "had-beens."

He was one of those whom fate had not marked out as deserving of special favours. He was, at least, honest enough to admit that he had had chances, but somehow things had not turned out right. He was also an educated man.

"Yes, for three years now I have lived this life. I came down to it—well, I won't say how. Perhaps it was my own fault, perhaps it was not! Here I am—but here I shall not be much longer—that's preferable!" When he said "that" he pointed to the river.

"But supposing you had a chance?" I asked.

"Chance? Who would give *me* a chance—whoever in this world offers such as I am a chance? Go up to the first well-dressed man you see in the streets and talk to him about a 'chance,' and he will probably give you over to the police. Chance? Ah! who's to give *me* a chance?"

"The Gov—" but I got no further, for at that word he turned on me fiercely.

"'The Government' you were going to say. The Government give me a chance!" and he uttered a hard, cynical laugh. "The Government! Why! perhaps you've never been in a casual ward—'spike' they call it in my level of life. Have you never tasted what civilised England calls 'relief'? I tell you that the present system makes more criminals than converts, for it's a take-all and give-nothing policy that's in practice at the present moment. No, I am nearly 'done.' There's no use in life for you when you are as I am. Once you're down—well! you're down, and none stretches out a hand to save you. Once or twice people have offered me work, but the conditions were too hard. I wouldn't consent to be labelled a pauper, to be pointed at as the object of someone's charity, so I am here still." And he turned his face to the river and looked over and beyond it, murmuring to himself "A chance!"

Assuming a cheery tone I tried to encourage him.

"You'll get a chance one of these days, and then you will wonder how you came to think life so blank and empty. Take heart, my friend, and think no more of 'that,'" and I jerked my thumb in the direction of the river.

For a moment he gazed at me, and a queer expression passed across his face, then he looked away and muttering something about "being hopeful," turned from me and shuffled off towards Waterloo Bridge.

*   *   *   *   *

That night the hunger-crowd was larger than usual. A large number of unemployed had drifted into London from the provinces, for I saw many new, gaunt, thin faces among them. The men were also in a queer temper. From what I could gather Socialist agitators had been at work among them, and a dangerous spirit was abroad.

The men that night numbered over twelve hundred (these figures I afterwards ascertained to be a little below the exact number).

Twelve hundred, with scarce a sixpence to their credit! Twelve hundred absolute destitute wrecks of once bright lives! Oh, it was a pitiful sight, I can tell you! The sight of so many outcasts together is one to stir the soul to its very depths. Even one poor wrecked life is enough to arouse the deepest feelings of commiseration, but twelve hundred, penniless and homeless, is a vision which burns itself upon one's memory, and is never forgotten.

*　　*　　*　　*　　*

Now, curious to relate, the Church Army officials, who distributed the tickets, had on this particular night, with the very best motives in the world, decided to begin the distribution *at the end* instead of at the beginning of the *queue*, this, in order to give the weaker men, who were sometimes thrust out of position by the stronger, an opportunity of getting the tickets for immediate meals and work. The intention was good, but it had disastrous results.

No sooner did the men in front perceive the alteration than they began first to murmur, then to commence a vigorous pushing and shoving, and finally set up a cry of "Mob 'em!"

Then came an ugly rush. Like an avalanche the crowd, hungry as wolves, swept upon the two defenceless men. With a cry to the police, who had already discerned something amiss and were making their way with all speed to the two men, the latter stood with their backs against the stone balustrades of King's College, and struck out right and left. They had no other means of saving themselves from serious injury. The more desperate of the crowd cried out "Chuck 'em into the river!" and once, indeed, it looked as if the threat would have been carried out, but the policemen joined in the fray, and in a little while order was once more established. The affair was afterwards carefully sifted, and it was found that the violent members of the crowd were the newcomers, who scarcely knew who the distributers were, and who, perhaps, were even more hungry and desperate than those who took the tickets nightly. Of the latter, my friend of Cleopatra's Needle was one. He, indeed, with others, had tried to push back the crowd that surged upon the two men. He, too, had taken the tickets often, and he, too, though he knew it not, had been watched as he chopped wood each night.

*   *   *   *   *

"John Chiltern!"

"Trade?"

"Nothing!" The answer came in deep tones of misery, careless misery. It was my friend of the Embankment.

We stood in front of the little office built inside the huge marquee which formed the Labour Tent.

"Come round this side, will you? I want to talk to you." I saw John Chiltern look at the man behind the window with a dubious, half-suspicious expression on his face. He hesitated, then went.

I walked to the further end of the tent, and took my place at the table for "meals." I had almost finished when Chiltern came to the door of the little office, and stepping out carefully closed it behind him. Then he was served with soup and bread, and came and took his place beside me. Covertly I glanced at him, and there I saw something that had been missing before—hope. I guessed what had happened. They had offered him a chance. My conjectures were not wrong.

"You're a bit of a prophet, my friend," said he presently, and in almost a whisper: "They've offered me regular work in a Labour Home. I'm going to-morrow at eleven o'clock to the headquarters at Marble Arch. It's almost too good to be true—I—I—" but here he could say no more, only his hand shot out towards mine, and we "gripped," for his "chance" had come.

CHAPTER X
THE CHURCH ARMY[14] AND THE CASUAL

THE story of the man whom I first met in the shadow of the Sphinx is not finished. There is a sequel to it, and in that sequel I

---

14. The Church Army, an evangelistic Anglican organization, was founded in 1882 with the express purpose of reaching out to the poor and dispossessed. In 1888 it inaugurated its "Labour Homes" intended to provide those willing to embrace the working world with food, work, and temporary lodging as a precursor to a fresh start in life. By 1911, there were 120 such Homes in London and the provinces. For a contemporaneous account of the Church Army, see Cecil, R. W. E. G. *The Church Army: What It Is and What It Does*. Oxford: Church Army Press, 1908.

shall try to show how the methods of the Church Army differ from those employed by the State—how their kindness and sympathy, which go hand in hand with offers of work, do more for the poor casual and out-of-work than the stony-hearted brutality of the Government Casual Wards and taskmasters. For therein lies the whole crux of this difficult question.

Individual attention, a recognition that some men are born naturally weak and unfortunate, and that others after a first fall have been allowed to sink lower when the State should have assisted them to their feet, is where the Church Army succeed in reclaiming men who have been given up for "lost" by the State. The truth of the matter is that *we do nothing* to help the man regain his former status. Once down—down for ever. The very word "relief" becomes unreal when one understands the way in which "payment" is wrung from the hapless casual who seeks a night's shelter in a Casual Ward.

Over and over again I heard men incite others, new apparently to the "spike," to commit crime if they wanted a "decent time." In prison one gets good food, a not uncomfortable bed, and warm clothing. In the Casual Ward, bread and water with an ounce and a half of cheese (once a day) as meals, which, with two or three dirty blankets and a wooden bench, are offered in exchange for seven or eights hours' hard work; useless work more often than not. The tasks are certainly not designed with the intention of benefiting *anybody*; indeed, I am sure that in many workhouses they are intended as means of *keeping casuals away* from the ward. It is right, of course, that the wards should not be made attractive, but between attraction and repulsion there is a wide difference, and the difference has yet to be learned by local authorities.

John Chiltern's outcry against a Government who would neither give him honest work to do nor in any way help him without "breaking" him, was entirely characteristic of the terrible conditions which face thousands of genuine unemployed, whose army is increasing year by year.

We have seen how the State treats a man when he is down. We know now what is offered to him when faced by starvation. Let us now see how private charity and kind-heartedness do more in a week than the State do in a year to alleviate the sufferings of the submerged—and this without detriment to their morals, one of the most difficult phases of this vast question. For to assist these men to help themselves is no easy matter. Indiscriminate giving, or giving *without some return* in the form of labour, is the very down-fall of those on the totter.

John Chiltern was to be given a chance. Once more the socie-ty of his fellow-beings—men striving to keep up their self-respect by honest work—was to be his. I have taken the trouble to follow his progress through the Labour Home to which he went on the morning following my last meeting with him in the Labour Tent.

He duly presented himself at the Home. At the very doors hands were stretched out to him, welcoming him by their friend-ly grip. No surly porter here whose very delight was to strike ter-ror into the poor fellows' hearts by a recountal of hard and cruel tasks. Words of sympathy were extended to John, and he was taken at once to the baths. There his clothing was taken from him, and as it was only fit to be burned, was replaced by a fresh, clean suit. Then he was regaled with a good, solid meal, for the Church Army know well that a man cannot work on an empty stomach, also that perhaps for weeks John might not have had a square meal. But he was told quite honestly that he must work. No prospects are held out to "Weary Willies" in these institutions of becoming less energetic; but firmly, though kindly, the men are told that in order to stay in the Home until they feel fit to take a job each man must do his best at the work set before him.

John's first task was wood-chopping. He probably found it very tiring at first. The constant bending over the chopping block must have made his back ache. But there was no nightmare held in front of him of imprisonment for a week or two should he not be able to complete a given task in a given time.

The Church Army Captains placed in charge of these Homes know whether a man is doing his best or not. Careful observation teaches much. And I daresay John Chiltern found it absolutely necessary to rest at times, for his arms and, in fact, every limb must have ached towards the close of his first day's work. But who can picture the joy he must have felt, when at the end of that first day he was shown into the little cubicle, which was to be his so long as it should be necessary and he did his work honestly! What a vision of long ago must have come to him as, with the Captain of the Home and the other inmates, he knelt before going to bed to thank the Almighty for once more leading him into the society and company of striving men! What a contrast to the Government Casual Wards! As he closed his eyes on that first night I can imagine John thinking of the time when as a boy he went to bed with dreams of what he would do on the morrow.

The second day passed much the same as the first, though the stiffness began to wear off and the colour now made its appearance in his pallid cheeks. He was given four substantial meals a day, eaten to the accompaniment of kindly words from the Captain of the Home. He is often called "Father."

Then, at the close of the day, the evening prayer of thanksgiving for work, food, clothing and shelter. And in this way the first week passed. But during this time John had been earning money; his work was not useless. He had been credited with a fair wage for the hours of labour passed during the six days. And now he finds that not only has he earned enough to pay for his week's lodging, but he has a shilling in his pocket to spend, and a little sum placed to his account in the Savings Bank.

Soon he began to feel himself a man of the world once more. Little by little his self-respect came back to him. He could not tell what it was, but the desire to live, an intense longing to make his way in the world reasserted itself, and surely, though gradually, John Chiltern was (it is perhaps not too much to say it) born again. His will and moral strength regained, the rest was easy. But it took many weeks before he felt able to accept a situation which the Church Army found for him. Then on a certain day he bid good-bye to the Captain—I am told almost with tears in his eyes. In his pocket he had a sum saved out of his wages in the Home. And occasionally he visits the place where he was assisted to his feet, and made to see that the life he was leading placed him almost beyond the pale of humanity.

John Chiltern's case was not an isolated one. Thousands of men of his stamp pass through the Church Army Homes year after year. They come of their own [free will];[15] they go when they wish to, though always advised to stay if the Captain thinks it would do them good. Some refuse to do the work and are turned away. A very large number leave of their own accord to take situations. Others who show special efforts to get on are sent out to Canada as emigrants, after a special trial on the

---

15. In the original: "freewill."

Church Army's Farm Colony. Of course they meet with disappointing cases. There are black sheep in every flock, but only those who carefully note the statistics given in their publications know what an enormous number of men benefit through the Army's humane method of treatment.

I particularly wish to point out that what struck me most was the entire absence of any desire to pauperise the men through over-assistance. Also that it is impossible for men to stay at the Homes unless they *do* work. And the way the men pull themselves to their feet, as it were, and soon acquire the desire to better their condition, is really marvellous. I have carefully investigated the workings of these Homes, and it seems to me that the Government might do very much worse than establish Homes and Colonies on a similar principle. Indeed, Labour and Detention Colonies are among the recommendations of the Poor Law Commissioners, though, in Prebendary Carlile's book, "The Continental Outcast,"[16] will be found an almost complete forecast of the recommendations of the Commissioners. After a careful survey of the various methods for the reclamation of the Casual now in vogue in the United Kingdom, the Labour Homes of the Church Army are far and away the most efficacious.

But they are unsuccessful with one class of Casual—the habitual loafer. For him there is only one place—the Detention Colony. As Englishmen, we do not like the idea of a man not having committed a crime being shut up within the space of walls—in grounds—unless he happens to be insane. But is not the habitual loafer an offender against the laws? Does he not contaminate those who are temporarily "down"? And is it not better that one man should be kept where he would not have an evil influence over his fellow-beings rather than being let loose on the community, breeding crime and influencing the weak-minded to "loaf," and make themselves a charge on others? How is it that we are so much behind the times in this question of Labour and Detention Colonies? Continental countries have ideal methods, and tramps such as we know them are seldom seen. But in England we harbour them, and give them every

---

16. Carlile, Wilson, & Carlile, Victor W. *The Continental Outcast: Land Colonies and Poor Law Relief.* London: T.F. Unwin, 1906.

opportunity of following nefarious lives. Without a doubt, if the habitual loafers were confined in Detention Colonies the lot of the unemployed would be ameliorated.

In the space at my disposal I have not room to fully describe the methods adopted by the Church Army in reclaiming the man, but that they *do* reclaim him is open to everyone to prove for himself. Personally I am sure that the Christian influence exercised by the Army's officers has much to do with the success of their efforts; for the Casual has a soul, he is human as we are, and the story of that Great Love which poured itself out upon the Cross at Cavalry in order to save the broken-hearted falls often on ears that have not heard it since childhood. Then at its sound the desire to be in the company of honest men comes back to the lost soul. It is a great theme—worthy [of][17] the attention of great men.

"Bear ye one another's burdens."[18] The Church Army do that, and in bearing the troubles of others find those who are willing to help the Army bear theirs. May it always be so, for it is a good work—a grand work!

---

17. Word omitted in the original.

18. "Bear ye one another's burdens, and so fulfil the law of Christ." Galations, 6:2.

Chapter Ten

A Vicar as Vagrant by George Z. Edwards,

with an introduction by Canon Denton Thompson

London: P. S. King & Son, 1910

INTRODUCTION

IT is with much pleasure that I accede to the wish of my friend and former colleague and write a few words of introduction to the following pages, which it is needless to say I have read with great interest.

They record an almost unique experience[1] of one who, with a view to increasing his knowledge of and his sympathy with the vagrant class, joined their ranks and became himself for a few days a tramp. It is only by such testimony that we can fully inform ourselves of the privations and sufferings, the degradation and misery which are incident to the lot of those who constitute this human wreckage in our midst. That there is urgent need for more [widespread information][2] on this and other phases of the social

---

1.   As the other texts in this volume, and many others from the period that are not included here, testify, Edwards's experiences were far from being "almost unique."

2.   In the original: "for a more widespread information."

problem is painfully evident by the astounding ignorance which prevails even amongst good and well-meaning people on the subject. How few there are who realise that one-tenth of the population, numbering over three millions, are "submerged" in a physical and moral morass, while on its verge millions more are struggling for the bare necessities of life, and, alas! in many cases struggling in vain, only to find themselves slipping into the abyss from which they would fain escape. The peril to the nation of this spreading morass is far greater than many suppose, affecting as it does every grade of society up from the lowest to the highest, while the groans of those engulfed are both an appeal and a challenge to the Church. It is my earnest hope that the reading of these pages will awaken and develop in every heart the sympathy of Christ, that sympathy which in His name and for His sake cannot but express itself in some effort to succour the weak, upraise the fallen, and rescue the perishing. None can, I think, deny that the problems of the unemployed, or the greater problem of the unemployable, are full of difficulty, and that they are the resultant of many co-operating causes. While I, for one, do not believe that their solution will be found in any single proposal for reform out of the many now being pressed upon the public conscience, I cannot admit that these facts afford any excuse for the widespread indifference on the part of many Churchmen to the deplorable condition in which millions of our fellow countrymen are living and apparently doomed to die. That the Spirit of God may arouse and inspire the Church to and with a sense of its duty in this respect is my daily prayer.

J. Denton Thompson.
The Rectory, Birmingham.

A VICAR AS VAGRANT.
A PARSON GOES ON TRAMP TO SEE.

I am a parson—but, I trust, also a man. I believe I am truly called to tell other men what they are, Who calls them to their works, and what strength they have for fulfilling their works.

But I have found it almost impossible to tell a man that he is God's child, that God is his Father and will care for him and give him strength to do what is right, when that man is out of work, his children starved with hunger and pinched with cold, and his home almost gone.

For I know that what that man needs is food, warmth, and work; and I know he cannot get food and warmth without work. How can I tell him of God? How can I tell him that God calls him? that God will forgive his sins, and give him strength for his duty, if I cannot give him work?

It is sheer cant to talk to men of their souls when it is their bodies which first need care.

Can a man be honest without work? Can a man be full of joy, love, and peace without warmth, food, and clothing? Can a man see his loved ones suffer—suffer so much!—without feeling savage, mad against that society which, by its callousness and indifference, has denied to him his rights of brotherhood and manhood too?

I will not talk cant. I will not evade my duty of loving, serving, befriending my brother by talking of God's love, of God's care, of God's home, when my first duty as a member of a great Christian nation is to see he has a home, a true home of his own.

So, for many a year I have wanted to feel the pinch of necessity, of need, of cold, of hunger, of being an outcast from society, that I, who am a parson, may be able to speak with more authority and conviction of the needs of my outcast brothers, and to urge upon all who have any power and authority the duty and necessity of social study and reform.

It was in the dark of an April morning in the year of our Lord 1910, when I set out disguised as a tramp.

My companion knew the road, the ways of the road, and the people of the road; for had he not of necessity spent many a month out of work, hungry, clammed to death on the road? He was a strong, powerful, well-built fellow, who could turn his hand to many a different job, any kind of farm work, carting, management of horses and cattle. He was, moreover, a good striker at smithy work, and could make many a thing in wire-working, such as toasting forks, flue brushes, photo stands, pan wires, and gridirons. He was also almost a professional boxer, pugilist, or rough-and-tumble fighter.

He was only 21, but had known more of the ups and downs of life than most. I felt more than safe in his care in whatever rough and wicked company we got. He was trustworthy—a true mate. I knew also that he was willing to take me, because he wanted me to be able to warn young men from taking to the road themselves.

As we left Southport we met six men who had spent the night on the road—six men forced to spend the night out on one road into Southport in the cold frosty weather of early April, who had probably been without food most, if not all, of the day before!

Before eight o'clock we had tramped through Ormskirk, and were soon well on our way towards Wigan, where we found our way to a common lodging-house—kip-house or doss-house—in which we thought we might be able to sit down and make ourselves a meal before tramping on.

Bread and cheese and a big bowlful of tea—no milk—was our fare, at the cost of 4 ½ d. for the two of us. Three or four of the dozen men in the kitchen were already drunk at that early hour, 12 noon. But my mate reminded me that it was pension day—the merriest day in the quarter for many a tramp.[3]

We hoped to get to Manchester that night, but after struggling on for some three or four hours more, through Abram, Leigh, Atherton, Tyldesley, nearly to Worsley, we sat down on a roadside seat for ten minutes to rest. But, fatal rest! When I got up I could not stand upright! I could not take a step without great difficulty, and it was quite impossible to stride—so stiff and footsore had I become.

Then it was that I learnt how men begin to beg. I had not a penny in my pocket, and I knew then that, if I had been alone, I could have gone to the nearest door to beg, nay, almost demand, some hot tea or some hot drink to quench my thirst, and also to entreat for money for a night's lodging.

Most men will not beg until forced by hunger or pain to do so, but once having learnt to beg, once having found out he can get relief and help for the asking, there is the tremendous danger of all too easily becoming little by little the professional beggar, unashamed, who, in a few short years, will laugh to scorn the offer of the work which once he would have held to be the greatest boon.

So, thoroughly exhausted after a [thirty-three-mile][4] walk, we got into a tramcar to fare to the centre of Manchester. For the

---

3. Under the terms of the Old Age Pensions Act of 1908 (8 Edw. VII, c.40, art.5), pensions were to be paid weekly in advance, although special arrangements could be made if necessary. It is not clear whether, or why, those in the lodging-house in Wigan received theirs quarterly.

4. In the original: "thirty-three miles."

remainder of our tour, during the whole of which I was eating very little but dry bread, I was tired out and somewhat in that state of body which all beginners on the road must experience.

We spent four days on the road as tramps, stopping each night at common lodging-houses, and tramping on the following day, often visiting doss-houses in the towns we passed through. We went from Manchester through Middleton to Rochdale, through Bury to Bolton, and through Chorley to Preston, and thence by train back to Crossens.[5] The doss-houses at which we stayed, and which we visited, were in no way exceptional in their character, except I hope, the "Penny Sit Up." Some were well conducted, others very much the reverse.

I now want to make men understand—what I have vividly learnt—that the stream of destitution on the road is continually recruited from young men—young men who, seeking work and finding none, become exhausted and penniless. Hunger, cold, and misery quickly drive them either to beg or to steal. In one of these ways they gather pence enough for the poor food and squalid shelter of the common lodging-house. Once there, they all too surely sink to the level of their companions and remain on the road for ever.

THE COMMON LODGING-HOUSE

We were tramps. My mate had just a few shillings in his pocket, so, hungry, footsore, and exhausted, we made our way to one of the large Manchester doss-houses. We entered the long darkly-lit room (all doss-house rooms seem darkly-lit) in which at that early hour of 5 P. M. there were already gathered about 200 men. Some in groups chatting and talking together; some busily getting their evening meal; some sitting tired out and miserable in their rags; and most of them keenly eyeing any stranger up and down.

The central point of attraction in a doss-house is the cooking stove—for is that not the source of a glowing delicious heat? The centre of a fragrant mixture of appetising smells? Of bacon and eggs, of herring and chop, and of many another morsel

---

5.   Edwards was vicar of Crossens, now a suburb of Southport.

crackling and frizzling each in its frying pan? The stove is generally a well-built glazed brick construction, coming right out into the room ten feet or more, with the fire at the end, and with some four or five feet width of a flat iron top, often quite red hot; also several large boilers from which boiling water can be drawn to make tea, and, overhead, a smoke and fume collector with racks for drying clothes. There are a number of frying pans, teapots or mugs, and big bowls—once enameled—belonging to the doss-house. You look around the tables, take up a mug and bowl that are not being used, wash them at the tap—no soap is provided—and brew your own tea, and if lucky enough to have a rasher of bacon for your meal you reach down a frying pan to begin the frizzling process, but mind you watch it well, lest, whilst you turn to make your tea or go to the counter to buy your pennyworth of bread, one cleverer than you cracks a couple of eggs in your pan over your bacon and curses you if you dare to touch his stuff!

For in this, the casual labourer's wretched substitute for home, you are surrounded by thieves and pickpockets, most of whom work in gangs, and will fight for each other in a row, in which you, a stranger, will have no chance whatever of redress.

But remember, this is *Home*, the only home to hundreds of thousands of our English lads! What is the charm of your home? A loving greeting from a loving wife, and bonnie bairnies[6] too. A little corner all your own. A place of peace and of refreshment, and of the delicious rest to weary limbs and tired brain of a clean sweet bed.

No welcome greeting to the inmate of the doss-house; no little corner all his own; no peace or spiritual refreshment here, and, most certainly no clean sweet bed! What a mockery of home! Truly England's greatest need is homes.

In the doss-house you eat in public; you wash in public; you sleep in public; you dress in public; and this always, whether you are well or ill.

You may be molested the first hour you enter; these men of the roads are used to fighting, brawling and stealing—it is their

---

6. "Bairn" is a term for a child commonly used in Scotland and parts of northern England.

ordinary life—and they can most easily involve you, force you, into a fight or brawl if they want. You are never safe from the insults of the drunkard, or the fingers of the thief, either by night or by day.

If you linger here many days, and especially if you are a greenhorn, you must become dirty. You will feel yourself growing dirty in body, and dirty in mind and soul. There is a sort of rough "sweep-up" cleanliness, but how can the doss-house keeper keep his beds clean? The filthiest old wreck on the road may have slept between the same sheets the night before, and what does he leave behind him? True you can wash your shirt and hang it over the stove, and watch it while it dries. Mind you watch it well! But you can't wash your trousers. Your washing, wash you ever so carefully, will never kill what may be multiplying there.

Your companions, too. You look at them; you ask about them; speak to them; who are they? Many of England's cleverest tradesmen are here; artizans and workmen of every sort—bricklayers, painters, joiners, plumbers, engineers, navvies and labourers as well. Through falling out of work, from misery, from drink, they first took to the road—they have now grown used to it; they have fallen so low, nobody cares, so there they will stop! They have become "content in their nast."[7]

But lower still, you are surrounded on every hand by [moochers][8] (professional beggars) and by thieves. These men in the main set the tone and spirit in all the thousands of common lodging-houses in the land. Their talk is about "marks," and the best houses on the road at which to beg. How "to pull a toff up" and tell him a good tale. (Truth is a forgotten language here.) How they fared in gaol; for most of these men have been in gaol, and come out with all the natural fear and dread of gaol gone for ever! And every tale they tell, and every sentence they utter, has

---

7.   Probably a misprint for "nest."

8.   In the original: "mouchers." Edwards uses both spellings.

its savour, its oath, its curse, or its blasphemy. Yet once they were not thus; once they shuddered at the thought of being such, as they felt themselves drifting down, and no one stretched out a hand to help.

But yet, lowest of all, the most degrading influence of the road is the women, for in many doss-houses both men and women are accommodated. Give a pal a copper to swear that *he* knows that you and the woman you bring are man and wife, and you may have your bed together. Only, if the doss-house keeper suspects you, he will charge you more. Poor women of the roads! They have lost their highest power to uplift, to purify, to ennoble man; they have gained a most awful power to shame men down to their own depths, to drag men down, down to drink and wanton devilry. Numbers of men in kip-houses live on the profits of prostitution by acting as bullies for these poor women.

Add together all these influences of the doss-house—its homelessness, its dirt, its varied inhabitants—particularly the mouchers, thieves and women—and to them add one more universally prevailing accompaniment, drink. Drink! their only joy, their only pleasure, their only heart's-ease from every pain!

And what do you do when you are tired, weary, despondent, exhausted (You never are so despairing, so desperate as they), but what do you do? Take a quiet rest by the fireside? *They* cannot! Music? *They* have it not! The soothing refreshment of little children, bathed and bedwards, with their good-night kiss and child prayers? These men never hear a gentle word addressed to them. Quiet prayer? How can these men pray? Why should they pray? They feel themselves God-forsaken! God-forgotten! They feel it bitterly, oh! so bitterly! Time was when life was as bright to them as 'tis to you, when hopes were high of noble happy manhood. *Then* they were thrown out of work. They sought work—WORK, not alms, but WORK; man's right and man's unceasing necessity. But their country refused it them, and let them drift on to the road. And so they were forced, forced to beg, to steal, to live with the lowest of the low, and thus become what they now are. Would YOU pray thus? Where are the hands of Christ stretched out to bless them?—our hands, Christ inspired? They see them not, they feel them not, for they know themselves to be outcast; outcast from man and, they think, from God Almighty too. And so they drink—is that not the poor man's quickest way to get out of Manchester?[9] To drink himself dead drunk?

At 10 o'clock we went to bed. You cannot go to bed except at stated times. One hundred and thirty or more sleeping around us. Boots under your flock[10] bed; you will want them in the morning. My mate tied his little money round his leg. Clothes tied on to the bed head, or under you, or between your rugs and coverlet. Naked we crept into bed—that is the wisest plan in a doss-house, for you will most likely have company in the night, and if naked you may not carry it all away. Sheets do duty for a fortnight; seven days at the top, seven days more at the bottom. There are [two][11] good rugs, a coverlet, and a flock bed.

Sleep? Who are these companions of the night? You watch them, as hour after hour they are let upstairs. Many fine, strong, well-built men they seem, but how thin! And look at their rags, poor worn garments! and some, one mass of filth indescribable. Who slept in my bed last night, you wonder? Your flesh begins to creep. You scratch; you listen to others all around scratching also. The drunkards roll in heavily and fling themselves down to sleep. You lie awake listening, and you find nearly all cough! cough! cough! the piteous hacking cough of consumption. Is the life of a tramp one merry round of song, "Under the greenwood tree"?[12]

---

9.   The observation that "drink is the quickest way out of Manchester" is commonly attributed to Friedrich Engels. Others suggest it to have been a Victorian cliché and "an oft-repeated maxim of this era;" Mason, Nicholas. "'The Sovereign People are in a Beastly State': The Beer Act of 1830 and Victorian Discourse on Working Class Drunkenness." *Victorian Literature and Culture*, 29, (March 2001), pp. 109-27, at 126. See also Shiman, Lilian L. *Crusade Against Drink in Victorian England.* New York: St. Martin's, 1988, p. 3.

10.   The *Oxford English Dictionary* defines "flocks" as "Powdered wool or cloth, or cloth-shearings, used formerly for thickening cloth."

11.   In the original: "too."

12.   A popular song based on a sonnet included in *As You Like It* (1599), Act II, scene 5. Thomas Hardy used the phrase as the title of a novel published in 1872.

Listen to him as with oath or tired fretfulness he coughs and coughs and coughs again, vainly seeking sleep. Do you wonder that he coughs? Wet by day, often wet by night; wet feet, wet limbs, wet body. Starved with cold, and starved with hunger, little wonder he is a fit and ready prey; and then an active propagator of one of England's greatest diseases—consumption.

Thus passes the long night, with fitful snatches of sleep. The policeman's whistle shrills again and again from the street. Yells as of one murdered pierce the air, but no one moves or turns; we are used to all that here! The morning dawns: 4.30—some dozen labourers are aroused to go and seek their casual task at the dock-yard gate; 5, more are awakened; 6, many more; and by 8 o'clock the majority have left their night's abode.

How long shall we allow this national disgrace—the compulsory herding together of gaol-bird, vagrant, moucher, thief, and all the hangers-on of a big city, with the respectable working man just left home seeking a job, and, more pitiable still, the young clerk looking for a new post? They must come to the doss-house, there is nowhere else so cheap; and coming, they learn evil, lose self-respect, and sink to the level of their evil surroundings.

WHAT I SAW—THE DRIFTED AND THE DRIFTWOOD

I wanted to see why young men on the road, who seek work and find none, go down so quickly in hope, in self-respect, and in power to work. I felt it my duty to see and to feel as far as I could, so that I might be able to fight against the wrong conditions which to-day are dragging down thousands and thousands of our finest manhood into degradation unthinkable.

I have seen two great classes of men on the roads and in all the common lodging-houses I visited.

In the first, the biggest and the greatest class, I have seen old and middle-aged men, professional mouchers, pickpockets, thieves, habitual beggars, and the hangers-on of the great cities, rag and bone pickers, shoe lace sellers and others. Taken as a whole, all these men drink heavily when they can, swear heavily always, hate and cannot abide regular steady labour and toil. Most of these men have been in gaol. A great number of them are known and watched by the detectives and police. They rarely go to the casual ward unless their clothes are alive with vermin. Their home is the doss-house, a constantly shifting home, with no furniture and no belongings whatsoever of their own, except what they carry as they tramp. They are the vagabonds and vagrants of England.

Were they always what they are now? No; they were once bright, smart, quick young fellows, with good characters, with the young man's usual ambitions and hopes.

Did they want to become what they are now? They loathed the coming evil, they fought against it as long as they could, they hated the swamp of evil into which they felt themselves to be sinking.

What forced them down to this loathsome life? In the majority of cases it was lack of work. Many yielded to some sort of crime or evil, such as drink, gambling, theft. But far and away the greater majority left home seeking for work, and went on looking for work, week in week out, till sick at heart and despairing—for it is a favour to-day to give a man a job, a job at which he fully earns every penny he gets—and few people realise the hopelessness and deadening effects of unemployment.

Whilst these men were seeking work they had to live very cheaply, which means they had to go to a common lodging-house with often no money for food or shelter, until they met with men who would and did teach them how to beg, how to dodge the police and the best houses to call at. These men were bad, evil men, who cursed with every sentence, who drank heavily when they could get drink, who knew all the evil and villainy which could be known. The young men looking for work had to spend their evenings with these fellows, had to sleep with them, had to learn from them, for they were starving. Do you wonder that soon, or perhaps after a long, long brave struggle, they became like them? They were treated as outcasts—they became outcasts! They were treated as thieves and vile—they became thieves and vile! and, my brother, you would become like them, if forced into the same degrading surroundings, into the same wretchedness and despair of body and mind.

These men didn't want to become vile and outcast from all that makes life joyous, any more than you do now. If twenty years ago you had been made to change places with one of them, he would have been "up," surrounded by all the delights of a happy home and you would have been "down," a wretched outcast of the streets, loathing and being loathed.

These men were not once what they are now; unemployment, starvation, and bad surroundings which they couldn't help, have made them what they are.

But there was another great class of men I saw, met, and spoke to on the roads and in the doss-houses—young men, mere lads, and middle-aged men too, who have only been on the road a few short weeks. Were these fellows criminal? No! Were they thieves or pinchers? No! What were they doing here, amongst the low company of the doss-house? They were seeking work—tramping from town to town seeking work—and of necessity spending the night at the doss-house since there is nowhere else so cheap. How were they existing? Many were famished, starving and just beginning, hunger-driven, to sing on the street for a few coppers or very timidly to beg. Poor lads!

Are these always going to be what they are now, honest, genuine seekers after work? Are these always going to remain temperate, kind, clean, hopeful lads, such as they are now? They cannot. Do what they will, they cannot. Down they drift, do what they can.

This is the most pitiable waste of our time! This is the sin, the wickedness, over which the churches should weep; for this they should repent themselves in bitterness of soul, since, whilst they have been busy sowing the seed of party strife to reap the Dead Sea fruit of sectarian bitterness, reform—that is to say, the business-like organisation of the life of our nation, its young men, has been forgotten!

Where, then, lies the fault? How is it that we witness to-day this national murder of youthful power and ambition? The fault lies in individual and national indifference.

"But they won't work," says one. It's a lie! They *will* work, they *do* work at the only pitiable work we as a nation have allowed them to do. They tramp and beg. We have allowed them, nay, compelled them to tramp and beg, and they have become professionals at the job; and, poor wretches, they will tramp on, beg on, for ever, until the day of doom! Do you say, "That isn't work"? Try it for yourself and see.

"But they won't work!" Just so! exactly what you would expect if you were not so thick skulled. Can a parson, or a commercial traveller, or a clerk, turn at once to navvying, or to coal-heaving, without becoming "work-shy," with a desperate sweat running off him, until at length he limps away from his all too strange and laborious work? And each of these men are well fed. WHY won't a tramp work? Because he can't! Strip him and examine him. Poor ill-clad wretch! Poor starved body! Poor fleshless bones! No well-filled stomach here; and lungs? listen to his cough! Take out and dissect his mind, moreover, if you can, and you will find a will-less, soul-less animality, just such as—if you were only wise—you would expect.

"It's their own fault!" says another. Which, in the majority of cases, is another ignorant lie. Have ye never read, have ye never believed that in England to-day there are hundreds of thousands of men, just such men as you and I, who never have and never will get regular, steady, life-giving, home-supporting work? Yes, the great majority of us are convicted of this condemning fact—unbelief and indifference to the condition and needs of the poorest of our land. How are we to alter it? We must clear our minds of cant and look facts, plain ugly facts, in the face—the fact of a continuous drift of young manhood down into the swamp of destitution and despair—the fact, moreover, that this downward drift is loathed and hated by those who know themselves to be drifting—the fact of the accumulated driftwood of past years of national neglect—the derelicts, the vagrant hordes of our roads.

The drifting must be stopped at the beginning of the long drift downwards; the driftwood, at first sight useless, mere wreckage of the ocean, must by long patience and mingled firmness be redeemed.

THE DRIFTING.
THE NEWCASTLE CLERK AND THE YOUNG BAKER.

The saddest, most pathetic sight on the road to-day is the large number of young men who are drifting down through lack of work. One that I spoke to was a clerk from Newcastle; he had lost his place through the bankruptcy of his firm; he had sought for work in his own town and the surrounding towns in vain. He had lived on his relations and friends until for shame he could do so no longer. And so one morning, with only a very few shillings in his pocket, he had started on the road to walk to Liverpool in order to seek for work there.

When I saw him on Saturday, April 2nd, at Rochdale, he had only left Newcastle some few weeks ago, quite a short time; but, although possessed of a pleasant appearance and manner, and only about twenty-three years of age, his chance of a job as a clerk was gone. I have been in business for nine years myself. I speak of what I know. No employer seeking a clerk would have looked at him twice with so many other men available. Why?

What was the matter with him? He had no collar, his linen was filthy, his clothes crumpled and soiled, unbrushed and untidy. He showed only too plainly that already he had begun to lose his self-respect. Had this lad done any wrong? No; his only wrong was that he had sought work and found none! No *wrong* here, surely! The lad wanted, still wants work, wherever he may be to-day—wants to earn his living; but his fatherland will have none of him, denies him his right to work, and so to live an honourable life.

But why had he thus let himself go down in looks and dress? Because he couldn't help it. I defy any penniless man to help it on the road. When a lad comes on the road seeking work he must live and sleep cheaply. He must, therefore, go to a common lodging-house. The first evening he spends there is a nightmare to him. The vicious, drunken companions, the beggars and vagrants of the roads, mouchers, pinchers, ex-gaol birds; the conversation, every sentence an oath; the suspicious eyeing up and down of the company. Maybe he is robbed the first night of food, of clothes, or of money. The bed in the open sleeping room, with no privacy of any kind, and the verminous sheets and bedding, are all a horror! There is a tap at which to wash, but no soap, and woe to him if he is fool enough to use a towel. Who used it last, and in what state was his face and skin? He is also tired, disheartened, disgusted, sick, perhaps, also—he will be soon—pinched for food, starved with wet, with cold, with hunger. Has this lad now any chance—whatever qualifications for work he may have had—has he any chance for successfully seeking employment as a clerk?

On Sunday morning I saw him again, taking a bit of breakfast. "Where are you off to this morning; which way are you going?" I asked. "Oh! I'm just going to do a bit of street singing," in a half-ashamed, half-defiant way. (I was an unknown tramp, of course.) "Street singing? Why, have you tried it before?" "Yes; last Sunday morning I was stranded in Manchester, had nothing to pay for my doss, no food. So I was desperate, and went out into some back streets singing, and got enough to pay my doss and my food." And so that Sunday morning he sang in the streets of Rochdale, and the next Sunday morning maybe he was singing in the streets of Halifax or some other town; next, Sunday somewhere else.

And you also—my so respectable, well-dressed friend—you

would do the same, where you were not known; when hunger had pinched and clammed you, when cold and exposure had made all your being shiver, when even exhaustion was driven back by the hungry, ravenous wolf within you; seeking food, shelter, and warmth, you then would do the same, and with a quavering, exhausted voice would go street singing to receive the pence of the poor, and the averted eyes and cold denials of the rich!

And so—like thousands of others—the young clerk from Newcastle took to the road, because there was nothing else to do. So, by one short step, he was thrown away from all good, helpful, wise counsel and influence. So he found himself, all unknowing, in the midst of one of England's licensed hatcheries of crime, a common lodging-house. There, driven by hunger, taught by evil companions, living a life he loathes, he is losing all good—his ideals, his manhood, his hope, his ambition, his power for work, his soul, his God; and he is gaining all evil, in a living, present hell of hopelessness and despair!

If you do not believe it, go without money in your pockets, and learn it for yourself. England will have to keep that poor lad on the road all his short life. Casual wards, prisons, asylums are all ready for him, for these are mighty England's only care and provision for her drifting, helpless lads.

I also met a young fellow in a Preston doss-house who had only been on the road for about a fortnight; he had tramped up with a companion from the Potteries, seeking work. He was a baker, and as quiet, sober, and respectable a young fellow as you could wish. But when I saw him he was tired, exhausted, and aching in body from exposure, hunger, and starvation. Two nights before he and his mate had no money for lodgings, and so had to spend the night out. They walked until they could walk no longer, and then—there was no other refuge near—lay down under the shelter of a hedge—just like thousands have to do each night in Christian England! When he awoke it was only with acute pain that he struggled on till, when the sun rose high and the passers-by thronged the roads at the entrance of Preston on that Sunday morning, all at once, without warning, down he dropped, as one dead, in a swoon from the exposure and starvation. Did any of the well-dressed throng sympathise? None! it was only two tramps on the road, and one had fainted; and, like the Pharisee and Levite of old, they passed, unheeding, by.[13] I myself felt the lad's head on the Monday night, in a Preston "kip"-house, marked with a great, ugly swelling right across the base of the skull; and yet in such a condition of mind and body he was seeking work!

But why should that lad, or any other lad, be compelled to thus insanely seek for work upon the roads?—and whilst seeking work become unfitted for work? If that lad—as many another—finds no work for six months, or twelve, what is he worth then? What can he be worth? He has learnt to live without working, and how has he lived?—by begging, by pinching, by stealing, by selling boot-laces! by telling a tale! He has been driven to lie, to steal, to swear, to drink, in spite of policemen, detectives, magistrates, and gaol, for the wild, ravening wolf of hunger and cold is fiercer than all these dread fears; and once sent to gaol for but doing what raw Nature makes us do, he dreads that terror no more. And then we wonder the "out-of-work" won't work! We wonder, with marvellous piety, why men should become "Weary Willies"[14] or "work-shy," when we ourselves might become worse than the worst of all if subjected, forced into the same degrading surroundings of the "kip"-house, forced to be outcasts from all uplifting society, forced from all hope and from all health work.

A NIGHT OUT IN PRESTON STREETS.

"A Night Out." The words are said lightly enough, and convey but little to most of our minds, but some hours passed in the clear star-lit night, with maybe the moonlight rippling across the waters, a silvery way to the far beyond. Some hours thus, warmly clad, after a good hearty supper and a bulky packet of sandwiches for the early dawn.

I speak of a very different night out. For weeks, through most of November, December and January, my mate had had no work, nothing whatever to do, and the little savings of the summer having vanished, he had been living at a common lodging-house, the

13. A reference to the parable of the Good Samaritan; Luke, 10:25-37.

14. See above, p. 232 note 2.

homeless labourer's wretched substitute for home. From time to time he had managed to pick up an odd job or two, just bringing in a few pence or shillings.

It was at Preston. For several days he had been living on 1d. a day, a ha'porth of bread, one big thick slice of white bread, and a ha'porth of "duck"—which is just all the odd scraps of all kinds of meat at the butcher's shop baked together in the oven. But yesterday he had to go without even that, and then only managed to get his night's lodging with his last three coppers through the kindness of the kip boss. With an empty pocket and a despairing, desperate heart, he walked about all day, seeking work and finding none. Ill-clad, the bitter raw wind pierced through his few garments into his very bones and being. Fits of cold shivering shook his frame from time to time, whilst a hacking cough told its tale of the past.

He turned into the doss-house for an hour or two in the evening, making belief he had enough for his lodging, until about 9.30, when he was turned out—out into the wet, chilly streets once more. He hangs about, and walks the streets in the centre of the town, trying to tell his tale to some of the passers-by, making another effort to see whether anybody will take pity on him or not. "Beg y'r pardon, Sir, but I've got no money for my night's lodging; would you give me a copper towards my doss." But there is none to pity him.

The city clocks strike eleven; soon the streets are full of expensively dressed men and women, with heavy gold chains, gold rings, gold bracelets and ornaments. He goes up to one after another, as well as he can, whilst evading the watchful eye of the policeman. "Beg y'r pardon, Sir, I've nothing for my lodging to-night; would you give a poor fellow a copper for his doss." And they look on him as on a dog, and either deign no reply at all, or tell him in impatient tones, "I've got nothing for you!"

Then is the time, my well-dressed friends, when you may feel thankful that the policeman is so close at hand, and that the poor starved beggar is so starved, so cold, so weak! If he had one-half the food and wine in him that you have, you would be knocked senseless on the road and robbed,—and do you cry "Shame!" Why shame? Why should you not also suffer a little sometimes, as well as he? Why should he bear all—all the misery of cold, hunger, starvation, hopelessness, fear and scorn?

The crowds have melted away, and the chances are getting less and less of that so much needed fourpence for shelter and food.

So, fiercely, my mate turns down into darkly-lit Leighton Street, a nice place (as he says) for begging money for lodgings.

"Is it true that it isn't safe for a well-dressed man to go down Leighton Street late at night?" asked a friend of mine; and the quick and ready answer was, "I've known the nights when if I'd met the likes of you there, and you'd refused me a night's lodging, I should have thought nothing of turning you upside down, and letting the money run out of your pockets; but, mind you, I should have left you so that you couldn't call out for help!"

And now 'tis midnight. Too late now to hope for help. The rain falls piteously, the pavements are wet and full of pools. A friendly doorway, with just a little shelter, looks inviting, so against that the outcast leans wearily, and seeks to forget his sorrows by a moment's sleep whilst he stands.

But 'tis not five minutes before tramp, tramp, and the bull's-eye[15] of the watchful policeman flashes on him. "Come on, my lad, let's have thee out of this. Keep a-going!"

"Keep a-going!" Oh, the bitterness of it! Keep a-going! Yes, but where? How those weary limbs and tired feet would "Keep a-going" did but the light, warmth, and love of a true home gleam out in the darkness miles ahead! Then he would "Keep a-going"! But why, why should he keep a-going, moving on, moving on to nowhere? Is this indeed a night in Hell, where souls lost through pride, fulness and fatness of living, are hounded on by the police of hell for ever? No, this is the grim reality of nightly experience in Christian England. For every night, on the streets of our big towns, the son of man to-day hath not where to lay his weary limbs and aching head.

And so, all through the age-long hours of night, until the dawn, the policemen keep him "going." If to escape them he turns out towards the open country, the town police follow him till the county police are met. If he turns back he is still followed. The policemen will often turn round and down a side street, but only a few minutes and round again, and if the poor beaten tramp offers to stop, "What are y'r hanging about for? Keep a-going."

---

15. A lantern with a single panel and a sliding door which could be adjusted to focus light on a given object. Generally used by police forces.

And if he doesn't mind what he says, he is perhaps locked up for "loitering with intent," and woe to him then if he happens to have about him an old key, or a penknife, or a piece of old candle, or a bit of wire, or a pair of pliers; as likely as not then he will get seven days, or fourteen days, or perhaps even up to three months in gaol.

And so down Gradwell Street he turns, up and down, down and up, up and down, till the starved brain had photographed by the dim light every stone, sett and grid therein. Up and down, down and up, till the footfall of the "knocker-up"[16] sounds in the distant streets, and the labourers heavily plod off to the work of another day.

Is this awful night at an end? May he now go home? Home? This poor man is homeless, an outcast, of less value, though strong and only 21, than a horse or a pig. His country has no need of him. His city can only keep him on the streets!

So wearily, footsore, cold, hungry, and exhausted he goes to seek work! The irony of it! And do you wonder that when the dockyard ganger sees him, although he wants a man, he says, "No, we're full up, Johnny!"

He turns away desperate, and should he meet a little girl going to the shop with money in her hand the temptation "over-gets" him—he takes the money from the child, and runs and runs until he gets some "stuff to eat." And do you wonder? Could you punish him?

Shall the poor ever cry in vain? Shall this drift downward never cease? Where, where is the man to-day who, to the tens of thousands of vagrants and casual labourers of our land, shall be as an hiding place from the wind, as a covert from the tempest, as rivers of water in a dry place, as the shadow of a great rock in a weary land?

"THE PENNY SIT UP," PRESTON, OR, "THE HOUSE OF DESPAIR."

The common or model lodging-house, the doss-house, or kip-house is, perhaps, the greatest source of moral contamination in our land.

---

16. Someone paid to rouse workers in the early mornings.

In the doss-house night by night, in the only living-room, the kitchen, for the whole long evening, there mix and mingle a motley throng. Honest fellows seeking work, professional beggars and thieves; prostitutes, cheap hawkers, and gaol-birds. They come here because it is the only place to come to, and it is comparatively cheap—$3^1/_2$d. or $4^1/_2$d. a bed are the usual charges in the larger towns.

I do not blame the doss-house keeper. He is a doss-house keeper. How can he turn the beggar with money in his pocket away? As in every business, so in this. Some are more honest and cleanly than others.

In Preston there are at least thirty-four common lodging-houses of one description or another, twenty-three of which take in women. Some are small and need not count for much; others, with from fifty to seventy beds or more. Preston provides, night by night, perhaps one thousand beds, not counting the casual ward in which the men and women of the road sleep.[17] The licensed common lodging-houses are under some sort of police supervision and inspection.

I do not know whether Preston is unique in one respect. I hope it is. It has a "Penny sit up." I call it "The house of despair." I have been there, so I speak of what I know. I went meaning to spend the night, one short night, there—short if you pass the hours of rest in refreshing sleep on a comfortable bed, but age-long if you spend it in this house of despair. I came out with a leaden weight upon my soul that men could sink to such depths of woe, and that we, we had thrust them thither.

This is not a bad dream. This is not the wild imagination of a heated brain. It is sober, solid fact. This house of despair is to be found in Shepherd Street, Preston. Its only recommendation is its cheapness; but how dearly you buy that cheapness! For one penny you buy the privilege of entrance—this admits you to a room about twenty-five feet long by eighteen feet broad.

You enter it in the evening, when the day is done. Already there are some twenty or twenty-five men there. The room is literally bare, with nothing in it, nothing! No fireplace, no stove, no hot water pipes, no sink, no water, no beds, no chairs, no blankets, no mattresses—nothing, nothing whatever for the furnishing of

---

17. The population of Preston was then about 125,000.

the room except a small, very small oil lamp, very dimly lighted, and four long wooden kneelers about two inches off the floor sloping upwards towards the back. Two of these at either ends of the room, and the other two running right down the middle of the room back to back. What are they for? This surely is not a house of prayer? No, these are pillows, wooden pillows, and presently the floor of this room will be covered with bodes lying feet to feet in two double rows down the length of the room.

When you enter some are eating their bit of food; but remember, there is no stove,[18] no warmth, no fire here, only a (washing) boiler in the yard, where you may get hot water. There are no cooking utensils; every man carries his own drum under his coat behind his back—just an old tin of some sort with a wire handle. When your food is eaten there is nothing to do but lie down on your length of the floor, some six feet by two feet, and then if your limbs ache with lying down on the hard boards sit up, and if you are privileged to have one of the select spots against the wall, you can lean against that if you will. If you are wet through you sit or lie in your wet rags till they dry, that is all!

Think of it! Ten, twelve, fourteen hours thus. Thirty to sixty men thus, night by night, in misery, wretchedness, filth of body, and starvation. The conversation is in the dull, hopeless undertone of exhausted men, except when it flashes forth now and again in the tone of revenge, hatred and bitterness against us who have condemned them to this. It is always heavily laden with oath or blasphemy, and is of begging, pinching, roguery, trickery, beastiality, at the best of the criminal courts, their prisoners and judges. The leaden weight of exhaustion and despair is only lifted when a man is dead drunk.

And so these men try to settle themselves to sleep. Sleep? Were human beings, God indwelt, ever meant thus to rest, in dirt, in degradation, in depression indescribable?

No clean horse-box with freshly-strewn straw, this! No well-drained pig-stye with abundance of bedding, warmth and food,

18. Author's footnote: "I have since spent a night here—the longest night of my life. There are plenty of hot water pipes, which I much regret I omitted to note in the darkness of my first visit."

this! No rat-hole, this, where father, mother, and baby rats may live together and seek their meat from God!

But a vermin-infested room, bare of aught but men's bodies clad in rags—bodies which are not washed or groomed or cleaned from one twelvemonth to another, except when forced to go to casual ward or gaol. Bodies which are half-starved, emaciated, lean. Bodies which carry the germs of horrible disease, yet which are untended, uncared for. Bodies which, because they are so poor, so poor in rich life blood, are thereby fit and proper food for the tramp's, the dirty beggar's worst enemy, lice. Little crawling, clinging, biting lice, which breed in twenty-four hours in the seams of your clothes next to your skin, and live upon you—biting, biting, feeding, feeding, like the gnawing worm of hell.

The atmosphere! Figuratively speaking, you could cut it with a knife! You yourself sleep next to an old decrepit man, who cannot always control his bodily actions; his trousers stink, stink; you will carry the stench in your nostrils for a week. Sixty thus, and if not quite thus, all unwashed, all with the smell of the unwashed. Add to this rank tobacco smoke of all blends, some unknown even to connoisseurs, such as "kerb-stone twist" (old chews), old cigar ends, "o.p.s." (other people's stumps), and old dried tea leaves. Add to this foul breath, some very foul, add also the stale atmosphere of the room itself when empty, and remember scarce any ventilation during the night except the occasional opening of the door into the yard, and you may think you imagine what you never will, till you experience it.

Thus the poorest of the poor live by night in Preston, thus the local authorities allow them to live, thus we Christian men through our ignorance, our party strife, and our fear of businesslike reform suffer it, and shame on us all.

It is the cause of this great national evil of needless degradation I wish to fight; not any one result, disgusting though it be. Yet be it known in Preston that the "Penny sit up" is a Lancashire disgrace—a disgrace to the soul and spirit of man, and not a cause for pious rejoicing.

My mate when stranded has gone to beg for bread to many a house in Preston, at which instead of being helped he has been told, "Take this ticket to the Shelter in Shepherd Street; we've nothing to give you; we send all our broken meat to the Shelter." Do these people know what the Shelter or the "Penny sit up" is like? Have they ever been there? Do they know that this broken food is placed in a basket on the floor of the room and scrambled for, in a wild mad rush of angry blaspheming men?

These are facts, indisputable—and one further,—do they know that these poor men, because they have slept the night in Shepherd Street Mission Shelter, and thereby, I suppose, touched the fringe of Christian sympathy, are refused admittance in the morning to a neighbouring doss-house of no great refinement, lest their living freight gathered the night before in Shepherd Street Shelter fall off them!

This Shelter has, I believe, been open now for some few years. Doubtless the owners and instigators feel they are doing a good work for the very poor, and this makes me hesitate in saying anything; but I am convinced such a place only brings men down permanently to a lower level than the doss-house, and encourages them to stay there. If in those years it has not been possible to put a fire in the room, to put in American cloth covered bunks like the Salvation Army have, to put forms round the room, to provide some rugs, to humanise and put a touch of home into the place, to light the place up with real Christian hope and effort—I say deliberately it would have been much better for everyone, to have closed the shelter long ago.

If Christian people can do no better than this, in God's name let them stand back; they put to shame the living Christ; and let the children of this world, who are often wiser than the children of light, be our guides.

TRAMPS IN CHURCH AND WHY.

"He hath put down the mighty from their seat, and hath exalted the humble and meek. He hath filled the hungry with good things, and the rich He hath sent empty away."[19] I have for many a year thought of the Magnificat as the Song of the Poor, but I never thought so more than on Sunday night, April 3rd, when with dirty clothes, dusty, unblacked shoes, open navvy's shirt, and an old scarf round my neck for a collar, tired and weary with long tramping and little food, I sat with my mate in Bolton's magnifi-

---

19. Luke, 1:52-53.

cent Parish Church. Then when we rose after the lesson to sing this song, "He hath filled the hungry with good things," the tears came unbidden to my eyes, my song was silenced, but my heart said, "God can, God will, for it is He who wills it. Oh, that the Great Deliverer would use me in this His great work of to-day!"

For three days I had lived with tramps, some honest, most not honest; some genuine work-seekers, but most men who would not stick at regular work for all you could give them. I also had tramped thirty-three miles the first day, and, unused to it, was tired, very footsore, and aching in every limb. I had slept with and amongst tramps, 130 or more in the same big room on the first night. Of course, no one knew me. I wished to go just as any other man would have to go who had to take the road, unknown, a pass-er-on. Why were we in church, then? Surely tramps of all men do not usually go to church. We went because I wished to see how two working-men in rough clothes would be treated in a large town church, because I wished to see whether the churchwardens and vergers would have any sympathy with the outcast tramp poor. How were we received? As we walked up the approach to the church feeling awkward and conscious of being eyed by the police-men and the well-dressed throng, a man of about fifty years of age quietly saluted my mate. "Good evening! Are you coming to church? Glad to see you; there are plenty of free seats; the verger will show you in." We entered, advanced towards the verger, who gave us books and showed us into the next empty free seat, with hassocks and seat rugs exactly like the rest. We took our seats, and looking round, I noticed to my great surprise that the same man who had spoken to us outside had come and seated himself next to my friend. It is not every man who chooses to sit next a tramp. After the service, as we walked out of the church, he asked us how we liked the service and the sermon, spoke very warmly of the vicar, and on saying "Good-night," asked my mate in a quiet undertone, "Are you all right for the night?" in a voice and way that meant that if we had been needing the fourpence each for lodging money he would have given it. Need I say that as we went to our humble doss-house I was glad?

What made me so glad? Just this. It is the Church's greatest work of to-day to welcome and befriend the working-man, the poor humble wayfarer of the roads, who has not and cannot have any change of clothes or "Sunday best." And more, it is the Church's greatest duty to fight for these vagrant tens of thousands, and to win for them homes. If Churchmen of old sold their precious chalices and golden communion plate to free the poor captive slave from his captivity, shall we not to-day be willing to sell our goods and give of our abundance that we may win back and redeem England's costliest treasure—human souls—from England's deepest, foulest disgrace, the vagrant, vagabond, workless stream which flows its sluggish course along England's broad roadways?

For there is a stream which flows past every man's door, flowing, flowing, a dark, muddy river along every main roadway of England, by night in greatest volume flowing in and through the multitudes of common lodging-houses and tramp wards of our land, partly also in open parks, under hedges, in farmers' hovels, barns, or brick-yards. A man never knows when he may drift therein. The firm's bankruptcy, the completion of the job, a change in machinery, some stock speculation at the world's end, and he is suddenly out of work. There is none at home. He seeks for work in vain. Friends bear with him long, but at last there comes a time when he feels he can stand it no longer. And so next morning he rises with the lark and off he goes. Where? On the road, of course—there is nowhere else to go. By midday he has tramped perhaps to the nearest town. He begins to search it for work; he is tired, footsore, sick at heart. Soon it is too late to ask at any more places, so he thinks of the night. Where shall he spend it? He must get a bed cheap; the few precious coppers he has must be made to last as long as possible. So he asks the way to a common lodging-house, or a workman's rest, or a model lodging-house, all variants of the same thing, where he will get a bed for *3d.* or *4d.* to put him over the night. He enters, pays for his bed, and sits horrified at the company, at the noise, at the dirt, at the sights, sounds, and language of his fellow-lodgers. There are skilled artisans of every sort, some of the cleverest men in England here, but men who are lost to all self-respect through casual labour, bad company, and continual drunkenness. There are strong navvies and labourers whose work is here and there, ever passing on; there are moochers—professional beggars and thieves, for most of England's gaolbirds are in England's common lodging-houses; and yet worst of all there are the multitudes of women tramps, women beggars, and prostitutes of the streets. All together (when it is a "doss" house where women are allowed) they mix, and as ever the bad influences are the loudest and the noisiest; there is nothing refining, nothing loving, nothing gentle, nothing hopeful here.

It was this that I wished to see, this that I wished to feel, not that I might be able to boast or talk about it, but that I might be able to so better work in helping men out of it, and most of all in changing the whole conditions of national life which makes and keeps our common lodging-houses the degrading, vicious influence that they are. For we must never forget the "doss-house" is a necessity. We cannot do without it, and it cannot be materially better than it is whilst we allow criminals, dissolute and wicked, of all ages, to mix and mingle freely, and form the chief influence in these the only homes of tens of thousands of honest men seeking work. I went to see the road—the road by day and the road by night, to feel the woes of this dull stream of humanity drifting downward. I have seen it, some of it, some little only, through Wigan to Manchester, through Middleton to Rochdale, through Bury to Bolton, through Chorley to Preston; and everywhere we met men drifting downward. We ate with them, we slept with them—young men just driven by stress on to the road, driven, not seeking for pleasure, but seeking for work, and driven on to the road by hunger, cold, and starvation to learn their first lesson on how to live without working. I have seen old men also, who are now scarce aught but driftwood, old, rotten, tottering into a drunkard's, beggar's, thief's grave; and in the Judgement Day the blame of their lives will be ours to bear. 'Twas not their fault they sank; they sought work and found none; they loathed the life into which they found themselves sinking, into which we as a nation pushed them, out of which we never allowed them to crawl. We have lived easily, delicately, or pleasantly; they have lived hardly, oh, so hardly! with what sense of degradation, despair, wretchedness, none of us know. 'Twill be our turn by-and-by to suffer and theirs to go at ease, for "that servant which knew his Lord's will, and made not ready, nor did according to His will, shall be beaten with many stripes; but he that knew not, and did things worthy of stripes, shall be beaten with few stripes. And to whomsoever much is given, of him shall much be required; and to whom they commit much, of him will they ask the more."[20]

20. Luke, 12:47-48.

I have seen women also, women on the road, women in the common-lodging houses. I watched one in the evening hour dressing to go out on the street. I noted the womanly care with which she re-trimmed the much-befeathered hat, put on her blouse, arranged her skirt, and then with a glance at the little bit of broken glass in the common kitchen, and a final touch or two, and with a light "Ta, ta!" to the little group of friends, went out— out into the night; the night when deeds of shame most frequently are done; went out also to earn her "kip," out selling her soul to feed her poor body. Think you women do this for fun? Think you, they love the life? Think you she first began it for a joke? All this, and much, much more in the kip-house; and I want to alter it. I want to change it! You smile! But say we all only wanted, willed to change it—it would be changed! Why should our lads and lasses thus perish? Why should the bairns[21] who have cost us so much thus perish?—far better they had never been born. Why should our sons and daughters—nay, sons and daughters of the Lord God Almighty, thus perish? Why? they perish but through our miserable party spirit, our callousness, our ignorance, and our wicked fear. We can at least all make our homes true homes, where growing lads and lasses may know they are more than welcome, for the home is ever theirs. We can all warn others to keep off the road. We can say, "Shun, avoid the road," for the road and the common lodging-house are the way to shame and degradation. We can all learn to discriminate—look at the tramp when he passes. Some are deserving, needy, starving. These will say the least and need the most. Help such with a cup of tea, a slice of bread and butter, a kind word, and perhaps a copper or two, and, oh, that it were possible, with work. But remember, most men on the road are not in a fit condition to work. Would you be, if miserable, half-starved, and ill? And also remember you can never be sure of a tramp's tale. A confirmed tramp, a three months' tramp, knows not truth[,][22] his only effort is to tell a good tale.

All young men, and men who have a vote, must and ought to study social reform, ought to read the reports of the Poor Law

---

21. See above, p. 284 note 6.

22. No comma in the original.

Commission[23] and study them, think over them, talk about them, claim the whole subject of the nation's action and refuse to ally it with any political party. I believe that destitution can be done away with. I believe that 80 per cent. of the vast army of vagrants can be redeemed. I believe that here is the work for all, for the individual, for the Church, for the corporate action of the whole nation. And I believe this because I believe the work is God's, and it is God Himself who calls men to this His work to-day.

WHAT MUST WE DO?

We must first try to realise the facts—above all, the great awful fact of the downward flowing stream of unemployed and casual labourers into the destitution and the degradation of the vagrant tramp.

It is most difficult to realise the vastness of this ocean of miserables, for we never see it in one mass, only in tiny wavelets, as one by one, or two by two, the ragged wretches splash against us on the shingle of our roads. Or, first starting, steal away stealthily from cottage home, town, street, one by one, to swell the great throng of seekers after work upon the roads.

Few people see even a casual ward full, or a crowded doss-house kitchen, yet there are about 25,000 professional tramps, and thousands and thousands more casual labourers, navvies, and others on the roads seeking work. The work-house casual wards alone provide accommodation for about 12,000 beds; for what an army must the hosts of doss-houses, workmen's rests and shelters provide?

Then we must seek the cause of this downward drift. What is it? There are two main causes producing pauperism and destitution—casual labour and drink. The first and the mightiest is the increasing volume of casual labour, work by odd jobs, the baneful employment by the day, with which we are all so familiar. The Commissioners of the Poor Laws appointed three groups of special investigators to discover what it was that was CREATING paupers.

---

23. The Royal Commission on the Poor Laws and Relief of Distress was appointed in 1905 and issued a Majority Report and a Minority Report in 1909.

"The outcome of those investigations was all the more impressive in that it was not what we anticipated. We do not exaggerate when we say that all these inquirers—numbering, with their assistants, more than a dozen, starting on different lines of investigation, and pursuing their researches independently all over the kingdom—*came, without concert, to the same conclusion, namely, that of all the causes or conditions predisposing to pauperism, the most potent, the most certain, and the most extensive in its operation was this method of employment in odd jobs.* Contrary to the expectations of some of our number, and of some of themselves, our investigators did not find that low wages could be described, generally speaking, as a cause of pauperism. They were unable to satisfy themselves that insanitary conditions of living, or excessive hours of labour, could be shown to be, on any large scale, a cause of pauperism. They could find practically no ground for believing that outdoor relief, by adversely affecting wages, was itself a cause of pauperism. It could not even be shown that an extravagant expenditure on drink, or a high degree of occasional drunkenness—habits of which the evil consequences can scarcely be exaggerated, and which are ruinous to individuals in all grades—were at all invariably accompanied or followed by pauperism. All these conditions, injurious though they are in other respects, were not found, if combined with reasonable regularity of employment, to lead in any marked degree to the creation of pauperism. Thus the regularly employed railway porters, lowly paid as they are, contribute only infinitesimally to pauperism. Even the agricultural labourers in receipt, perhaps, of the lowest money wages of any section of the wage-earners, do not nowadays, so far as they belong to the section in regular employment, contribute largely to the pauperism of adult able-bodied life. Again, though the average consumption of alcoholic drink among the miners, the boilermakers, the iron and steel workers, and many other trades appear to be enormous, these trades do not contribute largely to pauperism. On the other hand, where high earnings and short hours and healthy conditions are combined with the method of casual employment—as is the case with some sections of wharf and riverside labourers, and of the men who labour in connection with furnaces and gasworks—there we find demoralisation of character, irregularity of life, and a constant recruiting of the pauper army."[24] Or, as the secretary of Charity Organization says: "It is from the casual labour class that those who fall upon the Poor Law, relief works, or charitable funds are mostly drawn."[25] Or, as the Poor Law Majority Commissioners say: "There is a very general consensus of opinion that amongst industrial causes casual labour contributes more to pauperism than any other," and "There is little doubt that to regularise casual labour would do more than any one remedy to diminish pauperism of the worst type."[26]

The second awful cause of this downward drift is excessive drinking. Dr. Ralph H. Crowley, of Bradford, says in "The Drink Problem," after summarising the investigations on the relations of drink and pauperism of Chas. Booth, Alderman McDougall, and the Massachusetts Bureau of Statistics of Labour: "Were a careful inquiry to be instituted into the cause of pauperism through the country, it seems almost certain that drink would claim a proportion of one-third to one-half." He quotes also Dr. Sullivan, who divides alcoholic excess into (1) convivial drinking, which is gradually decreasing and is amenable to educational and religious influences; and (2) industrial drinking, which includes all forms of "misery drinking," such as that caused by overwork, insufficient or unattractive food, overcrowding, and the unnatural and harmful conditions

---

24. Great Britain. Commission on the Poor Laws and Relief of Distress. *Report.* Parliamentary Papers 1909 [Cmd. 4499]. xxxvii.1, p. 1,151. An author's note at the beginning of the paragraph gives the citation as: Poor Law Commission, *Minority Report II*, p. 195.

25. The Secretary of the Charity Organisation (sic) Society from 1875 to 1914 was C.S. Loch, who published widely on charity and social policy, and was a member of the Royal Commission on the Poor Laws from 1905 to 1909. We have been unable to trace this reference.

26. Commission on the Poor Laws and Relief of Distress, *Report*, pp. 223 and 224.

under which so many live.[27] He closes by saying that the drink problem must be recognised as a part of the whole social problem, and that we should be "careful of apportioning more especial blame, as we habitually do, to those who happen, through drink, to fall into destitution, and we may well give thought to the question, 'Were those upon whom the tower of Siloam fell guilty above all other?'"[28]

If this be so, that the greater part of the vagrancy of to-day is caused by lack of work, and work in odd jobs—casual labour—and an ever-increasing volume of evidence and experience make me accept this conclusion as true—if this be so, we must give up evading our duty by the all too frequent excuses, "They won't work," "It's their own fault," "They don't deserve help."

If this be so, we must fight the cause of this national sin. We must fight against casual labour as a national evil. We must fight against the unemployment we see all around us to-day. If unemployment is the evil, we must bring all our national resource, organisation and moral strength to do away with it.

For look at the effect of unemployment, or of casual labour; the lad is thrown out of work, he is forced out on to the road to

---

27. Ralph H. Crowley (1869-1953), was Senior Medical Officer of the Board of Education and for many years school medical officer of Bradford. See his "Alcoholism and Pauperism." In Kelynack, T.N. (Ed.). *The Drink Problem in Its Medico-Sociological Aspects by Fourteen Medical Authorities.* London: Methuen, 1907, pp. 199-210. Charles Booth surveyed 1,447 individuals in Stepney, St. Pancras, and Ashby-de-la-Zouch (Leiscestershire) in 1889, finding that around twenty-five percent of pauperism was caused by drink. Alderman A. McDougall studied 404 paupers in Manchester in 1883, and found that a little over half of all pauperism could be attributed to drink. The Massachusetts Bureau of Statistics of Labor found that nearly forty percent of paupers blamed their condition on their own "intemperance." Crowley acknowledges these sources as his authority. "Dr. Sullivan" is a reference to Sullivan, W.C. "A Statistical Note on the Social Causes of Alcoholism." *Journal of Mental Science*, 50, (1904), 417-32.

28. "Or those eighteen, upon whom the tower in Siloam fell, and slew them, think ye that they were sinners above all men that dwelt in Jerusalem? I tell you, Nay: but, except ye repent, ye shall all likewise perish." Luke, 13:4-5.

seek for work, he is forced by the search for work away from all the softening and helpful influences of his home, and into the common lodging-house, to mix with the vilest characters of the country.

He becomes hopeless, seeking work and finding none; loses his self-respect, learning to live by law-breaking, for whether he begs or whether he steals, he breaks the law; he begins to feel the police are his enemies and not his friends, and worse still, he soon gets the felling of being cast out—an outcast—not wanted by his fellow men. His friends don't want him, employers of labour don't want him, his fellow men don't want him, the decently dressed don't look at him, he is outcast, vile. There are few people who realise the hardening, the deadening, the degrading effects of such unemployment.

So he becomes State driftwood, social wreckage, either of the violent sort, as a thief, a burglar, or of the more cunning sort, an impostor, a beggar, or a begging-letter writer.

Do these fellows want to become thus? No. Do they want to go on the road? No. Do they like the company they find there? No. But they cannot help themselves; there is no one to care for them, to stand by them in their hour of need.

What is the remedy for it? What must we do? As individuals we can do but little. Yet we can look at the tramp as he passes by; he is a man, although he has fallen. Maybe it was not his fault that he fell. We can help the young especially, and encourage the lad seeking work. But most useful, let our voices be heard incessantly pleading for a sane reform of our national attitude towards the work seeker and the vagrant. Have faith in men; have faith in God, and know things need not be as they are to-day. Things are wrong and must be righted; each can do his part.

As Christian people, as a Church, what can we do? We can remember the fact that this is God's great call to-day; that it is our possibility and our duty to make destitution and beggary cease for ever.

Individual conversion won't do it. I mean that "saving of the soul" which some people think the Church's only business. Many a lad whom I have met and seen on the road has been individual-ly converted. Some were even wearing the sign and badge of the Salvation Army whilst they tramped; others had letters of recom-mendation from ministers of all denominations; and the pity of it is, these lads, having been converted once to some sort of love, hope, and ideal, are now by the evil surroundings into which they are unwillingly thrust being reconverted into hate, despair, and hopelessness!

But let those who think the Church's first and only work to be the saving of lost souls get themselves with all speed, into old clothes and old clouts, and no money in their pockets withal, and tramp, seeking for work; let them spend this night, and the next, and the next following in a mixed common lodging-house. Or if they cannot beg the needful for this, let them tramp the streets all night, shivering, exhausted, starved, tired out. Let them do this all week—but for one short week—and try to feel, as the tramp does feel, it MAY go on for ever!—and then they will either gain something of the hilarious mockery and blasphemy of the tramp towards all well-filled, well-fatted Christian Churches and souls, or indeed, in contrition and bitterness of mind for the past, know that Christ's work is still, as ever, to give meat to the hungry, drink to the thirsty, lodging to the stranger, clothes to the ragged, care to the sick, and life-giving work to all; and with work, and only with work, Hope, Hope, Hope—glad Morning-Star of a brighter day—for all earth's lost.

And yet as Churches we can do much—nay, we can do more than all, and we should, did we but leave out the spirit of bitterness and party strife and welcome and foster the marvellously increasing social aspirations of our age with fitting faith and hope. Every right man, surely every Christian man, must be an optimist. Let the optimism in us out, and it will multiply. Every Church should have its social study class in an entirely non-party spirit. Why may not Conservative, Liberal, and Socialist equally strive, each most sincerely, for the welfare for all? There might well be an emigration fund in each parish. Select some needy one next winter, feed him and train him and send him forth in the spring to the new and broader lands beyond the seas. Keep social problems to the fore, and for all local, ecclesiastical, municipal, and Parliamentary positions put in the best, biggest, sanest men, men who will think not so much according to the mere money value of the market, but in the higher value of the nation's manhood. For that which is morally right shall be seen not to be economically wrong in the end.

Especially must we remember that it is the duty of the whole Church to lead the way—to make the attempt—to devise means whereby the banished and outcast be not expelled for ever from wholesome life. Every county should have its labour colony, a city of refuge, whereunto he who had fallen in the strife of life might flee, and where he would always be received with strong arms of love.

Such a colony would be the home missionary work of the Church, continually calling for devoted lives to be given to the most difficult service of uplifting the fallen by comrade work and the tonic of hopeful love. A "great heart" must be at the head, the greatest heart that can be found, with a wise head, moreover. The thing most precious in this colony, nay, the only thing of priceless cost, will be Love, that love which inspires, which believes, which trusts, which laughs at impossibilities. We are not hindered by lack of money, but by lack of love. Such a colony in each county, with its ever-open door of hope, would give new heart and courage to every city pastor and slum worker. Such a colony would give new heart to true and worthy town councillors, members of watch communities, and police officers. The money which is now wasted in supplying useless casual wards and extra police cells would soon be voted hither; the work, as it became manifestly worthy, would meet with the generous support of the town and city fathers, and the lavish gifts of those hearts which ever open noiselessly at the magic touch of Love. Such a colony would provide the incentive, would give the basis by hard-earned experience, and would train the workers for further linking-up efforts by the local and national authorities themselves. And, be it know far and wide, this is the way in which Germany has so nearly solved her out-of-work and vagrant problem.[29] The good men of the Church led the way, the State wisely watched, supported, and followed.

For surely we all recognise that the great problem of unemployment, vagrancy, and degrading destitution is chiefly a collective and national work. We can only deal with the whole difficulty through legislation. It is the business of a Christian people to

---

29. Agricultural labor colonies were a feature of prisons and workhouses in Germany in this period. According to Simon Constantine, about sixteen percent of institutionalized paupers in Prussia were "engaged in agricultural work" in 1908, and the proportion was higher among prisoners; "Correction in the Countryside: Convict Labour in Rural Germany, 1871-1914." *German History*, *24*, (February 2006), pp. 39-61, at 43.

see that their laws growingly reflect the developing Spirit of Christ in their midst. The social conscience of England is aroused to-day as never before, in spite of all our lethargy; but our quickened conscience needs to be embodied in action, in legislation, in a new attitude towards the whole poor of our land.

Our only national remedies at the present are the tramp wards, the workhouses, the gaols, the asylums of our land, and a whole mass of blundering, unorganised charity.

Why are these expensive national methods of dealing with destitution useless? Because their only aim is to make the life of the tramp as uncomfortable, wretched, and full of disgrace as possible. Our present methods neither try to prevent the drift downwards by standing men who are seeking work, nor to lift up the fallen and give them a new start. The spirit, method, and aim of our present treatment of the poor is wrong, unscientific, and unchristian.

What, then, must we do? We must stop the drift downward. We must stand by men who are out of work. We must stop the vain and degrading tramping on the road to seek for work. What is our telephone, telegraph, and postal service for but to be used? And what is Government, with all its wonderful machinery, for, but to protect the best interests of the whole of the people governed?

Let periods of slackness of trade, and unemployment, be used as golden opportunities for the improvement of the workers. Let men be drafted off into technical schools, agricultural training colleges, and other like institutions, to further and complete their education as mechanics, plumbers, farm labourers and citizens. Then, when the demand for labour quickens, the men would go forth the better, the more intelligent, and capable for the well-used period of unemployment from ordinary business life.

This would stop the creation of a criminal class such as we see to-day, and would in largest measure stop the drift downward.

With a like spirit of kind, firm hopefulness we must, by magistrates' order, clear the roads and streets of the whole vagrant, vagabond class of beggars, loafers and wastrels. We must classify them. We must clothe them and fees them and doctor and heal their poor bodies, and their poorer souls also, with the glad gospel of Hope. Teach them a trade. Create new good habits of work and living, and as they regain strength of will and strength of body once more they, too, will gladly take their new-found places as honoured citizens of our land.

We welcome the new spirit moving in our midst, as evidenced by the National Labour Bureaux,[30] which should eventually, when trusted by both masters and men, prove of greatest value, especially if supported by a wise scheme of compulsory insurance against unemployment; as evidenced also by such a noble and sorely needed voluntary movement as the newly-organised National Association for Women's Lodging-Homes,[31] and the long tried efforts of the Church and Salvation Army.[32] There is room for all, there is need for co-operation and co-ordination amongst all, but there is no room for a party spirit which only pulls to pieces the efforts of others because they are the attempts of men of another political or religious creed.

The aim and object being clear:—(1) To stop the drifting; (2) To sweep the drifted off the streets and restore them to usefulness; (3) To employ every Englishman in honourable toil. This object being clear, we could do it! for it can be done. My purpose is to arouse men to this great duty, to which we are called—the duty of making destitution and beggary to cease for ever; to tell men *God* calls them to this work, and that it is not beyond the wit and power of *men* to accomplish it. This is God's call to-day! "If ye have faith as a grain of mustard-seed, ye shall say unto this mountain, remove hence to yonder place; and it shall remove; and nothing shall be impossible to you."[33]

30. Labour exchanges were created under the auspices of the Labour Exchanges Act of 1909 (9 Edw.VII, c.7).

31. Founded in 1909, to a large extent as a result of the efforts of the social reformer Mary Higgs; Chadwick, Rosemary. "Higgs [née Kingsland], Mary Ann (1854-1937)." *Oxford Dictionary of National Biography*, 27, (2004), pp. 78-79; [Higgs, Mary K.], *Mary Higgs of Oldham*. Wells: Clare, 1954. See above, pp. 32 and 216 note 10.

32. On the Church Army, see Everard Wyrall's account, above, pp. 273–278.

33. Luke, 17:6.

Index